Love and Attachment

Love and Attachment

Contemporary Issues and Treatment Considerations

Edited by

Carol Tosone, Ph.D.
and
Theresa Aiello, Ph.D.

JASON ARONSON INC.
Northvale, New Jersey
London

Copyright © 1999 by Jason Aronson Inc.

10 9 8 7 6 5 4 3 2 1

All rights reserved. No part of this book may be used or reproduced in any manner whatsoever without written permission from Jason Aronson Inc. except in the case of brief quotations in reviews for inclusion in a magazine, newspaper, or broadcast.

Library of Congress Cataloging-in-Publication Data

Love and attachment : contemporary issues and treatment considerations
    / edited by Carol Tosone and Theresa Aiello.
        p.   cm.
    Includes bibliographical references and index.
    ISBN 0-7657-0185-5
    1. Attachment behavior. 2. Intimacy (Psychology) 3. Love.
    4. Psychotherapist and patient. I. Tosone, Carol. II. Aiello,
    Theresa.
    RC455.4.A84L68 1999
    616.89—dc21   98–36489

Printed in the United States of America on acid-free paper. For information and catalog write to Jason Aronson Inc., 230 Livingston Street, Northvale, New Jersey 07647-1726. Or visit our website: www.aronson.com

This book is affectionately and respectfully dedicated to Dr. George Frank, Founder and Director of the Ph.D. Program at New York University Ehrenkranz School of Social Work, with much appreciation for his unwavering support and guidance to all his students.

Contents

PART II: DYSFUNCTIONAL ATTACHMENTS

PART III: ATTACHMENT IN THE THERAPEUTIC PROCESS

Acknowledgments

There are many people whose continued support helped bring this book to fruition. In addition to Dr. George Frank, whose kindness and wisdom guided this project, we are particularly indebted to our colleagues and friends at New York University Ehrenkranz School of Social Work: Dean Thomas Meenaghan; Vice Dean Eleanore Z. Korman; Associate Dean Lucretia Phillips; Dr. Eda Goldstein, Director of the Ph.D. Program; Dr. Judith Mishne, Chairperson of the Social Work Practice Area; Dr. Jeffrey Seinfeld, Chairperson of the Human Behavior Area; and all the faculty, particularly those in the Practice and Human Behavior areas where we teach. We thank them for their collegiality and fellowship. We would also like to thank the support staff at New York University Ehrenkranz School of Social Work, especially office manager Richard Lenert, for his meticulous attention to the detail of this manuscript.

We are grateful to Dr. Jason Aronson and Judy Cohen at Jason Aronson Inc. for their support and assistance in reviewing this manuscript. Barbara Guilfoyle, M.S.W., Director of Social Work at Calvary Hospital, deserves special mention for her editorial assistance.

On a more intimate note, Carol would especially like to thank her husband, Richard Connor Lutzy, for his infinite love and patience throughout all her professional endeavors. She would also like to thank the other special members of her family: her father, Albert J. Tosone, for his lifelong love, support, and practical wisdom; her sister and brother-in-law, Barbara and Nicholas Ambroselli, for their ongoing support and encouragement; her wonderful nephews and godsons, Nicholas Anthony Ambroselli, Paul Albert Ambroselli, and Michael Andrew Ambroselli, for keeping her young at heart (no aunt could be prouder or wish for more); and her exceptional and gifted stepdaughters, Jennifer Sue Lutzy, Jillian Marie Lutzy, and Rebecca Michelle Lutzy, for their generosity and understanding.

Theresa would like to commemorate the memory of Dr. Thomas Belmonte and Salvatore Aiello. She would also like to express gratitude to Dr. Larry Lockridge for his support and encouragement.

Contributors

THERESA AIELLO, Ph.D., is Assistant Professor in the M.S.W. and Ph.D. Programs at New York University Shirley M. Ehrenkranz School of Social Work. She is a supervisor for the National Institute for the Psychotherapies Child and Adolescent Program in Psychotherapy. Dr. Aiello is the author of *Child and Adolescent Treatment for Social Work Practice: A Relational Perspective,* which is forthcoming. Dr. Aiello was the recipient of the NYU Ehrenkranz School of Social Work Distinguished Professor Award. She is in private practice in New York City.

LOUISE CRANDALL, Ph.D., is Adjunct Assistant Professor and half-time dissertation advisor at New York University Shirley M. Ehrenkranz School of Social Work, and a member of the New York Freudian Society and International Psychoanalytic Association. She is in private practice in New York City.

ELLEN GRACE FRIEDMAN, M.S.W., is Adjunct Associate Professor and Ph.D. candidate at New York University Shirley M.

Ehrenkranz School of Social Work and the Department Coordinator, Department of Addiction Medicine at Saint Barnabas Hospital.

LISA GILMAN, M.S.W., is a Ph.D. candidate at New York University Shirley M. Ehrenkranz School of Social Work and a consultant for various social service agencies in the New York area. She is in private practice in New York City and Port Washington, Long Island.

JUDITH RAPPAPORT, Ph.D., is Adjunct Associate Professor at New York University Shirley M. Ehrenkranz School of Social Work, a member of the Postgraduate Psychoanalytic Society, and Supervisor, National Psychological Association for Psychoanalysis. She is in private practice in New York City.

FLORENCE ROSIELLO, Ph.D., is a faculty member and supervisor at the Institute for Contemporary Psychotherapy, the Psychoanalytic Psychotherapy Study Center, and the New York Institute for Psychoanalytic Self Psychology. She is in private practice in New York City.

LYNNE RUBIN, Ph.D., is a training and supervising analyst for the New York Freudian Society and the International Psychoanalytic Association, and a member of the Institute for Psychoanalytic Training and Research. She is in private practice in New York City.

JOAN MASELL SONCINI, M.A., Ph.D., is Adjunct Assistant Professor at New York University Shirley M. Ehrenkranz School of Social Work, founder of the Center for Intercultural Psychotherapy, and a multicultural specialist at the Institute for Contemporary Psychotherapy. Dr. Soncini is in private practice, specializing in intercultural psychotherapy.

DORIENNE SORTER, Ph.D., is a faculty member and supervisor at Blanton Peale Graduate Institute of Religion and Health and the Psychoanalytic Psychotherapy Study Center. She is in private practice in New York City.

CAROL TOSONE, Ph.D., is Assistant Professor in the M.S.W. and Ph.D. Programs at New York University Shirley M. Ehrenkranz School of Social Work and a Supervisor in the Group Therapy Training Program at New York University School of Medicine Department of Psychiatry. Dr. Tosone is author of several professional articles on the subjects of countertransference, short-term treatment, supervision, and women's issues, and has served on the editorial board of *Psychoanalysis and Psychotherapy.* She is in private practice in New York City.

SILKALY M. WOLCHOK, Ph.D., was a postdoctoral fellow in the Psychiatry Department and the Lauder Center at Memorial Sloan-Kettering Cancer Center. She is in private practice in Scarsdale, New York.

Introduction

Social work may well have produced the first American psychotherapists and, perhaps unwittingly, the first models of psychotherapy. With an emphasis on direct practice with the poor and the oppressed in a wide range of agency settings, social workers created paradigms for psychotherapy with populations previously deemed unreachable by traditional psychoanalysis. By incorporating the first English translations of Freud in their work in the early part of the century, they began to shape models for practice which continue to evolve.

This volume represents that continued evolution in the contemporary breadth and scope of clinical social work. Social workers in direct practice have always felt an alliance and identified with poor and disaffiliated populations. Although as a group social workers were often disregarded by other more "prestigious" mental health professions, many of the most prominent current interests in psychoanalysis evolved from social work values. The emphases on narrative, culture and race, and the socio-intersubjective field are just some of the social work ideologies that have impacted upon psychoanalysis and family therapy theories and practice.

This collection of essays places sharp focus on the most basic of human interactions—love and attachment—in all of their permutations, as well as the barriers that exist to achieving closeness. The specific social groups addressed here are inclusive as to gender, class, race, and ethnicity, all characteristics that reflect the complexity of modern life. In an increasingly technologically demanding society, intimacy and dependency become ever more daunting—perhaps even devalued—and are often lost in the demands of daily survival.

This volume is drawn from the work of the faculty, students, and alumni of the New York University Shirley M. Ehrenkranz School of Social Work Ph.D. Program. The chapters are divided into three categories: love styles in contemporary life, dysfunctional attachments, and attachment in the therapeutic process.

These chapters reflect the growing body of knowledge in developmental theory and attachment research. The rich confluence of psychodynamic theories that attachment studies have fostered is synthesized with techniques for working with specific populations. These writers speak to the wide spectrum of theoretical influences in psychodynamic work, including psychoanalysis in all of its voices; classical, ego psychology, object relations, self psychology, intersubjectivity; and family therapy, with their focus on systems and the larger scope of community, are also considered. The context of private and public direct practice mirrors the current state of relational life today in contemporary urban society.

Part I, Love Styles in Contemporary Life, addresses the problems of contemporary adult life in both internal and interpersonal didactics. Dr. Carol Tosone discusses the modern challenges of achieving intimacy, contrasting the nature of romantic attachments in avoidant, addictive, and transitory styles with mature object love. The paradox of achieving separation from the mother–child dyad concurrent with the task of forming a romantic union that is both reparative and sustaining is explored through the use of case illustrations. Dr. Joan Soncini focuses on the current development of clinical practice with intercultural couples. She explores the complex phenomena that bring intercultural couples into treatment, describing the essential therapeutic task as that of distinguishing between cultural and interpersonal or intrapsychic issues. Dr. Lynne Rubin presents a timely contribution to our understanding of how fathers and their infants relate and coexist. She reviews the existent literature on male development and in particular the influence of father love in helping children to develop enduring identification. Utilizing her own research, she examines the effect that paternal caregiving has on children, partners, and colleagues.

Part II, Dysfunctional Attachments, reviews the obstacles in contemporary society to achieving intimacy. Dr. Louise Crandall utilizes structural theory to explore similarities and differences among neurotic, borderline, and narcissistic patients in establishing and sustaining intimate relationships. She explores the implications of libidinal fixation points, ego problems, and superego pathology on problems and patterns of loving, examining the effects of the compulsion to repeat relationships from the past, and the resulting pathological identifications. In "Sexual Function and Dysfunction in Intimate Relationships," Dr. Silkaly Wolchok illuminates the complex components of sexual desire and the power of the interactive ingredient of intimacy. She also examines the organic and nonorganic sources of sexual dysfunction, providing relevant case vignettes. Lisa Gilman's essay, "Trauma's Influence on Love and Attachment," describes the post-trauma stress response resulting from sexual abuse as it impacts on the capacity to love. By integrating attachment theory with self psychology and object relations, Gilman underscores the idea that the therapeutic relationship is a reparative love relationship for traumatized clients. Professor Ellen Friedman examines the influence of addiction on intimacy. In "Intimacy Problems in Addiction," Friedman addresses the subjective personal meaning of drugs to addicted patients. Through extensive discussion of case material, Professor Friedman examines the contradictory wishes for both intimacy and the acquired "unfeeling" state experienced in the addict's "high."

Part III, Attachment in the Therapeutic Process, addresses the various manifestations of intimacy in the treatment relationship. Dr. Dorienne Sorter describes the integration of the attachment theories of Bowlby, Ainsworth, and Stern in her clinical work with schizoid patients. Dr. Judith Rappaport examines maternal love in the patient–therapist dyad, incorporating feminist and object relations theory in her discussion of a case. In the concluding chapter, "Transference Love, Eros, and Attachment," Dr. Florence Rosiello discusses the evolution of the concept of erotic transference, tracing it from Freud's initial observations of it as a hindrance to current relational theories that view it as a necessary component of treatment. Utilizing a two-person psychology in her work, Dr. Rosiello also addresses the erotic countertransference that can stimulate reparative intimacies in the psychoanalytic encounter.

Collectively, these authors enjoy a comprehensive understanding of love and attachment in all of its contemporary configurations. This book will assist social workers and other mental health colleagues at all levels of practice sophistication to both expand and hone their clinical skills, and in doing so to help their clients in the process of growth, love, and attachment.

PART I

LOVE STYLES IN CONTEMPORARY LIFE

1

Illusion, Disillusion, and Reality in Romantic Love

CAROL TOSONE

"Love is an endless mystery, for it has nothing else to explain it," wrote the Hindu poet Rabindranath Tagore. For centuries, poets, philosophers, and pundits alike have pondered the anatomy of romantic love. Despite its central importance to human existence, romantic love has managed to elude a precise definition. Idealists tend to view love as the key to the meaning of life, while cynics often describe it as a temporary insanity.

Regardless of one's perspective, mutual romantic love often serves as the basis for selecting a partner. Yet in the fast-paced American society of today, with its emphasis on individualism, the goal of finding and maintaining a compatible relationship is difficult to achieve. In psychotherapy, single patients may be unwilling to marry until they find partners who possess all of the characteristics they find desirable. Only then, they believe, will happiness be assured. Marriage, as the consistently high divorce rate attests, does not guarantee happiness. A common complaint among married patients is that they knowingly settled for relationships out of a sense of insecurity and now do not have the courage to leave. For many of these patients, the primary treatment goal is to leave their barren marriages in search of happiness.

Why is romantic love so central to human existence and happiness? While the poets have attempted to answer this question for millennia, psychoanalysts' attention to the subject remains in its infancy. Perhaps this is fitting given that Freud (1905, 1914), Bowlby (1958, 1969, 1973, 1980, 1988), Bergmann (1980, 1988), Benjamin (1988), Kernberg (1995), and others focus on the mother–infant dyad as the prototype of later love relationships.

This chapter examines the nature of romantic love, beginning with a review of Freud's ideas, followed by a discussion of Bowlby's attachment theory, and concluding with a comparison of the different types of romantic attachments, including avoidant, addictive, transitory, and mature object love, using case vignettes to illustrate these relationship patterns.

FREUD'S VIEWS ON ROMANTIC LOVE

Beginning with "Three Essays on the Theory of Sexuality," Freud (1905) identifies the mother as the first love object of the infant. He maintained that "the prototype of every love relationship is the child sucking at the mother's breast. The finding of the love object is in fact a refinding of it" (1905, p. 222). According to Freud, sexual development is diphasic. That is, it occurs in two waves, the first beginning between the ages of 2 and 5 and the latter starting with puberty. The final outcome of sexual life is determined with the achievement of genital organization. In between these phases, a repression and split takes place during the latency period, such that passionate sexual trends are separated from affectionate ones with the former undergoing repression.

Freud (1912) traces the origin of the affectionate trend to the earliest years of childhood when, out of a self-preservative instinct, the child directs his or her affection toward a primary object who provides nurturance and nourishment. These affectionate feelings have an erotic component, which is diverted from the primary object, becoming autoerotic. In latency, the affectionate current is reinforced by the repression of the sexual aim. With the advent of puberty and its accompanying instinctual pressures, the affectionate trend is recombined with the powerful sexual current. Reunification makes it possible to love a new, nonincestuous object choice. If these currents fail to fuse, the person is unable to experience both passionate and tender feelings toward the same object because of unresolved oedipal conflicts. In this case, the genital stage of development has not been attained. (Genital organization is characterized by the synthesis of the component instincts under the primacy of the genital zone, in the service of reproduction.)

In his paper "Instincts and Their Vicissitudes" (1915), Freud reserves the term *love* for the "relation of the ego to its source of pleasure" (p. 135), a state which is possible only after fusion of the component sexual instincts. He recognized, however, that love could not be explained simply as an instinct, or as a duality of trends. He offered that love has three paired opposites: loving and hating, loving and being loved, and loving and indifference. Here Freud shifts from an instinctual to an ego perspective.

In addition to the parent as model for a later love object, Freud proposed that the self can serve as an object choice. In his paper "On Narcissism" (1914), Freud contrasts anaclitic and narcissistic types of object choice. In his previously mentioned paper, Freud (1905) postulated that object choice is based either on an anaclitic or a narcissistic model, the former chosen because the love object resembles the person's parent and the latter because the love object symbolizes the person's relationship to him- or herself. In their extreme manifestations, narcissistic love is characteristic of persons who use others in an effort to enhance their self-esteem, while anaclitic love is characterized by intense dependency on another.

In his later paper, Freud (1914) expands the notion of narcissistic object choice to include what the person was, is, and would like to be (the projection of one's ego ideal), as well as having components drawn from someone who was once part of the self. This last idea refers to the mother's narcissistic love for her child, and allows the person in love to restore his or her lost unity. Freud also contrasts male object choice, usually of an anaclitic nature, with that of females, which is generally narcissistic. He notes that this distinction is a schematic one, with both modes of object choice able to combine in any individual case.

In regard to the ego ideal, Freud saw its origins as largely narcissistic and as the target of the self-love enjoyed in childhood by the actual ego. If the ego ideal is projected onto the love object and the love is mutually expressed, then the dynamic tension between the ego and its ideal is excluded as long as the experience of being in love lasts. For Freud, love involved a transformation of narcissistic libido into object libido. He describes love as the highest form of development that object libido is capable of, when the person seems to yield up his or her entire personality in favor of the object. This transformation, coupled with the projection of the ego ideal, helps to explain the idealization of the love object by the person. It is important to note that, in contrast to falling in love, mourning involves the transfer of libido from the object into the ego (Bergmann 1980).

Bergmann (1988) considers that Freud's major contributions to the understanding of love were formulated within the topographic frame of reference and, as such, that his ideas on love are analogous to dream theory. That is, the prohibited oedipal longing provides the impetus for love, and the person with whom one falls in love serves in a role akin to the day residue of a dream. The person is generally not aware of the similarities between the new love object and the prohibited one, a situation that attests to the success of a censorship force reminiscent of dream work. When one falls in love, a dreamlike state ensues, with reality testing being temporarily diminished and projection and displacement prominent. As the ego restores its powers, the person moves toward experiencing the real qualities of the love object. Bergmann (1980) observes that the transition from falling in love to evaluating the future of the relationship is a difficult one for most lovers to make.

According to Bergmann (1980, 1988), Freud did not unify his ideas on love into one coherent theory, as he did with dreams and sexuality. Instead, in separate papers he addressed such questions as why one falls in love with a particular person and the metapsychology of love. In "Group Psychology and the Analysis of the Ego" (1921), Freud attributes a central role to the ego ideal both in amorous fascination and in submission to leaders and hypnotists. Freud proposed that "the object serves as a substitute for some unattained ego ideal of our own. We love it on account of the perfections which we have striven to reach for our own ego" (p. 112). In essence, the love object enjoys a certain degree of freedom from criticism and is valued more highly than other objects. The object has been put in the place of the ego ideal.

Freud's ideas on love, and particularly on the importance of the original mother–infant unit, have influenced later psychoanalytic authors.

ATTACHMENT THEORY AND ITS APPLICATION TO ADULT ROMANTIC LOVE

John Bowlby (1958, 1969, 1973, 1980, 1988) concurred with Freud on the importance of the mother–infant bond. However, unlike Freud— who viewed anaclitic attachment in terms of the infant's oral investment in the mother—Bowlby maintained that attachment behavior was primary, and independent of the need for oral gratification. His theory on the primacy of attachment was based on observations of infants and young children who were separated from their mothers for varying periods of time. Because of similarities between human infants and other primate infants, Bowlby also included ethological studies in the development of his theory.

His own observations and those of other researchers led Bowlby to conclude that attachment is the basis of self-confidence, security, and happiness. When an infant is in the presence of mother and secure in this attachment, the infant demonstrates interest in exploring the environment and in establishing contact with others. However, when mother is not available, the infant becomes preoccupied with reestablishing contact with her and interest in other activities is significantly diminished. The infant attempts to regain her attention by various means, including vocalizing, crying, and actively searching for her.

Bowlby (1973) maintained that confidence in the availability of attachment figures, or the lack of it, builds up slowly throughout childhood and adolescence and tends to persist relatively unchanged. In essence, people develop mental models of themselves and their relationship partners that are closely interrelated and likely to proceed in a complementary fashion. These mental models largely determine the nature of a person's feelings and relationship patterns for life.

For Bowlby, all important love relationships, whether between a mother and infant or adult lovers, are attachments. As his often quoted statement implies: "attachment behavior . . . is a characteristic of human nature throughout our lives—from the cradle to the grave" (1988, p. 82). He also describes the connection between attachment and strong emotions as follows: the formation of a bond is falling in love, maintaining a bond is loving someone, and losing a bond is grieving over someone. Additionally, the anticipation of loss arouses anxiety and anger.

Shaver and colleagues (1988), in comparing the features of infant–caregiver attachment with adult romantic love, note significant parallels. They derive facts about attachment from Bowlby and other developmental researchers. Noteworthy among their comparisons are the following: (1) Mothers and infants engage in prolonged eye contact, are fascinated by each other's features, and touch each other. Similarly, lovers gaze into each other's eyes and are excessively preoccupied with the face of the other. They too enjoy frequent touching. (2) Mothers and infants coo at one another and develop their own language, much of it nonverbal. Lovers also develop their own verbal and nonverbal language, and names for one another. (3) Infants share toys and discoveries with the mother, while lovers give gifts and share their experiences with one another. (4) A distressed infant seeks physical contact with mother; a lover wants to be held and comforted by his or her partner in times of stress. (5) When feeling insecure, an infant may be vigilant for cues that the mother approves or disapproves, just as lovers who feel insecure in a relationship are often sensitive to cues of being loved and are dependent on such cues. (6) Last, there is a hierarchy of attachment for both dyads. While the infant can be attached to more than one person at a time, there is usually one key relationship. Adults can also love more than one person, but intense love usually occurs only with one partner at a time.

The separation experiences for persons in both dyads are similar. When an adult love relationship ends, the partners' responses are comparable to separation distress in infants. Bowlby (1979) describes the infant's reactions to maternal separation that begin with protest and resistance to the soothing efforts of others, are followed by the infant's sense of despair and passivity, and end with a defensive detachment in which the infant initially avoids the mother if she returns. At times of separation and loss, adults also experience strong emotions, such as crying, anger, and anxiety.

Ainsworth and her colleagues (1978) applied Bowlby's ideas on attachment and separation to their observations of mother–infant pairs. They concur with Bowlby's point that the mother's attentiveness and sensitivity to her infant's needs are conditions essential for a secure early relationship. Based on their observations, Ainsworth and her associates delineated three types of attachment, referred to as secure, anxious/ ambivalent, and avoidant. The secure infant is confident of the mother's accessibility and responsiveness; such experience has been repeatedly confirmed by contacts with her in different contexts. The anxious/am-bivalent infant is more prone to crying and anxiety on separation from mother. Unlike the secure infant, this child is unable to use mother as a secure base. The avoidant infant mirrors the rejecting behavior of the mother, and detaches from the mother as a means of protection.

Ainsworth and colleagues (1978) do not refer to varying intensi-ties of attachment, but rather to the specific quality of each attachment. Their three-category scheme has been applied to the study of adult ro-mantic love by Hazan and Shaver (1987), who refer to corresponding qualities of adult attachment as secure, anxious/ambivalent, and avoidant, respectively. Hazan and Shaver describe the avoidant lover as jealous and fearful of intimacy. The anxious/ambivalent lover is also jealous, and is obsessed with the availability of the love partner. The secure lover, by contrast, is comfortable with intimacy and not preoc-cupied with abandonment issues.

Hazan and Shaver's styles of romantic attachment bear similari-ties to certain diagnostic groups that represent varying levels of psy-chological development. For instance, their description of avoidant lov-ers is consistent with descriptions of patients who fall into borderline and narcissistic diagnoses, whose approach to love could also be cat-egorized as transitory. Anxious/ambivalent lovers often demonstrate certain masochistic features in their approach to love, such as being repeatedly drawn to unavailable partners. Their relationships are highly dependent and often addictive. Secure lovers have attained a genital level of development, which will be referred to as *mature object love.*

The features of these diagnostic groups, and their characteristic responses to falling in love, passion, and "chemistry," are delineated in more detail below.

ROMANTIC LOVE: DEVELOPMENTAL AND
DIAGNOSTIC CONSIDERATIONS

Idealization is a core feature of romantic love. When a person experiences "love at first sight," the ego functions of judgment and reality testing are temporarily impaired. The person idealizes the love object and is unable to assess the lover's actual qualities for a period of time. How successfully one makes the transition to realistic assessment depends on the developmental level achieved and other considerations. Those who are dealing primarily with issues from the rapprochement subphase (Mahler et al. 1975), for instance, may experience love as a constant cycle of fighting, breaking up, then making up. As the lovers reunite, their desire is to connect on a deeper emotional level than had occurred earlier, and so to undergo a symbolic resolution of the rapprochement crisis. Transitory, avoidant, addictive, and dependent lovers are also attempting to master trauma of preoedipal origin. For those dealing with oedipal issues, the search for a partner involves the perpetual quest for reunion with the lost oedipal object.

Transitory Lovers

Transitory lovers are often described by such colloquial expressions as "picky," "Don Juan," or "Jezebel." The "picky" or avoidant type of transitory lover has difficulty trusting others and rarely allows the experience of intimacy. As the curmudgeons of love, avoidant persons tend to be skeptical about the longevity of romance and find it nearly impossible to meet a suitable partner.

It is important, of course, to distinguish avoidant behavior from the inability to find an appropriate partner. The social and professional advancement of women in recent years has made it difficult for many women to reconcile achievement with romantic needs. McGrath and colleagues (1990) comment that single professional women may be rejected by men because their accomplishments pose a threat to male self-esteem. Indeed, clinical observation supports the perception that some men experience both conscious and unconscious envy of women who have equal professional status. Thus, a man who maintains a traditional view of marital norms may often choose a partner whose status is inferior to his own.

Truly avoidant persons become anxious when others move close, and easily feel smothered in relationships. Fairbairn (1954) describes schizoid individuals as having difficulty expressing love due to the steep anxiety it engenders. For such persons, unconsciously, expressions of love, connection, and intimacy connote the destruction of the other. On a conscious level, the person may offer a variety of reasons for the absence of an intimate relationship. "Love never lasts anyhow," "All the good ones are taken," and "I don't have time for a relationship" are familiar rationalizations.

An example that clearly illustrates the avoidant lover was offered by John Tierney (1995) in the *New York Times Magazine*. In an article entitled "The Big City: Picky, Picky, Picky," Tierney describes a casual dinner with a single male friend in a New York restaurant. During their conversation, all heads turn to admire a stunning, statuesque blonde woman who walks toward a table alone. While Tierney stares admiringly, his friend glances briefly, declaring "your basic blonde." When Tierney protests, his friend insists "she's not even a real blonde, you can see her roots." Several minutes later the woman is joined by her husband, Alec Baldwin. By having dismissed Kim Basinger as flawed and unappealing, Tierney's friend epitomizes the successful and talented cosmopolitan who remains baffled as to why he has not found a potential mate. Tierney attributes his friend's response to the "Flaw-O-Matic," which he humorously describes as "an inner voice, a little whirling device inside the brain that instantly spots a fatal flaw in any potential mate" (p. 22).

As Tierney demonstrates, avoidant lovers have a keen ability to identify flaws that they perceive to be fatal in a relationship and hence avoid investing in the courtship. *Perception* is the operative word, because outer reality is distorted to suit an internal unconscious need to avoid closeness with others. Rather than acknowledge their own avoidance as destructive, avoidant lovers attribute the impairment to others. Consciously, they escape intimacy, and on an unconscious level the equation of love with destructiveness remains unaltered.

Transitory lovers of the Don Juan and Jezebel type, by contrast, have the unconscious goal of seducing and abandoning. Person (1988) asserts that they are driven by a need for power and domination, and are incapable of sustaining a loving relationship. They are skilled at eliciting love but are inconsistent in its reciprocation. Diagnostically, they exhibit borderline and narcissistic features, especially in the quality of their idealization of the love object.

Borderline patients, according to Kernberg (1995), are prone to develop primitive idealizations that are not based on the real qualities of the love object. The unrealistic nature of the idealization often leads to the destruction of the relationship in that it does not tolerate ambivalence or conflict. When they fall in love, borderline personalities tend not to perceive the love object in any real depth, and are readily disappointed. Kernberg also notes that such idealizations can change abruptly, transforming the idealized love object into a persecutory one. Persons with borderline personality organization generally have a history of similarly failed relationships.

An example that illustrates the fragile nature of the borderline patient's idealization is the case of Margaret, an attractive professional woman in her mid-thirties who frequently began sessions with the pronouncement "I'm in love." I found myself thinking "again?" Each new lover was "totally different." "He's the real one, not like those other fakes," she would say, referring to her two ex-husbands, a former live-in boyfriend, and countless dates. Her object relations were often split, with the current boyfriend as the idealized love object and the previous ones as persecutory. She would go on to enumerate the latest lover's attributes, qualities that to me seemed similar to her early perceptions of previous lovers. There was a "magical connection" in the initial meeting that lasted for much longer than expected. But her blissful experience of symbiotic merger was short-lived; with each new partner, minor differences and disagreements were construed as relationship-breaking cruelties. Treatment focused on her need to devalue the previously adored and idealized love object, as well as working toward helping her to identify her own contributions to the self-destructive pattern.

In contrast to borderline patients, who are able to develop an intense attachment of some duration, the involvements of narcissistic patients tend to be shallow and transitory. Kernberg (1995), who has written extensively on the subject, observes that narcissistic patients often search for love objects who are perceived as desirable by other people.

Their idealizations are not of the lover as a total person, but are limited to his or her body surface. Kernberg adds, "Such a body or person stirs up unconscious envy and greed in narcissistic patients, the need to take possession of, and an unconscious tendency to devalue and spoil, that which is envied" (1995, p. 68).

Sexual desirability can create the illusion of falling in love. Once the need for conquest is gratified sexually, however, enthusiasm for the desired object wanes. The person may experience a rapid decline in sexual and personal interest. An unconscious process occurs whereby the previously desired sexual object is devalued. Unconscious greed and envy are projected onto the object, making the narcissistic patient fear exploitation. The narcissist enacts the pathological grandiose self while projecting the devalued part of the self onto the partner. Kernberg explains that this process reinforces the patient's need for "freedom."

Indeed, narcissistic patients can feel stifled by the love object. Kernberg contends that such persons tend to be sexually promiscuous, which can indicate unconscious guilt over the inability to establish a stable, gratifying relationship. Because such a situation would symbolize the fulfillment of an incestuous oedipal relationship, the narcissist instead desires admiration, not love; he or she experiences the partner's expectation of reciprocity as invasive and exploitative.

When the narcissistic personality does fall in love, the idealization of the love object usually centers on physical attractiveness, wealth, or prestige, qualities to be admired and incorporated as part of the self. According to Kernberg, the movement from fixation on body surfaces to the capacity for experiencing concern, guilt, and reparation toward the object is a determining factor in the narcissistic personality's ability to love.

To illustrate, Roger, a 50-year-old divorced male patient with narcissistic traits, routinely placed personal ads in a local newspaper. At first, his ads stated modest requirements for the respondents. Then, after each brief and unsuccessful relationship, he would expand the ad to rule out factors that had led to the demise of the previous relationship. For instance, his request for a woman with "no children at home" proceeded to "no children at home or college," and finally to "no children of any age, or pets."

Roger relished the power of deciding whom, among the fifty or so responses to each ad, he would deem desirable enough to meet. The few select women who "made the cut" were attractive, accomplished, and often elusive. His brief association with them buttressed his sense of self-worth. Once these women were "hooked," Roger found ample reason in each situation to leave. It was generally something or someone who interfered with the degree of attention he received from his partner. Exploration revealed that when these women gave attention to others, whether to their children, pets, or career, Roger experienced it as a cruel withholding of affection and as a reflection of his lack of worth. In an unconscious expression of retaliation, it was Roger who would abruptly withdraw and lose interest. There were "plenty of fish in the sea" and Roger was determined to find one worthy of his interest.

Throughout his childhood, Roger's mother had repeatedly frustrated his longings for physical contact and affection, leaving him with a feeling of rage and despair. As his mother rebuffed him, so too Roger now coldly rejected each partner. Similarly, in treatment, my vacation was unconsciously experienced as a cruel and sadistic act, one that withdrew support when he most needed it. Consciously, he questioned the need for a therapist when his problem was merely finding a compatible partner.

Exploration of the transference at the point when he most wanted to leave revealed that the patient had difficulty acknowledging his attachment to me. I was "selfish," as were the other women in his life. Further exploration led to insight regarding his feeling unimportant and abandoned when his girlfriends attended to the other people and obligations in their lives. Perceived withdrawal of affection was reminiscent of wounds inflicted in childhood by his mother. The patient gradually developed an ability to tolerate the brief lapses of attention from his girlfriend.

Roger's repeated failures in maintaining a relationship and his nagging sense of loneliness provided the impetus for his continuing treatment. With time, he developed a greater ability to experience feelings of concern and love for his most recent girlfriend. He also became more appreciative of her kind and thoughtful manner, attributes that would have gone largely unnoticed in earlier relationships. In short, the patient had advanced from his preoccupation with beauty and devotion to a more mature way of relating to a partner. Roger was developing a capacity to love.

By contrast, in his earlier dating days, Roger relished the conquest of "winning over" an attractive and accomplished woman. Once assured of her devotion, he rapidly lost interest and began pursuing other women. Jessica Benjamin (1988) offers a useful explanatory model for understanding his behavior. Adopting an intersubjective perspective, Benjamin asserts that the individual develops in and through relationships to other subjects. She continues, "The other whom the self meets is also a self, a subject in his or her own right . . . we are able and need to recognize that other subject as different and yet alike, as an other who is capable of sharing similar mental experience" (1988, p. 20).

The need for "mutual recognition," that is, the yearning to recognize as well as be recognized by the other, is key to achieving intimacy. Roger would enter into a relationship with another subject in need both of mutual recognition and connection. When he "wins over" the woman, he feels in control of the relationship and able to determine its destiny. In fact, when Roger wins control of the other, he actually loses. He loses the experience of the woman's subjectivity. Once the other person is objectified, true recognition and connection is no longer possible.

Benjamin's intersubjective perspective complements the existing intrapsychic model proposed by Kernberg (1995) for understanding the narcissist's approach to love. Benjamin (1988) notes that it is essential to grasp both the internal world of the unconscious and the external reality of capacities that emerge in the interactive field between self and others. Describing childhood development, Benjamin explains that the child who experiences others as extensions of him or herself must dread the emptiness and loss of connection that results from their powerful omnipotence. The child can use the other only when she or he perceives it as an external entity in its own right. The object's independent existence must survive the child's fantasy attempts to destroy it.

Likewise, in adult love relationships, when someone "wins over" a partner, as Roger did, the victory is experienced as hollow. The true goal is not to win, but to lose—in the sense of not being able to manipulate and subjugate the person to one's own wishes. Unfortunately, however, narcissistic personalities are often drawn to lovers who need to submit to and adore the other in order to gain access to power. This results in a common pairing, the masochistic-narcissistic couple. Benjamin (1988) notes that it is often the woman in the submissive role who, by virtue of her own surrendering of subjectivity, loses the sense of connection to the other. Benjamin further notes that intimacy and independence are interrelated processes. Intimacy occurs between two persons who can experience a sense of connection without obliterating their differences. True intimacy cannot take place in the masochistic-narcissistic configuration.

Addictive Lovers

The masochist in the masochistic-narcissistic pairing exemplifies the addictive lover, one who is drawn to "challenging," unavailable people. The masochist longs for an idealized partner and often projects those qualities onto partners who are not desirable, and readily falls in love out of a need for attachment and commitment; dependency may masquerade as love. Peele (1988) contends that addicted lovers experience love as accidental and capricious, something that can disappear at any moment and that needs to be cherished whenever present. Their sense of the world is painful, and, as Peele observes, they tend to gravitate to the music of romantic love, which mirrors their pain more than pleasure. One patient, for example, spent hours listening to songs of unrequited love.

Altman (1977) describes the vicissitudes of love, particularly the tendency to transform joy into pain and sorrow. This process is pronounced in the masochistic-type attachment. Glickauf-Hughes and Wells (1995), writing on the masochistic-narcissistic dyad, emphasize the interactional nature of the process. While masochism occurs in both genders, its manifestation in love relationships is often reported by women. The masochistic woman is attracted sexually to an idealized man who initially provides a whirlwind romance, then may reject or abuse her. The exciting object is transformed into a rejecting one with short periods of gratification followed by long periods of yearning.

It is often difficult for the masochist to accept that the previously caring person is now critical and rejecting. The narcissistic partner is perceived to have the necessary narcissistic supplies and the masochist searches for the right thing to do to get the partner to respond favorably, believing that she has some control over the relationship. Glickauf-Hughes and Wells (1995) note that the masochist's belief in the availability of the partner is reinforced by the sporadic attention of the narcissist. Their dynamics interlock, as narcissists have a propensity for projecting unwanted parts of themselves onto others while masochists tend to introject aspects of others that are not part of themselves. In essence, the masochist internalizes the burden of badness that resides in the object. In becoming bad oneself, one purges the object of its badness (Fairbairn 1954).

In their adult love relationships, masochists reexperience the narcissistic injury created in childhood by the parents. Through pleasing and submission, masochists attempt to win the love of an admired, yet critical partner (parent substitute). They seek love relationships where they are nurtured and gratified as a child would be by a parent, not as an adult in equal partnership with another adult. They surrender their power to the partner, but also hold that person responsible for their sense of security. Masochists tend to be caretakers in relationships, treating others as they wish to be treated themselves. Caretaking assures them a sense of interpersonal control and security.

According to Glickauf-Hughes and Wells (1995), masochists are developmentally arrested at the stage "on the way to object constancy" (Mahler et al. 1975). Masochistic character organization is reflective of fixation "at a level of separation-individuation where good self and object representations are differentiated but bad self and object representations are not" (Glickauf-Hughes and Wells 1995, p. 16). Many were raised in chronically unpredictable environments where they were rewarded and punished for the same behavior. Developmental research supports the hypothesis that mothers who were inconsistent in their displays of affection often raised children who were not highly exploratory. These children were preoccupied with issues of abandonment.

As Berliner (1958) postulates, the preoedipal child is loyal to an early love object who also serves as a source of pain and sadism. The child, fearing both the loss of the object and of its love, neglects its own developing sense of self in favor of satisfying the sadistic object. The child introjects the sadism of the love object in an effort to meet the needs of a painful parental figure. As adults, masochists fear being alone and prefer connection to a painfully perceived love object, one who is idealized and adored.

Both Benjamin (1988) and Kernberg (1995) emphasize the masochist's search for a highly idealized yet unattainable partner. Submitting to an idealized figure, although painful, ensures the masochist access to power. Benjamin describes "ideal love" as a form of masochism that is rooted in the female child's relationship to her father. The father serves as a knight in shining armor who provides a means to freedom and self-realization. Benjamin notes that when the girl's identificatory love for her father is thwarted in childhood, it can lead to self-abasement and unattainable yearning in later life.

Victims of domestic violence often report childhood histories of inconsistent and neglectful parenting. Beverly, an unemployed mother in her early thirties, would repeatedly return home after violent arguments with her husband. Although he had a predictable pattern of abusive behavior, she insisted each time that he did not mean to hurt her. Beverly was dependent on him emotionally and financially, and did not feel "complete" unless by his side. Following the pattern of her unhappy childhood, she was particularly attuned to his unmet needs. He hurt others, she convinced herself, because he was so brutally neglected as a child. Both she and her husband were raised in families where the fathers were alcoholics.

Despite their faults, Beverly idealized both her father and her husband. She fondly recalled her father accompanying her on the first day of school, while dismissing his frequent fights with her depressed mother. Similarly, with her husband she emphasized the early days of the courtship when he often brought her flowers. Essentially, she internalized the early aspects of the relationship, and now feels that the abuse she endures is the necessary condition for receiving his love. The "chemistry" she experienced initially with her husband reflects her desperate need for affection and connection, things that were sorely lacking in her childhood.

Beverly and other masochistic patients are capable of an in-depth relationship, but it is generally of a painful nature. In treatment, such patients tend to be predisposed toward feeling unrequited love in the transference. Their need to suffer provides the impetus for the formation of the erotic transference. Glickauf-Hughes and Wells (1995) suggest that the therapist needs to tolerate and to help the patient work through sexual feelings within the analytic frame of treatment; that is, the "as-is" nature of the transference provides the vehicle through which the patient can address these feelings and develop a capacity for mature object relations.

Mature Object Love

Individuals capable of mature object love, in contrast to transitory and addictive-type lovers, are secure in their attachments to others. Branden (1988) enumerates the characteristics of such persons in successful romantic relationships: they express their love affectionately, verbally, sexually, and materially; they are comfortable with mutual dependency and are not preoccupied with abandonment issues; and they are not afraid to get close to others. Essentially, in mature love relationships, one is capable of maintaining feelings of intimacy, passion, and commitment (Sternberg 1986, 1988).

Successful couples tend to idealize their partners, but the idealization occurs in the context of an integrated, whole-object relationship, with the corresponding capacity for experiencing concern, guilt, and reparative trends. In a way distinct from narcissistic attachments, in which the object is idealized but rapidly devalued, and from masochistic attachments, in which one idealizes the object at one's own expense, the mature person idealizes the body as well as the total person and value system of the love object (Kernberg 1974, 1995). These are the couples who report feeling close to one another, both affectionately and sexually, and who believe that they could not be happier with anyone except their partner.

In a mature love relationship, feelings of tenderness and concern reflect the integration of love and aggression, with love as the dominant affect. The capacity for tenderness, coupled with mature idealization and passion, constitutes an advanced developmental level of functioning. Bergmann (1980) maintains that love is fueled by symbiotic longing, but can be realized without fear only when the separation-individuation subphases have been successfully negotiated and there is an established sense of identity with intact ego boundaries. He suggests that three interrelated factors need to be present in a happy love relationship:

1. Simultaneous refinding of the early love object on a number of levels of development.
2. Improvement on the old object by finding what one has never had in childhood.
3. A certain amount of mirroring of the self in the beloved. Those who suffer from self-hatred will shun partners who remind them of themselves, or aspects of themselves, and therefore will not tolerate the mirroring that is part of any happy love (Bergmann 1980, p. 75).

The integration of these elements represents not just a repetition of the past, but rather a new integrative achievement of the ego.

When refinding the object, there is also an activation of past pathogenic internalized object relationships in the partner. Through mutual projective identification, each partner is inducted into the role of a past figure or figures, with the hope that the partner will respond reparatively and differently than had occurred in the past. Kernberg (1974, 1995) notes that couples can experience conflict between the conscious wishes for the relationship and the unconscious activation of past internalized object relationships, with the result that they may establish a compromise formation between these needs. Person (1988) optimistically emphasizes the transformative nature of love relationships in mastering past traumas.

Refinding of the object also involves the unconscious search for the oedipal object of desire. While the object must not consciously arouse guilt, it does provide the feeling of attainment of forbidden, unachieved childhood wishes. Passion is an essential component of mature love and involves the overcoming of oedipal inhibition. Persons functioning on a neurotic level of development have the capacity to fall in love and maintain a stable relationship, but there is often a degree of inhibition of genital sexuality. Such patients are unable to combine sexual and tender feelings for their partners; they may experience premature ejaculation or frigidity with their spouse, but be able to perform successfully with a partner outside the marriage (Kernberg 1995).

In the context of mature object love, passion implies intimacy and shared rebellion against social convention. Kernberg (1988) notes that the social group maintains a latency-age mentality toward sexuality and that there is ongoing opposition between the group and relationship of the couple. The happy couple defies the envy and resentment of the excluded others. In fact, couples who maintain the elements of danger, secrecy, and transgression, key organizers in the oedipal constellation, also maintain the mystery and illusion necessary in passion.

Kernberg (1995) also postulates that the mature couple acquires a superego system of their own making, in addition to their respective individual ones. As observed by Chasseguet-Smirgel (1985), the ego-ideal aspects of the superego, when projected onto the love object, can serve to enhance self-esteem. Love of an idealized object and its reciprocation enhance the couple's ability to link idealization with sexual intimacy and to establish a deep, mature relationship.

The question often arises as to whether passion is a lasting or fleeting emotion. Passion, the state of intense longing for a love object, needs to be distinguished from sexual promiscuity, in which sexual objects are interchangeable. In passion, possession is never complete. Teasing, withholding, and separation help to maintain it, while familiarity, predictability, and repetition serve to undermine its fragile state. Viederman (1988) emphasizes the paradoxical nature of passion, noting that even with its intense intimacy, all is not revealed. He believes that passion involves elusiveness, impenetrability, and illusion. Contact and confrontation support reality and can undo the illusion.

Benjamin (1988) describes erotic union as the ultimate expression of mutual recognition. The attunement of the lovers' bodies and minds is so complete that they momentarily lose boundaries without the loss of self. At the height of orgasm, self and other are fused and the ego is capable of tolerating a brief extinction of self. Both Bak (1973) and Kernberg (1995) remind us that the French expression for orgasm is *la petite mort*—meaning "little death."

Mature loving couples derive pleasure and gratification from the orgasm of the other partner. Each is able to identify vicariously with the ecstasy of the other, and so to experience two types of fusion. Kernberg (1995) attributes this ability to the psychological bisexuality that occurs in both genders. There is a sense of experiencing both genders simultaneously, of briefly overcoming the barriers that separate the genders. Erotic desire involves both transgression and aggression, because the latter occurs in the service of love. In mature object love, couples possess the capacity to fall in love and are able to establish a gratifying sexual relationship with concomitant expressions of intimacy and idealization. Their ongoing private rebellion against the conventions of the established social group serves to reinforce their bond and fuel their passion.

CONCLUSION

People in the throes of romantic love may not be able to tell whether it is based on reality, illusion, or the more likely combination of the two. If partners feel competent, lovable, and deserving of happiness, they are more likely to choose mates who support their self-concept. Then the experience of love at first sight and chemistry will be based on intuition, not pathology. Paradoxically, as we try to analyze love to its component parts, we must be careful that we don't lose the qualities that make it unique. In short, our therapeutic task is to help romantic love maintain its mystery.

REFERENCES

Ainsworth, M., Blehar, M., Waters, E., and Wall, S. (1978). *Patterns of Attachment: A Psychological Study of the Strange Situation.* New York: Wiley.

Altman, L. (1977). Some vicissitudes of love. *Journal of the American Psychoanalytic Association* 25:35–52.

Bak, R. (1973). Being in love and object loss. *International Journal of Psycho-Analysis* 54:1–8.

Benjamin, J. (1988). *The Bonds of Love: Psychoanalysis, Feminism, and the Problem of Domination.* New York: Pantheon.

Bergmann, M. (1980). On the intrapsychic function of falling in love. *Psychoanalytic Quarterly* 49:56–77.

——— (1988). Freud's three theories of love in the light of late developments. *Journal of the American Psychoanalytic Association* 36:653–672.

Berliner, B. (1958). The role of object relations in moral masochism. *Psychoanalytic Quarterly* 27:38–56.

Bowlby, J. (1958). The nature of the child's tie to his mother. *International Journal of Psycho-Analysis* 39:350–373.

———— (1969). *Attachment and Loss: Volume I: Attachment.* New York: Basic Books.

———— (1973). *Attachment and Loss: Volume II: Separation.* New York: Basic Books.

———— (1979). *The Making and Breaking of Affectional Bonds.* London: Tavistock.

———— (1980). *Attachment and Loss: Volume III: Loss.* New York: Basic Books.

———— (1988). *A Secure Base.* New York: Basic Books.

Branden, N. (1988). A vision of romantic love. In *The Psychology of Love*, ed. R. Sternberg and M. Barnes, pp. 218–231. New Haven, CT: Yale University Press.

Chasseguet-Smirgel, J. (1985). *The Ego Ideal.* New York: Norton.

Fairbairn, W. R. D. (1954). *An Object Relations Theory of the Personality.* New York: Basic Books.

Freud, S. (1905). Three essays on the theory of sexuality. *Standard Edition* 7:125–245.

———— (1912). On the universal tendency to debasement in the sphere of love (Contribution to the psychology of love, II). *Standard Edition* 11:177–190.

———— (1914). On narcissism. *Standard Edition* 14:69–102.

———— (1915). Instincts and their vicissitudes. *Standard Edition* 14:109–140.

———— (1921). Group psychology and the analysis of the ego. *Standard Edition* 18:69–143.

Glickauf-Hughes, C., and Wells, M. (1995). *Treatment of the Masochistic Personality: An Interactional-Object Relations Approach to Psychotherapy.* Northvale, NJ: Jason Aronson.

Hazan, C., and Shaver, P. (1987). Romantic love conceptualized as an attachment process. *Journal of Personality and Social Psychology* 52:511–524.

Kernberg, O. (1974). Mature love: prerequisites and characteristics. *Journal of the American Psychoanalytic Association* 22:743–768.

———— (1988). Between conventionality and aggression: the boundaries of passion. In *Passionate Attachments: Thinking about Love*, ed. W. Gaylin and E. Person, pp. 63–83. New York: Free Press.

———— (1995). *Love Relations: Normality and Pathology.* New Haven, CT: Yale University Press.

Mahler, M., Pine, F., and Bergman, A. (1975). *The Psychological Birth of the Human Infant.* New York: Basic Books.

McGrath, E., Keita, G., Strickland, B., and Russo, N. (1990). *Women and Depression: Risk Factors and Treatment Issues.* Washington, DC: American Psychological Association.

Peele, S. (1988). Fools for love: the romantic ideal, psychological theory, and addictive love. In *The Psychology of Love*, ed. R. Sternberg and M. Barnes, pp. 159–188. New Haven, CT: Yale University Press.

Person, E. (1988). *Dreams of Love and Fateful Encounters: The Power of Romantic Passion.* New York: Penguin.

Shaver, P., Hazan, C., and Bradshaw, D. (1988). Love as attachment: the integration of three behavioral systems. In *The Psychology of Love*, ed. R. Sternberg and M. Barnes, pp. 68–99. New Haven, CT: Yale University Press.

Sternberg, R. (1986). A triangular theory of love. *Psychological Review* 97:119–135.

——— (1988). Triangulating love. In *The Psychology of Love*, ed. R. Sternberg and M. Barnes, pp. 119–138. New Haven, CT: Yale University Press.

Tierney, J. (1995). The big city: picky, picky, picky. *New York Times Magazine*, February 12, section 6, p. 22.

Viederman, M. (1988). The nature of passionate love. In *Passionate Attachments: Thinking about Love*, ed. W. Gaylin and E. Person, pp. 1–14. New York: Free Press.

2

Clinical Practice with Intercultural Couples

JOAN MASELL SONCINI

INTRODUCTION

In the United States we have seen a shift from "like marrying like," that is, marriage among people of similar race, religion, and cultural background, to increased numbers of interracial, interfaith, and intercultural marriages. This chapter will focus on intercultural couples, defined simply as couples whose partners are from different countries and, therefore, from different cultural backgrounds. Intercultural couples who seek couples therapy in this country generally have issues that concern the decision whether to marry; painful and confusing conflicts based on some combination of cultural, intrapsychic, and/or interpersonal issues; the disharmony created by different cultural values regarding, for example, child-rearing techniques, religion, gender roles, and appropriate behaviors; and boundary issues with in-laws or the extended family.

Americans increasingly pursue opportunities to study, work, and travel abroad. Our civil rights movement and legislation in the 1960s legalized marriage between different races and cultures. As reported in the U.S. Census Bureau's August 1996 report, the foreign-born population has reached its highest level since World War II. The topic of a growing debate, U.S. immigration laws have permitted increased numbers of foreigners to permanently enter the country (Holmes 1995). People clearly have more opportunities to meet each other and fall in love.

However, when backgrounds are different, whether on racial, religious, and/or cultural grounds, adjustment and compromise are particularly problematic and conflictual, according to many respected authors (Barron 1972, Cretser and Leon 1984, Gordon 1964, Ho 1984, McGoldrick and Preto 1984, Romano 1988, Tseng et al. 1977).

Let us take a couple, Miguel and his fiancée, Helen, and look in on their first session in premarital couples therapy. As background, Miguel was a doctor in his native Mexico. Helen, a midwesterner, met Miguel in Monterrey, Mexico, where Helen had spent the summer studying Spanish before returning to her last year of college. Now living in the United States, Miguel drives a cab while he struggles painfully to improve his English in order to pass the qualifying examination to practice medicine in this country. As the initial excitement of falling in love in Mexico had somewhat waned, the couple became aware of their numerous differences, not to mention the fact that both sets of parents expressed deep concerns and, at times, even prohibitions about the marriage.

As the couple arrives for the first session, the therapist notes the following heated exchange:

> *Miguel* (to Helen): "What? You think that's right? *Es absurdo. No tienes razon*! Listen to me. Put on my glasses and you'll *see* that I'm right and you're absolutely wrong!"
>
> *Helen*: Miguel, *you* just don't see. Why don't *you* put on *my* glasses and you'll see that I'm right!"

The couple is in crisis due to rising disagreement, conflicting views of reality, and fears that their decision to marry may be a mistake. Miguel, as often happens with intercultural couples, agreed to explore couples therapy only under duress, barely hiding his disdain of the process. He explained that in his native Mexico, psychotherapy was only for crazy people, "*locos.*" He didn't see the sense in talking with a total stranger. However, hoping to work things out with Helen, he would comply with her ultimatum: therapy or no marriage.

Their original comments had to do with the precipitating factor that forced them to face their differences. Helen had changed since her return to the United States with Miguel, who had never been to this country. She had become more critical, more sure of her rights and gender roles (supported by the surrounding culture). Recently, when Miguel became incensed about their diet, complaining that he missed Mexican food, Helen had exploded, complaining to him about what she termed his "male, macho chauvinism," and threatened to break their engagement.

Miguel and Helen are not sure whether to marry or not. Their initial session indicated several areas of conflict. Unlike couples from the same cultural background, these two see life through very different lenses. A major point that I emphasize is that *having diverse interpretations of reality is normal for intercultural couples, for their perceptions are born and developed in different cultural settings.* Thus, when conflicts arise, the couple should not be surprised. On the contrary, they need to be prepared to anticipate and to talk over their differences, especially in the early years of adjustment to their relationship. Falicov (1986) refers to this period as the "cultural transition phase" and states that the couple's developmental task is to "arrive at an adaptive and flexible view of their cultural similarities and differences," including a balance of individuated values, a capacity to negotiate conflicts, and the creation of a "new cultural code," one that integrates parts of both cultural heritages (p. 448).

In this chapter, I wish to help clarify the issues of intercultural couples, their needs in seeking therapy, and some special considerations in treating them in therapy. Hsu (1977) points to the need to enhance knowledge, skills, and techniques for therapists working with intercultural couples:

> In general, it is widely accepted that difficulties are more likely
> to occur in intermarriages and that it takes more effort to make

an intermarriage work. In spite of such information, however, little guidance has been given to partners in intercultural marriages and very few suggestions are available for the mental health professionals who are apt to be summoned to help when difficulties arise. [p. 121]

INTERMARRIAGE, ON THE RISE: GOOD OR BAD?

With the increased number of intermarriages, also known as exogamous or out-marriages (more unfriendly terms), there have been many changes both in the way people perceive and treat these married couples and in the research and literature on the subject. American views have swayed back and forth, preferring either a "melting pot" of cultures or respecting differences. Some see intermarriage as deviant, a threat and a danger to retaining cultural identity, or, in contrast, as exciting, enviable, enriching society, evidence of reduced prejudice and bias, and so on.

An Exercise in Cultural Identity

In intercultural couples therapy there are three (perhaps four, if there is a co-therapist) people in the room, and this means the presence of at least two, if not three or four different cultural backgrounds. Before attempting to treat these couples, the therapist needs to explore his or her own cultural identity and views on intermarriage. Clearly, this is part of a larger topic: countertransference. But, for the moment, please think about how you personally would answer the following questions: Are you yourself in an intermarriage, with differences of race, culture, class, and/or religion? How about your parents, friends, and siblings? What are the first words that come to mind when you see a biracial, interfaith, or intercultural couple? Finally, have you ever treated an intercultural couple in couples therapy, and have you noticed any differences between therapy with intercultural versus monocultural couples?

In the process of answering these questions, I hope to have teased your curiosity and awareness about your own thoughts and feelings about marriage between two people of different backgrounds. Can you imagine, to give an example, treating a Chinese man married to an American woman, when the latter, in a fit of rage, denounces her husband for not only paying extensive attention but also financial support to his family of origin? Would you, if you are also American and/or also female, be moved to side with the wife? Or could you begin to explore with the couple the cultural significance of family, the role of the Chinese son, and the presence or absence of underlying, unconscious meaning for the wife, perhaps of feeling uncared for or unloved, perhaps reenacting her feelings of playing second fiddle to her siblings or a parent when she was young?

How would you react to Miguel, introduced above, who ridicules his American fiancée for failing to carefully prepare meals for him? Of course, it would be easier to listen to him, to empathically try to understand him, if he did not raise his voice. Working with intercultural couples demands a special coolness, a neutrality, and a capacity to contain anxiety rather than acting it out. This is far easier to attain if we anticipate the challenge and always ask ourselves: "Is this a problem created by cultural differences, by interpersonal or intrapsychic problems, or by a combination of both?" "What am *I* feeling?" and, finally, "What is each person and/or the couple dyad putting into me or getting me to do?"

Benefits and Contributions of Intercultural Marriage

Among the advantages one may observe among people who intermarry is that they frequently tend to prepare more thoroughly for their marriage than other couples, in response to unsolicited advice and opposition from friends and family: sort of a "We'll show them!" attitude. Following this preparation, the couple may become more self-reliant, determined, and committed to make it work.

During one of the interviews for my doctoral dissertation on this subject, one husband, interculturally married, eloquently expressed a positive view of his intercultural marriage:

Being married to someone of another culture has given me an opportunity to grow, to see my own capacity and flexibility in trying to understand another person's cultural values, beliefs, and customs. I daily have to deal with and to respect my wife's differentness. From this, I have a broader opportunity for learning and growth. And, of course, it's never boring! [S. Ahmad, personal communication, February 12, 1995]

The preceding statement reflects how this successful intercultural marriage offers a greater degree of self–other differentiation than may be found in a monocultural marriage; differentness may aid in clarifying boundaries, something helpful for any marriage.

UNDERSTANDING SOME SPECIAL ISSUES OF INTERCULTURAL MARRIAGE

Motives for Choosing a Mate: Healthy versus Not So Healthy

Motives for marriage range from the positive ones of personal growth and expansion—for example, when one seeks an exotic and exciting spouse, enhancing one's sense of specialness or uniqueness—to unconscious defensive motives, such as emancipation from and rebellion against one's childhood background and family who are perhaps viewed as deficient, overcontrolling, prejudiced, or intrusive.

Paris and Guzder (1989) attribute the higher risk of divorce in exogamous marriages to the power of unconscious reasons for marrying and to unconscious dynamics within the couple. Expanding on this discussion, Cottrell (1990) points out that a couples therapist working with intercultural couples needs to thoroughly explore and determine the couple's primary motivations for marriage, as this is essential in understanding the underlying foundations of the marriage, and in helping assess the couple's strengths, not only for adjusting to cultural differences and working through conflicts, but also for participating in the process of therapy.

Phases of Intercultural Marriage

All marriages pass through several stages of adjustment to a comfortable level of intimacy, from development of the self as an individual and a partner to development of the couple as a dyad with tolerance for frustration and conflict. However, particularly in the case of the intercultural marriage, couples have additional tasks, including an initial realization and acceptance of their cultural differences, and gaining an understanding of and working through them on the way to making necessary adjustments.

Before marrying, couples tend to focus on their romantic differences and similarities, often denying any unpleasant differences. They are like a "wonderful international cocktail," made up of the best ingredients of traditions, customs, art, holidays, cooking, language, music, and friends (Romano 1988, p. 16). How long this lasts depends upon the magnitude of the couple's differences. These may, paradoxically, have attracted them to each other initially, yet may later come to represent a source of tension and conflict. When the couple comes face to face with upsetting differences, they may experience what object relations theorists call "the return of the repressed," namely, aspects about the spouse that they previously have ignored or denied (Frank 1989).

Resolution may be attained by fighting, postponing, denying problems, distancing, or—on a more positive note—confronting differences and then seeking solutions or compromises that work for both partners.

Typical Areas of Conflict

The following complex collage of issues is meant to give the reader a sense of how culture influences one's beliefs and values. When one choses a person of another culture as a partner, the potential for misunderstanding and disagreement rises greatly and, therefore, the couple will be best off if they can anticipate and understand this reality is *normal*—and so will the couple's therapist. Subsequent evaluation will determine the extent to which the couple's specific issues are more serious.

Tseng and colleagues (1977) observe that couples may experience very trivial differences, such as deciding who is responsible for taking out the garbage, how to celebrate a birthday, or how to properly entertain, as major ones, or, on the other hand, the differences may indeed be major, such as questions regarding gender roles and status, religion, ownership of property, and child-rearing practices.

Major issues

External issues are created by environmental confirmation or hostility, pressures that either hold and support the couple or leave them with a sense of social isolation, marginality, and alienation (Bizman 1987, Cottrell 1990, Cretser and Leon 1984, Hutter 1990, Markoff 1977). Likewise, the environmental response affects how foreign-born partners negotiate the process of acculturation.

Internal issues generally emanate from incompatible worldviews, defined by Ibrahim and Schroeder (1990) as

> the beliefs, values, and assumptions that mediate communication, relationships, modes of problem-solving, decision-making, and the lifestyle of the client. Worldviews are culturally based variables, that tend to be *implicit* [italics added], and to some extent we believe *unconscious.* . . . [They are] influenced by ethnicity, culture, religious or spiritual beliefs, language and semantics, educational level, social class, age, lifestage, lifestyle preferences, and gender. [p. 194]

Two dangers I wish to emphasize originate in the tendency of couples to *minimize* or *maximize cultural differences*. In the former instance, the couple may *deny* any cultural differences, due to their determination to show the world that their issues are not cultural, particularly when family and friends have objected to the marriage on those grounds (Falicov 1986, Romano 1988). In the latter case, the couple *blames* the easily visible cultural differences for everything that goes wrong, at times using this as a defense against looking at more serious underlying issues.

Couples often rigidly adhere to an ethnocentric belief that "my way is the only way to be," as seen in the initial dialogue between Miguel and Helen. Different worldviews often support misunderstanding of intentions and the meaning of behavior, as, for example, when one partner perceives as a rejection the respectful restraint seen in the behavior of an Asian spouse, or as a threat of violence the passionate excitement of a Hispanic spouse.

Crohn (1995) defines six areas that have particular power to create cultural conflict, and notes that each member of an intercultural couple enters the marriage with a mixture of attitudes, composed of a first, a middle, and a least-valued form:

1. Time: the value of punctuality; a present, past, or future orientation; rushing to make every minute count versus a more relaxed attitude about time;
2. The nature of the universe: trust in the inherent goodness of man and destiny versus a distrust of others and pessimism;
3. Cohesiveness of the family: belief in and valuing cooperation and interdependence versus independence of the individual;
4. Emotional expressiveness: expressing versus holding in one's emotions, particularly anger;
5. Interpersonal relations: a hierarchical society, such as Japan, respects age, authority and tradition as most important; a cooperative or collective society, such as Mexico and Italy, focuses on the needs of the group before those of the individual; and an individualistic society, such as the United States, places the individual, his needs, his independence as primary;
6. Gender roles: last, but certainly not least, is the major issue of different perspectives on gender roles. U.S. couples are adjusting to the evolving and changing nature of gender relations. What happens when you combine an American woman with, say, a Japanese man; an American man with an Indian woman? [Crohn 1995, pp. 78–102]

Let us observe an "East–West" couple from Hawaii: Koko, a Polynesian, and John, a Caucasian. For Koko, the family comes first, whereas for John, it is the individual and his or her needs. John chose Koko because he fell in love with her and she with him. But her family was shocked and displeased with her choice, which was perceived as a rebellion. As a traditional family, they expected Koko to agree to a prearranged marriage, thus respecting the supremacy of the extended family *within which* the new couple would have a specific and well-structured place (Markoff 1977). In addition, John considers Koko to be in an enmeshed relationship with her family, whereas Koko feels that John doesn't care much about his family, as he rarely visits them. John tells his wife she should be more independent and have her own ideas and values about various aspects of life; Koko is surprised by how much John differs from his own parents' lifestyle. When and if they have children, this dynamic may create strife between the spouses over how much to promote dependence or independence in their children.

In the United States there has been growing attention to the way men and women differ in communicating styles. If monocultural couples suffer from such communication problems as are discussed in *Men Are from Mars, Women Are from Venus* (Gray 1992) and *You Just Don't Understand* (Tannen 1990), imagine adding to this equation *different* cultural backgrounds, native languages, personalities, levels of education, and life experiences. Language itself can be highly ambiguous, especially in nonverbal communications, as observed in gestures, postures, style, physical proximity, and touch that often have distinct meanings in different cultures.

Emotional expressiveness also differs from culture to culture. There can be quite a contrast between, for example, a more formal and controlled Englishman versus a Hispanic, who is used to speaking out loudly, even angrily. McGoldrick and colleagues (1982) explain that

> couples often react to each other as though the other's behavior were a personal attack rather than just a difference rooted in ethnicity. Typically, we tolerate differences when we are not under stress. In fact, we find them appealing. However, when stress is added to a system, our tolerance for difference diminishes. We become frustrated if we are not understood in ways that fit our wishes and expectations. [pp. 21–22]

Perel (1995) notes that certain life-cycle events, especially additions (the birth of a child, weddings) and subtractions (divorce, retirement, death), are often stressful and conflictual. These issues necessitate renegotiation of previous agreements, often in a surprisingly emotional environment. Cultures vary as to the norms of how to bring up children. A collectivist society may encourage dependency on the family and community, whereas an individualist society supports autonomy and sharpened ego boundaries (Mann and Waldron 1977).

Stereotyping is a particularly onerous problem, even within the intercultural couple. "You're Asian, so of course you think that way; just like your parents!" "You're French and that's why you never do/always do . . ." Stereotyping disregards individuality, and it tends to be prejudicial. Hand in hand with stereotyping is its pernicious relative, ethnocentrism. When this negative stance exists within the intercultural couple, the scene is set for disaster. Conversely, openness to explore and understand the worldview of a spouse from another cultural background allows for enhanced understanding and harmony.

Minor issues

Tesler-Gadow (1992) observed conflicts around food and eating habits, friendship patterns, the use and treatment of money, cleanliness, decorating, recreation, holidays, and pace of life and work. Romano (1988) adds to this list issues including place of residence, politics, in-laws, social class, modes of dealing with stress, and response to illness and suffering. I have a theory, humorous and seemingly superficial: ask an intercultural couple what and how they eat, and you will learn a lot about how well they function together. As an example, I asked my hairdresser, a New York Jew, what his Filipino wife and he generally eat. He smiled and responded: "Well, you know, we mostly eat Filipino or Asian food, as my wife really prefers it and, as for me, I like it tremendously and really don't care that much to eat American food. She's also the one to have left her country, so I figure it's important for her to feel a tie to her culture" (R. Stuart, personal communication, January 20, 1996).

Listening to his response, I am not surprised that their marriage has endured so happily for almost eighteen years. Eating habits vary from culture to culture: frozen dinners versus handmade pasta; Japanese ritual tea ceremonies versus a hot dog on the run in Central Park; dinner at six p.m. or at ten or eleven—and so on.

The issue of acculturation to a new country generally has an impact on the couple at one time or another. Here, several factors are prominent: language proficiency, whether the move was voluntary or involuntary, and whether the individuals can continue to live as they lived before in their country of origin with regard to profession, education, and socioeconomic level.

It is of particular importance here to recognize that going to a doctor or a psychotherapist is a culturally influenced decision. Although it is accepted as increasingly normal in some cultures, others view as shameful the need to resort to professional help, rather than depending, first and foremost, on oneself, one's family, a spiritualist, a faith healer, or God. In many cultures, such as Miguel's, only "crazy people" go for psychotherapy or counseling.

How Do Intercultural Couples Adjust to Differences and Resolve Conflict?

Attitude seems to be the key to success in couples work, and it is something that can be observed on a continuum: on the healthier side are empathy, flexibility, and tolerance, in contrast to the less healthy side of rigid ethnocentricity, as in "my way is the right way."

Tseng and colleagues (1977), Ho (1984), and Romano (1988) explore the issues of intercultural couples from the more optimistic perspective of adjustment rather than from a focus on problems. Solutions to cultural differences reflect very different dynamics and results. One method, which Tseng and colleagues refer to as "*One-way adjustment*," is a solution in which one partner basically gives up his or her culture in favor of the other's. Used to avoid conflict, it has drawbacks, in particular the denial of one partner's cultural identity or of any cultural differences at all.

A second solution consists of compromise and agreement; accepting culturally bound beliefs, values, and customs; allowing room for negotiation; building enhanced understanding founded upon respect for differentness, which is not seen as disloyalty; and having an awareness of individual needs and values. Romano (1988) calls this the "ideal intercultural marriage model" (p. 124).

Ho (1984), Tseng and colleagues (1977), and Romano (1988) list several ingredients for successful adjustment and conflict resolution: an ability to tolerate confusion and anger, to hear the other's views, and to be flexible and open to change; a general liking and respect for the other's culture; a sense of humor; and, last but certainly not least, the support of families and friends.

ISSUES THAT BRING INTERCULTURAL COUPLES INTO THERAPY BASED ON THEIR TYPICAL PROBLEM AREAS

Premarital Therapy

Hsu (1977) identifies areas of particular sensitivity that need to be addressed when couples come in for premarital therapy, in particular the opposing or conflictual worldviews of the couple. He encourages the therapist to take an active role in alerting these couples about the inevitability of experiencing cultural conflict as a normal situation.

McGoldrick and Preto (1984) use premarital therapy to offer techniques to help maintain contact with the partners' respective families, especially when one or both are oppositional; to explore gender and marital roles, the meaning of "family," and expectations about how a husband and wife fit into the extended family; and to expand knowledge, fascination, and respect for the cultural backgrounds and rituals of each partner, enhancing acceptance of difference.

Child-Rearing Concerns

The arrival of the first child often brings a resurgence of old conflicts over culture, both because of pressures from in-laws and from the spouses themselves. People often encounter their own early childhood experiences upon anticipating parenthood. As these are quite different experiences in the intercultural couple, they may create a strong, unexpected emotional environment.

Couples who seek therapy regarding this issue realize a need for help either before the child is born or when the child starts to ask questions, perhaps at age 6 when he or she goes to school. Depending upon the mix of the parents the questions may be: Who am I? Am I American, or French, or South African? Am I white, black, Jewish, Muslim, or Catholic? (Perel 1995).

Parents are now forced to make decisions concerning, for example, religion, holidays, how to achieve desired behaviors in children, and so on. Perel (1995) also wisely points out that parental harmony and agreement on these questions are the keys to their children's well-being. McGoldrick and Preto (1984) additionally emphasize the importance of integrating the two cultures, something that is supported by the couple's maintaining open access to their two families of origin. Thus, the couple can model for their children a pride and respect for their cultural roots.

SPECIAL TECHNIQUES AND CONSIDERATIONS IN INTERCULTURAL COUPLES THERAPY

Beginning Sessions—Some Basic Background Information

This section offers some observations about working with intercultural couples in therapy, with some cautions about the beginning sessions. Ho (1990), an experienced intermarriage therapist, wisely warns: "If [the therapists] are not adequately aware or sensitive to the complex dynamics of the multiracial or multiethnic system, therapists may unknowingly drive away their clients after the initial session" (p. 47).

The intercultural couple's therapist must realize that one spouse may be far more comfortable with therapy than the other. This knowledge will help guide the therapist's understanding and support his or her ability to deal with different levels of anxiety in the initial sessions and, in addition, encourage the therapist to take the time to explain how therapy works.

When an intercultural couple enters therapy, both the therapist's and the couple's ethnicity, race, class, culture, and gender will be highly visible and identifiable as similar or different. These differences mean that particular attention must be paid by the therapist to maintaining an objective stance and demonstrating his or her desire to remain neutral to the couple during the initial sessions, particularly to avoid being accused of being prejudiced against or allied with one of the partners.

Returning to the issue of worldviews, Ibrahim and Schroeder (1990) explain how they determine what is perceived as healthy or unhealthy. When working with an intercultural couple this becomes particularly complicated, for in the therapeutic triad there will be two or three worldviews (that of the therapist and the two partners), in addition to other complicating factors such as sex, personality, and life experience. It is important to understand not only our own value systems, but also those of both clients, paying close attention to exploring their worldviews as *individuals*, rather than incorrectly categorizing or stereotyping them according to ethnicity, race, religion, or class.

The therapist's own worldview may lead him or her to greatly disagree on many issues, and often in doing so to reflect the reality of one of the spouses. Within the sessions, enhancing the partners' understanding and respect for each other is a prelude to exploring various alternatives or compromises, and to expanding horizons beyond any one particular cultural stance.

Cultures vary greatly in their ideas about the relationship between clients and therapists. Unlike more egalitarian cultures, traditional societies tend to respect authority, with the result that the therapist will be expected to be wise, to know the answers, and to give advice to be followed obediently by the client.

Some men may feel uncomfortable expressing personal problems to a woman therapist, expecting wisdom and authority only from a male counselor. Other men may not wish to discuss private marital matters in public or with any outsider. A man may feel shame about both his needs and his inability to handle his wife and their problems.

When the therapist encounters a patient whose worldview conflicts with his or her own, the scene is set for strong emotions, countertransference reactions, and acting out. Rendering this scene more complex is the presence of the other partner, who may share a world view that is similar to the therapist's.

To give an example, when making a case presentation to a group of professional psychotherapists, I described an interaction between an intercultural couple. One of my colleagues responded both angrily and adamantly: "But you have to tell the husband he can't do that! Tell him he's in America now, and his behavior is outrageous here!" I was quite surprised and taken aback by her vehemence and responded innocently, holding in my anger: "But if I told him that, he would leave therapy and never come back. Besides, I feel that it's important to explore how his culture supports his behavior, and then to work through to an understanding and a new way of responding to his wife." On reflection, I saw that my colleague's reaction represented my own split-off (to maintain neutrality), negative feelings when dealing with this foreign-born spouse.

PHASES OF THERAPY WITH
INTERCULTURAL COUPLES

Engaging the Couple

Therapy with intercultural couples shares similarities basic to any couples therapy: the need to form a therapeutic relationship, first individually and then with the couple as a whole, and the need to build understanding, confidence, and trust in the ability of the therapist (and the therapeutic process) to help the couple. However, there are some special considerations. With intercultural couples, there is often a clear disparity between the partners, as one member (usually the foreign-born partner) may be skeptical, nervous, shameful, negative, or even antagonistic to the idea of therapy, *depending upon his or her culture's level of comfort and experience with the idea of seeking psychotherapy!* The therapist must show an ability to leave his or her own cultural framework and to be open to explore and learn the cultural background of each spouse, seeking an understanding of each partner as an individual, rather than as a stereotyped member of a cultural group.

Caution is needed to avoid triangulation, or the perception of the therapist colluding with one spouse (especially with the spouse who shares the same gender or culture), to create a common front against the other partner. Triangulation may result from the therapist's countertransference reactions to an uncomfortable or even oppositional spouse, perhaps one who may be feeling extremely uncomfortable with the process of therapy.

Identifying and Defining the Problems

In addition to the typical assessment process in couples therapy, based on intrapsychic and interpersonal issues, it is also essential to identify cultural components or differences.

Falicov (1986) found that those intercultural couples who experienced distress in their marriage often had an unbalanced view of their cultural similarities and differences. Such couples either *minimize* or *maximize* cultural differences, often as an unconscious defense.

Thus, the intercultural couples therapist learns to listen with a "special ear" in order to distinguish between cultural and interpersonal or intrapsychic issues while continuing to assess other problems or issues. I hypothesize the following continuum (Figure 3–1), *with most problems deriving from somewhere in the middle—that is, from several sources:*

Figure 3–1.

Source of Problems Continuum

All culturally derived . . . . . . All interpersonal/intrapsychically derived

---

Developing therapeutic goals takes time, as we explore together, and gradually tease out and define those problems and issues that undermine happiness and understanding. To elaborate on this important concept, *a culturally derived issue*, for example, might take into account the situational stress of acculturation. Toward the middle of the continuum lie *interpersonal couples issues*, with cultural conflicts in the foreground or the background, depending upon how the couple views (maximizes or minimizes) cultural differences. In this middle ground, the therapist begins by questioning whether differences in the couple's cultural background and worldviews create conflict, in particular regarding issues of gender roles, power, child-rearing, communication, and intimacy. Moving over toward the right side of the continuum, the therapist explores *interpersonal conflicts*, especially the defensive reenactment of previous object-relations conflicts within the present family. Finally, of course, *intrapsychic personality traits* influence the extent to which an individual can successfully be part of a couple dyad, and therefore must be included in assessing the couple.

Ho (1990) reminds us to keep in mind the context surrounding the couple: culture, family, individual, and environment, all of which influence the partners. For example, being an interracial or intercultural couple is far easier in Hawaii than in a small Southern town not used to, fearful of, or openly hostile to such diversity.

The Intervention Phase

It should be noted that different cultures are accustomed to employing quite different strategies to resolve conflict. For example, contrast a

British American's belief in self-sufficiency with his Asian wife's expectation that a person of authority (the therapist) is expected to give advice and guidelines to be followed. Observing what works and does not work in the culture of each of the spouses, and modeling respect for learning and understanding, the therapist can offer new ideas and ways of observing reality, while still supporting each individual's style or approach to tackling problems.

Intercultural couples therapy combines traditional couples-therapy techniques, *whether they are systemic or psychoanalytic object relations*, with special attention and sensitivity to understanding ethnocultural backgrounds, as well as psychoeducational techniques. Special components emphasize (1) helping the couple to clarify and respect their similarities and differences of values, expectations, and standards within the marriage by enhancing each partner's curiosity, interest, and respect for the other partner's way of understanding or viewing reality; (2) reducing rigid ethnocentrism; (3) teaching improved cross-cultural communication strategies; (4) viewing cultural conflict as a *normal* phenomenon, rather than proof of pathology or lack of caring; and (5) working with the couple to create a safer space in which they can explore ways to resolve disagreement by mutual compromise.

The Ending Phase

Both evaluation and termination in intercultural couples therapy have a cultural component, insofar as the newfound understandings and adaptations must be *culturally owned* by the couple. For example, Ho (1990), generalizing, shows how endings are idiosyncratic: the Irish *tend* to end abruptly, avoiding praise; British Americans *may* end abruptly when the "business" is done; a Jewish spouse *may* end unwillingly, complaining, yet maintaining newfound understanding and growth; a person of collectivist culture, attempting not to burden the therapist, *may* terminate prematurely, and so on.

Goals for intercultural couples therapy can be divided into three levels: *intermediate goals*, which contribute to a climate for continued therapy and help to furnish the basic needs in situational stress; *instrumental goals*, which aid in achieving the ultimate outcome; and *ultimate goals*, which directly deal with the couple's primary motives for seeking therapy, such as the relationship itself, child-rearing practices, in-law relationships, and related issues (Ho 1990).

In therapy, progress in improving relations, learning new ways of dealing with and resolving conflict, and gaining empathy must be attained in ways that are culturally acceptable for each individual. One example, among many, is the client from a collectivist culture, with a strong "present orientation," who may not want to recall the painful past or look forward to the future, but who will seek active advice from the therapist, whom the client views as an authority.

CONCLUDING REMARKS

"There are many roads to Rome." In intercultural couples therapy, the therapist's flexibility and openness to learning and respecting how each member of the couple understands reality models the essential ingredient and technique for marital success for the partners themselves. In a recent example of my practicing flexibility, I followed the advice of Ho (1990) and treated an African-born wife individually when her husband's negative cultural view of psychotherapy precluded his continuing therapy. It was a difficult choice for me, as the couple's issues seemed the focus and, therefore, couples therapy was the treatment of choice. Happily, the wife made progress toward an enhanced sense of her own capacity and power, which she then applied to improving the couple's understanding and harmony.

Conducting intercultural couples therapy, and meeting the need both to maintain neutrality and control for biases and countertransference reactions, is hard work for the therapist. Nevertheless, it is also challenging and tremendously fascinating.

REFERENCES

Barron, M., ed. (1972). *The Blending American: Patterns of Intermarriage.* Chicago: Quadrangle.

Bizman, A. (1987). Perceived causes and compatibility of interethnic marriage: an attributional analysis. *International Journal of Intercultural Relations* 11(4):387–399.

Cottrell, A. (1990). Cross-national marriages: a review of the literature. *Journal of Comparative Family* 21(1):151–168.

Cretser, G., and Leon, J., eds. (1984). *Intermarriage in the United States.* New York: Haworth.

Crohn, J. (1995). *Mixed Matches: How to Create Successful Interracial, Interethnic, and Interfaith Relationships.* New York: Faucett Columbine.

Falicov, C. J. (1986). Cross-cultural marriages. In *Clinical Handbook of Marital Therapy,* ed. N. S. Jacobson and A. S. Gurman, pp. 429–451. New York: Guilford.

Frank, J. (1989). Who are you and what have you done with my wife? In *Foundations of Object Relations Family Therapy,* ed. J. Scharff, pp. 175–186. Northvale, NJ: Jason Aronson.

Gordon, A. (1964). *Intermarriage: Interfaith, Interracial, Interethnic.* Boston: Beacon.

Gray, J. (1992). *Men Are from Mars, Women Are from Venus.* New York: HarperCollins.

Ho, M. K. (1984). *Building a Successful Intermarriage between Religions, Social Classes, Ethnic Groups or Races.* St. Meinrad, IA: St. Meinrad Archabbey.

———— (1990). *Intermarried Couples in Therapy.* Springfield, IL: Charles C Thomas.

Holmes, S. A. (1995). Surprising rise in immigration stirs up debate. *New York Times,* August 30, pp. A1, A15.

Hsu, J. (1977). Counseling for intercultural marriage. In *Adjustment in Intercultural Marriage,* ed. W. S. Tseng, J. McDermott, and T. Maretzki, pp. 121–131. Honolulu: University of Hawaii Press.

Hutter, M. (1990). Introduction to cross-national marriages. *Journal of Comparative Family Studies* 21(2):143–150.

Ibrahim, F. A., and Schroeder, D. G. (1990). Cross-cultural couples counseling: a developmental, psychoeducational intervention. *Journal of Comparative Family Studies* 21(2):193–205.

Mann, E., and Waldron, J. (1977). Intercultural marriage and child rearing. In *Adjustment in Intercultural Marriage,* ed. W. S. Tseng, J. McDermott, and T. Maretzki, pp. 62–81. Honolulu: University of Hawaii Press.

Markoff, R. (1977). Intercultural marriage: problem areas. In *Adjustment in Intercultural Marriage,* ed. W. S. Tseng, J. McDermott, and T. Maretzki, pp. 51–62. Honolulu: University of Hawaii Press.

McGoldrick, M., Pearce, J., and Giordano, J. (1982). *Ethnicity and Family Therapy.* New York: Guilford.

McGoldrick, M., and Preto, N. G. (1984). Ethnic intermarriage: implications for therapy. *Family Process* 23(3):347–364.

Paris, J., and Guzder, J. (1989). The poisoned nest: dynamic aspects of exogamous marriage. *Journal of the American Academy of Psychoanalysis* 17(3):493–500.

Perel, E. (1995). *Intermarried couples.* Paper presented at the meeting of the Family Therapy Network Symposium, Washington, DC, March.

Romano, D. (1988). *Intercultural Marriage: Promises and Pitfalls.* Yarmouth, ME: Intercultural Press.

Tannen, D. (1990). *You Just Don't Understand: Women and Men in Conversation.* New York: Ballantine.

Tesler-Gadow, B. (1992). *Intercultural communication competence in intercultural marriages.* Unpublished doctoral disseration. University of Minnesota. Minneapolis, MN.

Tseng, W., McDermott, J., and Maretzki, T., eds. (1977). *Adjustment in Intercultural Marriage.* Honolulu: University of Hawaii Press.

3

When Fathers Take Care of Their Children

LYNNE RUBIN

"Some time ago at AT&T," writes David Whyte (1994), "I found myself working with a roomful of particularly thoughtful managers. We were looking at the way human beings find it necessary to sacrifice their own sacred desires and personal visions on the altar of work and success. One manager, a woman, wrote the following lines: 'Ten years ago . . . I turned my face for a moment and it became my life . . . ' (Whyte 1994, p. 231)."

These few words of poetic astonishment followed one employee through years of professional choices. Not long ago, her gender would have been likely to evoke, at the least, tangential attention: *male* and *management* were paired—nearly equated—in corporate life. But these twenty years have marked stunning changes in how, where, and by whom business is performed, and some of this evolution has prompted major changes in work and family life. Indeed, every effort to define a family, parent, or caregiver enlists intelligent defenders. And as for work—by law, if not by tradition—men may now take parental leave. Gender-neutral "family leave" is now regulated by legislation, not corporate conscience. Just as work versus family has been a tortured choice for many women, so many young fathers are now wondering whether they will regret having turned their energy away from their families for professional gain.

Life is changing both at home and at work for working parents. This chapter will consider how certain of these changes have made room for the expression of the unique and unexpected caregiving skills that men possess, and suggest why it has been so hard for fathers and babies to develop an unselfconscious way of being with one another, and how the traditional workplace interferes with the possibilities of caregiving fatherhood. It will trace the psychological development and normal, expectable struggles of men, and consider ways that physiology and society conspire to make fatherhood a hard role to define. Finally, it will describe the experience of ten employed men who took several weeks of parental leave to be caregivers for their small babies.

INTRODUCTION

"Radical differences of soul and nature" once substantiated the vast institutionalized differences between the sexes. Laqueur (1990) describes gender views two centuries ago:

> The uterus and the ovaries which defined the woman consecrated her maternal function and made of her a creature in every way the opposite of her companion. . . . Men and women evolved in two distinct worlds and scarcely encountered each other—except during reproduction. Strong in her generative power, the woman reigned as mistress of her home, presided over the education of her children, and incontestably embodied the moral law that determined good manners. To the man was allotted the rest of the world. He was in charge of production, creation, and politics, and so the public sphere was his natural element. [cited in Badinter 1995, p. 7]

Two hundred years later, gender issues are different but tensions between men and women are still marked, and biology—fundamental genetic differences—is still blamed for strained relationships between men and women. Since the beginning of the twentieth century, women have been demanding the right to vote, to divorce, to be educated, and to be outspoken and political—demanding, that is, access to prerogatives and power once granted solely to men.

The need for physical strength in order to farm, to hunt, to fight, and to protect the family and govern their children had given men indisputable value. Then men's work moved from farm to city, and they worked and traveled away from home. With the change, *women* were assumed to have the superior child-rearing sensibility. Home and children became mother's responsibility and father's value was equated with job and income; father maintained strong prerogatives and economic clout despite his often scarce physical presence (Griswold 1993). Escalating divorce, diminishing family bonds, and increasing numbers of women functioning in formerly male roles caused President Theodore Roosevelt to warn that the American race was "committing suicide." He founded the Boy Scouts to counter the coddling of boys by their mothers and ". . . turn male children into manly men" (Filene 1974, quoted in Badinter 1995, p. 24).

Through two World Wars, women excelled in factory and frontline work. Nevertheless, this seemed insufficient evidence that many gender-based assumptions about a woman's physical limitations were ill-supported. When soldiers returned to reclaim their places, many women retired from "men's work." Advantaged postwar American families in a boom economy shaped what to this day we call "traditional" roles: good mothers stayed home to raise the children, good fathers paid the bills.

But the world was too much changed to halt its altered spin, and by the mid-1950s women were "only" housewives in barely half of American families. By 1990, about half of the mothers of children under the age of 1 were in the labor force. Among employed mothers with preschool children, close to 70 percent held full-time jobs (Gerson 1993).

Even with women strongly represented in the workforce, female anatomy was considered evidence of obvious, perhaps singular, caregiving superiority. Mother could work as many hours as father, but father was still imagined to be comparatively extraneous to the emotional development of his small children. As a result, fathers were virtually ignored in early infant-development research: the earliest fatherhood research was conducted by questioning mothers about fathers

(Pedersen 1985). Further, these presumptions about biological barriers to male parenting ignored the fact that a significant minority of the world's fathers *do* actively participate in intimate caregiving.

Before 1970, little was written concerning the child's need for "fathering." Then, in one of the earliest psychoanalytic references to the boy's specific need for a father, Loewald (1951) wrote: "Against the threat of maternal engulfment the paternal position is not another threat of danger, but a support of powerful force" (p. 14). It had been assumed that father was fungible, interchangeable with other helpers. Then in 1971 Abelin confirmed that an infant could recognize its father *specifically* during symbiosis, which generally occurs between the second and third months of life. Yogman and colleagues (1976) had demonstrated that infants only three to five months old were able to discriminate between their parents, and to respond to them differentially.

Herzog's (1980) study of little boys with sleep disorders, all of whom had recently lost fathers through divorce or separation, was strongly suggestive that a little boy needs his father both physically and emotionally. Father helped him to formulate a sense of himself, to complete his separation and individuation, to form a core gender identity, and to modulate his libidinal and aggressive drives. *Father hunger* became Herzog's term for the "state that exists when these needs are not being met" (p. 222).

To this day, even as women work in huge numbers in what were formerly "male" professions, there is a persistent if at times covert conviction that fathers cannot responsibly attend to a child. David Popenoe, associate dean of social studies at Rutgers University, substantiates this view by stating that women's voices are more soothing; that women are better able to read a child's signals before he or she can talk. Popenoe (1993) told *Time Magazine* that "Parenting of young infants is not a natural activity for males" (p. 45).

This notion ignores findings from the last twenty years of infant observation that consistently demonstrate that fathers are, for example, "able to feed their newborns as effectively as mothers, handling the small, irritating problems and disruptions of daily feeding with skill and empathy" (Parke and Sawin 1980, p. 367). Parke and Sawin found that a father's sensitivity and response to an infant's sneeze, spit-up, or cough while feeding was just as marked as mother's; that the amount of milk consumed by the infant is almost identical with fathers as with mothers; and that the play style of primary caregiving fathers is similar to the play style of primary caregiving mothers, although fathers smile at babies less (p. 366).

But some feared the effects of adding attentive adults other than mother to the child's intimate world. Bowlby (1958) had warned that to interfere with the child's natural tendency to "attach to his mother was to run the risk of abnormal development" (p. 358). This was an informed and important warning that applied to hospitalized and institutionalized babies and toddlers who indeed longed for consistent and familiar caregivers. But it fit too well with the presumption that there was a hierarchy of relationships, one that needed mother at the sole start for optimal development. It also implied that mother was intrinsically the indispensible caregiver.

Over the years, it has become increasingly difficult to maintain the idea that a father is inconsequential in his baby's early weeks. Brazelton (1987) and others demonstrated that infants imitate adults, including persons other than mother. Brazelton and others strongly supported a father's presence in his baby's life. Research by Schaffer and Emerson (1964) and later Kotelchuck (1972) observed that young children formed relationships with other-than-mother with very positive results. Lamb (1981) and Yogman (1982) showed that babies, apparently oblivious to the gender of the caregiver, "attach" to those who significantly invest in their care. They found that while babies most typically prefer mother in the first year, they include other familiar loving figures. They found that a baby's primary attachments change over time, as determined by its age and sex, and psychological, physical, and biological needs (Badinter 1995, Lamb 1981, and Yogman 1982). They determined that fathers were more positive than neutral additions: Spelke and colleagues (1973) found that, "[infants] whose fathers had greater caregiving involvement with them at home experienced less separation protest than those whose fathers had minimal caretaking involvement . . ." (p. 86).

In 1956, in a paper presented to the Chicago Institute for Psychoanalysis called "Cultural Forces, Motherliness and Fatherliness,"

Josselyn issued a plea for a less demeaning role for fathers. She observed that while "motherliness" is an expected and acceptable developmental role, "fatherliness" is neither. One comfortable way to differentiate males and females has been to admit few shared characteristics. In this way, "female" traits rule out "masculinity." For many, the expression of tender love in a male—even toward one's own infant—is demeaning evidence of repressed femininity, and further, "tenderness, gentleness, [and] the capacity to empathize with others" are not seen as *human* characteristics, but rather are restricted to normative females (p. 269). A father with an aptitude for the kind of intimate nurturance that includes changing diapers and doing a baby's laundry is seen as less of a man. Many men *and* women are discomforted by men spontaneously doing those things with young children that women have done to an admiring audience since childhood: speaking a special language, in a special voice, with a special expression, at a special distance, to a baby they love.

Fathers are expected in childbirth classes and the delivery itself, and have found themselves immensely drawn to and engrossed in their newborns—but they were often prompted to repress and suppress outward indications of their responsiveness. That is, they ignored or denied their spontaneous *engrossment* in their fascinating infants (Greenberg and Morris 1974). In fact, quite soon after the birth—in part because they did not comfortably speak in the familiar female language of infant-love, in part because of tradition and division of family turf— men were discounted as potentially reliable and intuitive caregivers. Early dismissed as disinterested, inept, careless, or even laughable in the nursery, many new fathers default to the remembered, distant father of their own childhood.

Freud had very early ascribed great importance to the father–child relationship (Machlinger 1981), and later (1930) wrote, in "Civilization and Its Discontents," that he " . . . could not point to any need in childhood so strong as that for a father's protection" (p. 59). Similarly, in 1951 Loewald wrote: "[The] creation of the father-gods is an expression of the need for help and protection from the father . . . " (p. 15). With belated but convincing data like Loewald's "Ego and Reality" (1951), Mahler and Gosliner (1955), Benedek's "Fatherhood and

Providing" (1959), Burlingham's "Preoedipal Infant–Father Relationship" (1973), and Abelin's attention to the father's role in differentiation and individuation (1971, 1975), the specific and crucial role of the father began to develop a literature and be recognized as a given of its own. When the women's movement of the 1960s and the economic realities that followed put middle-class families in search of trustworthy, affordable child care, fathers were more likely to be offered a share in the job.

GENDER IDENTITY

If fathers are allowed the broader caregiving prerogatives that many researchers—and mothers—are now supporting, how will the children fare? Will a nurturing father dilute the masculinity of his son and encourage "maleness" in his daughter? Some families are comfortable with parenting where gender boundaries are not closely guarded, but "regular" families still worry. According to David Lynn (1962) they have no cause for concern. Lynn's research reveals that a father's greater nurturance plus high participation in child care increase "masculine" traits in his son from preschool to college age (p. 166).

Lamb (1987) and Biller and Borstelman (1967) found that when fathers and sons have an amiable relationship, the boy will more likely emulate his father and the sex-role standards of the culture. This was the case regardless of the father's "masculine" interests and preferences. Biller and Borstelman (1967) found that fathers of preschool boys who set limits facilitate the boy's masculine development only if there is "an already established affectionate relationship" (p. 274). Further, father's nurturance more than father's punitiveness "appears to facilitate masculine development." When they measured fathers' sexual anxiety, it was *negatively* correlated with the amount of time a father spent caring for his infant (p. 273). Indoctrination into sex roles seems to begin at birth.

Copying, imitating, and identifying are early tasks of the infant, and some people fear that the "maternal" qualities of a caregiving father will hinder the little boy in his functioning beyond the nursery. Indeed, it appears that both sexes have buried at their core the early ministrations—the life-giving, protecting, feeding, comforting imago—

of both parents. If this internalized caregiver is only mother, it is likely that her qualities will be deeply ingrained in her children. But there is room for multiple styles of being satisfied and entertained, and it would seem that only more security can come from two willing caregivers. Ross (1974) suggests that it is the *activity* of both caregivers that has enduring attraction for children:

> Above all, the boy appears to strive to be active like his parents, first the mother and then the father. . . . In this respect, the mother generally appears more powerful and effective; an identification with her no doubt persists throughout life, buried beneath the superstructure, as it were, of subsequent identity formation. Whatever the implications for the current controversy over "male" and "female" social roles, the hypothesis [is] that the maternal image is at the unconscious core of the boy's and the man's identity. [p. 36]

Gender-specific behavior is not as clearly defined for children as many adults would find comfortable. Irene Fast (1978) suggests that in the early processes of identification a young child excludes neither male nor female characteristics in forging a personal identity. Until around the second half of the second year, a child does not identify him- or herself or others as singularly male or female. Kubie (1974) proposes that the child's unconscious drive is not to relinquish his or her gender, but rather to supplement and complement it: to have both—all the admirable qualities of each loved and feared parent.

Childbearing is typically viewed by both boys and girls as a powerful *activity* and an enviable achievement—no matter that it is biologically destined to be mother's feat. The boy may well assume that his anatomy is universal and that mother, too, has a penis. He wants to be like mother and have a baby with her, to share one with her, and in time to give her one. He identifies with his active mother whose very power deeply influences his early wish to be like her, and to bear children as she may (Van Leeuwen 1966). He is the passive counterpart to his mother, hoping she will give him a baby to love as he has felt loved.

Although I refer here to the relevant and consistent "male" in a little boy's life as "father," brothers, grandfathers, uncles, teachers, and other men whose presence is significant in countless ways also become part of the child's composite definition of maleness. It seems unnecessary for that male to be present in an intact family or at home most evenings; perhaps his very scarcity gives each exchange a deeper value. Similarly, the term *parents* is not intended as a legal definition. What is considered here is the impact of those responsible adults whose investment the child feels and who are connected to him in relevant, affect-laden ways.

In the earliest months, mother and caregiver function as a synchronous unit. It is not mother's gender that determines her usual synchrony with the infant: when father is the primary caregiver, the infant and he are similarly attuned (Pruett 1987). Over time, the infant looks out from the early dyad; he or she detects differences between his parents. By the "practicing subphase" of the separation-individuation phase (Mahler 1966), the toddler is able to turn away from the primary caregiver for the other's uniqueness.

In the years when the child is between 1 and 2½, the father can greatly assist in the interrelated processes of individuation and consolidation of core gender identity. Abelin (1980) understood the child's energetic turn toward father at this time as an effort to leave mother's orbit: father's involved presence invites the child to eschew the comforts of regression and the tempting reengulfment of the rapprochement subphase.

By the end of his second year the boy clearly recognizes the countless differences between mother and himself. But how can he leave the intrinsic familiarity of her smell, her touch, her knowledge of him without another safe and accepting place to be? If he has a father who has been familiar from his early days, who knows him in countless ways through countless behaviors together, and who welcomes his growth, he grows toward an *other* with its many compensations: then, separation from mother means expanding his sense of the world as a place populated with others who will love and relinquish him when need be. Throughout his growth, the little boy is assessing his prerogatives and absorbing societal expectations. The risks of being one sex or the other, the rewards of identifying with qualities of each parent, and the possibilities of having it "all" are enacted in games, plans, and fantasies.

Freud (1940) explained the child's "cloacal" theory of birth as ema-
nating from anal urges and from the boy's belief that both sexes possess a penis. It was logical to imagine that babies were born through
the anus, and that boys, too, could therefore have the babies if they
wanted. The boy may imagine his feces to be babies and he may re-
tain them in fulfillment of his fantasy. He may assume that excretion
is akin to childbirth, and in these similarities he is allowing himself
the prerogative of delivering children, too.

In time, his love and admiration for father brings the little boy to
images of coupling with him: these are images that in an adult would
appear to be homosexual fantasies replete with feminine identifications.
But often they are more complex, and now, as this little boy is picturing
love in the only ways he can, he imagines taking mother's place in order to be loved by father. His view of himself still bears remnants of
his easy identification with her.

He is fascinated with bodies of both sexes, but as the boy reveals
his wish to bear a baby, he must also increasingly acknowledge that to
do so would require relinquishing his own intact body, his specific genitalia (Kestenberg 1956, Ross 1977, Van Leeuwen 1966).

Burgeoning phallic narcissism encourages the boy to tend to the
task of consolidating a valued male body image. He "adopts other masculine behaviors and attitudes, as we see significant evidence of the boy's
taking on father as an ego ideal" in order to further move into the positive oedipal phase (Tyson 1982, p. 182). "[He], too, wants to be intrusive, erect, angular, mobile, and of course, phallic" (Ross 1977, p. 335).
In the normative paradigm, the little boy—manifestly accepting that he
is unable to be female without serious consequences to his body and
his expected roles—becomes reconciled to and appreciative of his penis. Phallic pride, aims, anxieties, and aggressiveness substitute for his
early overinclusion of acceptable sexual behavior. Increasingly, the little
boy wants to be loved by mother for his "male" qualities, to relinquish
genderless dependency in return for her devotion (Tyson 1982, p. 182).

To fully appreciate the normalcy of the little boy's maternal yearn-
ings, it is helpful to understand that not all of the little boy's wish to
have a baby is the aggressive, competitive completion of a life lived in
early envy. There is the very important issue of mastery. The child has

experienced gratification and also withholding at the hands of his mother. Now, in the reversal of a passive experience, he is eager to have the opportunity himself. He wants to take care of his needs, to feed himself, and, in identification with his mother, he wants to care for himself and his *own* baby. He can identify with her activities without continuing to identify with her gender. He has lost mother as a complete caregiver, and now he wishes to replace her in his own life and in the life of another. Therefore, his ego ideal may well include the ability to nurture another as he was nurtured—likely with traces of both parents. In certain respects, the identification with mother's activities demonstrates that disidentification may never be complete, just as total obliteration of this identification is not a necessary component of "health."

The boy incorporates important features of father, including more astute perceptions of father's specific procreative role and ability, in order to "assimilate" and become like him. He is quite accurate in his observation of gender differences and he focuses hard on the sexual interaction between his parents. Now his love and admiration are spiced with the envy and jealousy of a lover ignored. The weight of his hostility makes him fear retribution from the father he also deeply loves. He cannot rage at the man he needs, fears, and loves; one solution is to become like him—at the expense of his previous ambivalent sexual self. His identity has been increasingly connected to his gender; if it relies too strongly on this equation, any threat to his masculinity will threaten the dissolution of his self in its most fundamental form. The threat is dissolution of his identifiable self and must be, therefore, fierce.

Loewald (1951) made an important distinction between the positive nonhostile relationship of son to father and the later oedipal rivalry. He understood the loving identification with father to be entirely masculine, a resistance against maternal engulfment and the backward spiral that would call for him to trade his maleness for the familiarity of his early mother. Blos (1974) traced the little boy's love for his father from its origin in the dyadic stage of his object relations to its "repressed, more or less unaltered, state until adolescence" (p. 56). Blos describes the early father–son relationship not as a time of combat, aggression, competition, and fear, but rather one with room for love, admiration, and encouragement. Indeed, Freud (1914) described the paternal imago as one "which, as a rule, is no longer remembered . . . [but] none is more important for a youth or a man than that of his father. . . . A little boy is bound to love and admire his father, who seems to him the most powerful, the kindest and the wisest creature in the world" (p. 243).

In the most opportune resolution of the oedipal struggle, the boy puts the goal of a self-loving ego ideal above the fear of an archaic and tyrannical critic (Ross 1979). Similarly, Jacobson (1950) considered the resolution of the Oedipus to be more the result of loving one's father than fearing him. Jacobson saw the little boy's realization that he cannot bear children as a blow for which phallic identification and pride were comforting compensation. And indeed, the preoedipal boy—no less than his sisters—will cuddle, love, cradle, and disdain his transitional object in a fine imitation of the parenting he has seen and experienced.

A school-age boy has sexual interests, but they are manifestly focused on a range of activities and people that increasingly excludes his parents. Reaction formations disguise his old maternal inclinations: he replaces preoedipal and oedipal wishes to have or be a baby with the familiar activities of a little boy who is "disgusted" with babies and with little girls. Now many little boys, having abandoned conscious and unconscious wishes to bear a baby, become interested in animals and in multiple and extensive collections that require careful nurturing. The boy may wholeheartedly depreciate those females he had so recently befriended: teasing and disparaging help maintain a distance from his early procreative, "feminine" goals (Pruett 1991). The competence that accrues from the rewarding and successful activities of academics, sports, interest in the natural world, and his increasing physical strength help him fashion a self-perception socially appropriate to his gender. He becomes a worker and player; he is identified with his talents and physicality.

When the young boy enters puberty, his imaginings become more sexually explicit; boys find comfort in the proximity and potential restraint of a "good-enough" father. It is a developmental paradox that the violence of the boy's adolescent revolt against father is in proportion to his earliest—now repressed—deeply felt paternal attachment. Prepubescent father love becomes the catalyst for adolescent combat. There seems no safe place at home: unacceptable incestuous impulses push the adolescent boy right back to the narcissistic cathexes of prepuberty: he becomes what Pruett (1985) calls a "young dude" (p. 435). The slovenly, oppositional, teenaged anal-phase tendencies operate in tandem with the active, phallic, maternal imago whose procreativity and power were at once threatening and awesome. It is a tumultuous time in which fierce conflictual identifications are tried and denied access to consciousness, until at last the adolescent can make a safe commitment to the outer world of adult men.

The young man who emerges from this crucible of identifications, disidentifications, and physical growth has traits he cherishes and traits he abhors or denies. Typically, those traits from important men in his life are socially more acceptable. He builds on them, displays them, and chooses work, attitudes, and pleasures commensurate with them. Often, the culture requires that entrenched "female" identifications estrange him from his ideal self. If the awe and envy of women have not been resolved in new generative plans in his life, if mother's "abandonment" of him for father and for the adult world have left too raw a memory, if he is acceptable to men he honors only on condition that he reveal no traces of his mother's love, he may fill his adult life with choices that are primarily valued for their apparent *difference* from typically female choices.

If father has been distant or absent through work or war or divorce or personal style, the little boy can only imagine his part in the abandonment, and add fantasies to the realities of the loss in his estimation of himself.

The boy may choose to stay in mother's domain because leaving her would revive the experience or fantasies of abandonment, and remind him that he may be abandoned by her, too. Lacking a father's presence, he and mother may mother each other. He may suffer from his unchecked libidinal access to her with inhibitions or excesses. He may become a man who learns to protect himself from ever again being the exclusive province of a woman, even (or especially) one whom he loves. He may dread the intimacy that permits reengulfment, entrapment, and the consequent loss of all that is different and specifically male. The strength of his distancing may be proportionate to his submerged wish to return to the mother he loved, now tempered by his fear of the castrating consequences. The real and imagined reasons for a father's absence, as well as the boy's age and developmental phase at the time, are all relevant in determining his understanding of his and his mother's loss.

The need to disparage women, the need to hurt and abandon, or to love and marry but with subtle distance, are all deeply influenced by the boy's freedom and ability to love his father, and to love and leave his mother. The resolution of this complex task will in turn greatly influence his intimacy with his own children. If his father (or other important men in his life) is a loving, actively nurturing parent, the little boy can considerably relinquish his entrenched maternal identifications and still maintain his ability to love generously as a male.

WORK AND FATHERS

Most fathers equate being nurtured with being mothered, and they learned quite young to consciously disparage that role. But in the work world, nurturing can be offered by managers, mentors, and supervisors. In this form it can be received well by adult men; the wish to be fathered does not end at the end of adolescence. Indeed, managers and supervisors who take an interest in a man's work, and who mentor and encourage without fear of being replaced by their grown-up charges, can fill the hunger for a loving father. Just as an adult has an opportunity to repair or relive nurturing relationships in important and different ways as a parent, so does the opportunity recur when one has a "boss" or is one.

Men are now legally entitled to unpaid parenting leave. But while the legal roadblock to paternity leave has been lifted, day care still generally begins when legislated maternity leave ends, because most fathers are reluctant to take the parental leave due to them. It is significant that James Levine (1991), director of The Fatherhood Project, testified before a select Senate subcommittee that "the number of men reporting a significant conflict between work and family life has increased sixfold, from 12 percent in 1977 to 72 percent in 1989" (Levine 1991, p. 4). Why then don't more fathers take leave? Few men trust that the workplace will respect their professional dedication if they request a child-care leave. In fact, management does often observe that an employee with no ostensible interest in caregiving is pouring his energy into the workplace, and in turn is more of a "worker" than a father—perhaps even more of a man.

Gender-neutral leave is usually offered within a baby's first year. While this allows parents to keep babies out of day care longer, few families can afford consecutive leave for two parents. Where the corporate culture is genuinely supportive—often because management personnel have young working wives and babies themselves—more men take the chance. "Family friendly" companies like Johnson & Johnson, IBM, Aetna, Levi-Strauss, AT&T, and Eastman Kodak offered unpaid parental leave for many years before President Clinton signed the Family and Medical Leave Act in 1993. Where companies disseminated the leave-taking literature, made paperwork easier, treated the benefit as working-time off—not a subversive vacation—men took leaves in greater numbers. At Eastman Kodak, considered to be one of the most family-centered large corporations (Catalyst 1986), 7 percent of men (compared with 93 percent of women) had taken family leave in the prior six years. At less-responsive companies, days off for a newborn were usually labeled sick leave or vacation (Pleck 1993).

At one time, fatherhood was quantifiable: a failed father was one who couldn't financially support the needs and valid aspirations of his family. Now, many men are pressed to be part-time caregivers and only fractional financial providers. In return for sharing the financial support of his family with a working wife, a man often loses decision-making prerogatives. In turn, today's family is often forced to overcome its dated, gender-based distribution of child-care expectations.

THE CHILDREN

The realization that one has failed at fatherhood elicits for many men the most shameful remorse (Lansky 1992). Even so, men who *wish* to intimately father their children are more common than the number of men who act to do so. Are the losses only for the father (Gunsberg 1982)? Radin (1976) and Lamb (1981) have found that children with highly involved fathers are cognitively more developed and higher achieving academically; they have more empathy, they are less inclined to hold stereotypic gender beliefs, they are better adjusted socially, and they feel more control over their lives.

Kyle Pruett followed the development of youngsters whose fathers were primary caregivers for several years of their young children's lives. Pruett (1983) suggests that the fine growth of children whose fathers are significantly involved in their caregiving is in part the result of both parents doing what gives them pleasure—parenting and working—and in part due to the opportunity for the child to have the input of two interested parenting adults. A little boy who is raised by one parent receives only one view of himself. Two involved parents offer alternative views that may moderate an estimation that is too high or too low.

At the four-year mark, Pruett's (1983) young subjects were neither cognitively nor emotionally compromised. They were secure in their gender identity and very flexible in their conception of what constitutes maternal as opposed to paternal activity. Their fantasies were organized around the caregiving father who was a procreative and nurturing force like the mother in the traditional family. They were more curious about and interested in their fathers' role in procreation.

A little boy whose distant father does not satisfy his need for male companionship may be left to wonder why he is not more lovable. He loses the opportunity to learn firsthand about his half of the world. If his experience with mother was ego-enhancing, his loss may be less wounding. If it has been significantly deficient, the two lacks may be insurmountable. If the first important man in his life rejected him, he may well duplicate in an active form what he experienced in his helplessness: he may not know how to accept love and return it to those he most admires. He may have problems with authority at work and in society, and wonder how much he needs to give of himself and how constant he can expect others to be.

TEN WORKING MEN AND PARENTAL LEAVE

In 1994, I interviewed ten men who had taken parental leave before the passage of the Family and Medical Leave Act. These men chose to remain home with their infants when their wives returned to work.

For two to six months, nine of the men were primary caregivers; the tenth shared the care of new twins and two older children with his wife. Not one of the fathers had ever consciously imagined being alone at home with a new baby—feeding it defrosted breast milk, learning its moods and signals—but they all soon became exclusively enveloped in the baby's world. Their well-paid wives liked working. They expected their husbands to do a good job. They openly encouraged the intense relationship they saw developing between husband and baby, and expected that their husbands would be good caregivers. The men flourished in the freedom to be successful and also to make the same mistakes as any caregiver new to the task. Most couples knew before or soon after the birth that they wanted to postpone day care as long as possible: by the end of the child-care leaves, all parents were grateful for this delay and regretted that it had not been longer.

What kind of men were these? Every one was successful and well rated at work. Most had graduate degrees; all were engaged in creative aspects of science or engineering, in teaching, or in law. Some had fathers whose parenting they admired and wished they had seen more of as children (nearly all of the wives had fathers of this description). Some were men who had vowed since youth that as fathers they would do it differently. Their fathers were difficult, exhausted, distracted, or frightening; most described their fathers as absent in spirit; many were also absent physically for long periods.

These men were raised in the 1950s, when fathers worked long and hard and were the disciplinarians of last resort. But mother's physical presence prevailed. While these mothers did not work out of the home at least until the children were of school age, the men described them with great admiration. They respected their energy both inside and outside of the home. Many of the men were awed now, as parents themselves, by their mothers' ability to run the family and raise the children virtually alone. Several had older sisters whom they referred to as "second mothers"; one described his sister as having replaced the father he felt he didn't have.

These men seemed to identify with the energy of *each* parent, both at work and at home. Their mothers taught them nontraditional tasks—perhaps imagining the flexibility and opportunity they would have wanted for themselves. They themselves married women who were more likely than they to play games like soccer, and they in turn were more likely than their wives to be good cooks. Most of the wives had themselves had mothers who had worked and fathers whom they loved but saw too little of.

They were the men who chose to ask for a parental leave that was due them (as it was to their wives), but which few male colleagues requested. Those with corporations had the leave-time option in place for several years before their request. In these instances, the culture of the corporation was publicly supportive of leaves and jobs were ostensibly secure. Nevertheless, human resource personnel were frank in confirming a subtle risk in status and a compromised view of commitment to their career for those men who took leave. One participant was a dorm counselor and taught at a prestigious boarding school where the female administration was eager to "teach" the students by example about the potential for fathers as caregivers. All but two leaves required extensive planning for both colleagues and supervisors. Every couple stressed the need to put money aside for the financial strain; more than half of the wives earned as much or more than their caregiving husbands. These men also volunteered to talk about their caregiving experience; they felt they were "pioneers," but wished there were "more pioneers"; they wanted to encourage every new father to have their experience.

Perhaps it was no coincidence that the supervisors who received the men's requests for family leave were most often described as fatherly men who, at the time of the request, expressed regret that *they* had not had leave time to be with their own young babies (although two supervisors were women with children). Perhaps these ten men were tacitly encouraged to request the leave, sensing that they would have managerial support to buffer the resentment of colleagues. Returning to work, their confidantes became working mothers with whom they shared child-care concerns. They disparaged male colleagues who were inept or reluctant caregivers, who called themselves "baby-sitters." The father who had the least formal education and was in a production department had the only reported unpleasant workplace experience: his supervisor blamed his leave on Hillary Clinton and, perhaps not coincidentally, his co-workers called him "Home Alone" for a year after the leave. This said, he remarked that he would take another leave if necessary; he felt the leave changed his relationships with all his children, and that it optimized his connection to his baby girl.

The marriages of these men were remarkably friendly and close. Nearly all lacked the expectable level of competition or criticism between parents or partners. Several described their wives as their "best friends." They were awed by their partners—perhaps as they had been by their mothers—for their ability to plan ahead and to manage the household. Though they took responsibility for a wide range of direct child-care tasks, it was still typical that their wives remembered that a child's birthday was coming and planned the children's wardrobes (though some men prided themselves in being able to shop for their children, knowing their sizes, and choosing wisely). All of the men in this group also used their wives' approval of their choices as the measure of a job well done.

Laundry was often a task still directed by their wives, and they frequently traded that chore for another. The men felt that their style of play was more active and creative, but that they and their wives were equally empathic. In all but one instance, the men were resigned to their wives' being more able to plan ahead: it was the wives who knew how to approach human-resource people about details of the leave. The men wondered whether it was women's magazines, intuition, societal expectations, or greater intelligence that gave women this edge. In the one instance where the leave-taking father claimed to be the better manager at home, he felt it was his wife's lower self-esteem and not the quality of her parenting skill that fed her view of his superiority. None of the men suggested that identifying with their caregiving mothers—now grandmothers—had given them the inclination to parent, but nearly all of the men said that watching their wives taught them a great deal about parenting.

This group was not representative of working-class men: every volunteer was Caucasian, American born, and middle-class. Every couple owned a home and none of their parents had been divorced. Their work gave them pleasure and pride, and was therefore neither grueling nor dreaded. Rather, their work was a perpetual test of their talent. Nearly all were distracted by the downsizing in their companies: part of the courage required to take parental leave was in acknowledging the risk in the face of an uncertain economy. Nevertheless, aware as they were, every man said he would take another parental leave if he were to have another child, and he would recommend it to every new father. They all urged that prospective leave-takers make financial plans well in advance to cover the leave.

Several of their own fathers and fathers-in-law were initially skeptical, purportedly worrying about what the choice would do to their sons' future prospects in the company; what would their supervisors think of such a worker, such a male? Male colleagues wondered what would happen to the balance of power in the family. Some female colleagues worried (to the subjects' wives) about giving up some traditional turf. But the men's own mothers were encouraging from the start. Their siblings and their spouses were supportive and proud of them, and their marriages were reportedly strengthened by their experience. They felt they understood parents at work in ways they never could or would have, and as supervisors they felt more generous as a result. Further, each felt immense, and sometimes renewed, loyalty to the company and co-workers who supported their leave choice.

These men were accustomed to being promoted. Now, in the uncertain economic climate of the early '90s, downsizing was pruning their ranks. Their jobs felt far more tenuous than when they were hired. But while they were somewhat worried that a stagnant professional future or unemployment could result from their parenting leave, they regarded these possibilities as less calamitous than becoming distant fathers. Parental leave was a choice that each man recognized might put him at future risk professionally, and not one regretted it.

These men wanted, and perhaps needed, to live out the part of their male role that went beyond mating behavior. Until the moment their wives' bodies showed the unique role they were about to play as a parent, the men had assumed they could be equal partners in parenting. Several recalled their sad resignation to the fact that their pregnant wives were already "getting to know" their baby-to-be. It may be that taking parental leave was one way to equalize the opportunity to be an involved parent and to share in the baby's affections. In this way, they were able to balance their need to *provide* with the longing to *nurture* the infants they co-created. Long working hours had kept their fathers from them and they were eager to stop the cycle of distant parenting.

WORKING MEN AND WORKING FATHERS

In many ways, these ten caregiving fathers have integrated traditional masculine and feminine longings and have thus far flourished under their expression. They married women who invited their participation, who were neither excessively competitive nor possessive with their babies, and who valued their own work opportunities. Ultimately, the men felt elevated by their competence at traditionally feminine nurturing responsibilities.

Perhaps the enactment of the wish to be the primary caregiver for the duration of the parenting leave, and to remain a sharing caregiver, has partial foundation in what Van Leeuwen (1966) and Jacobson (1950) have alluded to as "pregnancy envy," and what Kubie (1974) explained as "the drive to be both sexes" (p. 354). Several of these men described pregnancy and childbirth as the moment when they finally realized that they could never be an "equal" parent, indistinguishable in relevance from their wives. Perhaps through their intimate caregiving, the men overcame the disappointment inherent in having to relinquish certain gender-specific tasks: they could not conceive, bear, or nurse an infant. They chose an attainable if not an equivalent identity: to be a nurturer, an equal provider and protector, overtly sharing the intimate care of their babies.

These men identified with the nurturing activities of their caregiving mothers or older caregiving sisters. They also identified with the activity and goals of their hard-working fathers. With their own patient caregiving, some repaired memories of too-harsh fathers; some repeated early, fondly remembered, but scarce pleasures with their fathers.

Every one of them wished the leave had been longer, and lamented that they still can't spend more time with their infants. Work seemed easier to them than what they had just left, but caregiving seemed to fill a place in their lives they didn't know was even available. They felt different from friends who were more traditional fathers: they felt closer to their children, more involved in most aspects of their children's lives.

Early in their leaves they felt awkward in the playground and super-market as parent-in-charge; by the end of the leave they were more embarrassed for the people who mistook them for "baby-sitting" fathers.

The men were grateful to their companies, but on returning to work found they were changed; many had altered their lives in ways that would allow them more time with the children. One man arrived late almost every day, having dropped the children off at day care first, and skipping lunch or breaks if need be. He was a supervisor and worried at the example he was setting; he was even teased by his subordinates—but he felt willing to take the risks in order not to rush his baby and toddler as they packed up in the early morning. Even the most ambitious, highly placed manager now left work in time to pick up his baby at day care and start cooking dinner. He brought work home rather than work late, and now judged his group members by what they accomplished, not just by how many hours they clocked. It is not possible to know what part of the changes reported were due to fatherhood and what part to the power of the leave. Nevertheless, it may be instructive that this father made none of these changes after the birth of his first child, also a son, when his wife, and not he, took a nine-month leave.

How likely is it that corporations will encourage men to take the leaves mandated by the Family and Medical Leave Act? Noble (1995) writes that managers and chief executives may verbally acknowledge that people are important assets, but that financial officers see people who take leave "as a cost to be contained" (p. 43). Such disparagement of "people issues" outside of human resource departments doesn't bode well for men who might be caregivers. Men who have achieved management positions typically have older children. Men typically make policy and set corporate culture. Corporate decision makers who do not have full-time working wives, and do not share hands-on responsibility for a child's needs may not be sympathetic to the difficult choices of men who are.

Can the corporate benefits be documented? Michael McAndrews (1992), of the *Hartford Courant*, interviewed Denise Cichon, a senior consultant in Aetna's Work/Family Strategies Area, who says that "Aetna has received significant benefits in return for its flexibility. . . . It gives us an edge in recruiting, cuts training and replacement costs, and aids in morale (p. 36)." Several supervisors commended these ten men for learning to work faster and manage their time better after their child-care leave. Most men weren't sure whether their professional improvement was due more to the impact of fatherhood or the leave, or to fatherhood enhanced by the leave, but each of the men returned to work feeling more mature, more reliable, and more valuable as a father, husband, and employee.

The urge to nurture doesn't disappear at 9:00 A.M. Each of these men, in his own words, substantiated what has been written about the stresses of parents who work: when one has little control over the demands of a job, when schedules are rigid and allegiance is judged by hours, not excellence, morale may well suffer. With preparation and the proper equipment, one can often work as well at home caring for a sick child as in an office. When a phone is the only connection between a feverish child and a worried parent, productivity is not the obvious priority.

TREATMENT ISSUES

Men, married and not, often come to treatment to lessen the pain of loneliness, isolation, unstable self-esteem, and failed employment. Since mothers have so long taken responsibility for child-rearing, the impact of the father is an often overlooked clue to the patient's complex development. But as treatment deepens, father's impact can become more evident. Similarly, in their absence and in the style of their presence, the men in a patient's world reflected an image of himself. Through the imago a man often learns to live his life in order to meet those expectations. Some of the expectations were for failure, some for success. Many men cannot rise above the unsuccessful father who did—or did not—love them. Others spoil grand chances to excel, designing a disappointing compromise that demonstrates that they *can* win—but then they lose, sparing *other* men the pain of loss while satisfying their own harsh superego. Some fight supervisors with a feistiness reminiscent of adolescence. Some relate uncritically to inappropriate leaders. Often the style of a man's relationships will be modeled on how his fatherly figures nurtured him.

When men marry, they choose women who bear traces of both the good and bad memories of mother; there are also composite memories of father in these mates. Should their wives conceive, long-buried feelings of envy and anger from their own youthful wishes may intrude on the marriage. From father's latent example, some men learn to ignore or disguise maternal wishes, but then gain weight for nine months in silent and unconscious identification with their wives. They may feel embittered at the woman's starring role in pregnancy and see no part for themselves as parents of a newborn. They are usually expected to attend the birth, take a day or two off (counted as vacation days), and return to work as though their lives had barely changed. If their wives had a similar background, they will most often make no unusual preparations to involve the father in the crucial early days of their baby's life. Father, in turn, will not have the opportunity to understand that his life as a father has really just begun, that he, too, at the birth of his child, can choose to be responsible in whatever measure for the infant's early needs.

Male and female therapists need to recognize the shadow of the paternal imago and to deepen the patient's understanding of its relevance in his issues. Reworking a conflicted relationship with his mother *and* father may help free the male patient to be his own best blend of male and female, father and mother.

THE FUTURE

This chapter is about babies and their employed fathers—but what of the vast numbers of newborns born to young unmarried women whose partners have slim prospects of employment and its vast benefits? And what about men whose employers are not bound by current legislation to allow family leave, or who would retaliate in ways that make the risk too great for most men to overlook?

Joseph Pleck (1993) has found that fathers who take longer leaves show greater involvement with their children, that early infant involvement generally leads to a quantitative and qualitative lifelong difference in a father's family investment. Men must be encouraged to spontaneously use their child-care talents and instincts. They need to correct misconceptions about their ineptness in the nursery. They need to hold and love and walk a crying baby with an understanding that, given a familiarity between themselves and their infants, they are no less able to soothe than a mother. Being "good at" fatherhood may interrupt the cycle of poor self-esteem for many men. And a young man who is well fathered may in turn assimilate nurturing capabilities that good mentors *and* good parents need.

From the child's perspective, the ultimate aim of involving fathers in child care is to have the benefit of two unique sources of energy and love. From the mother's perspective, father may balance her work and home life. From the father's perspective, parenting is an additional source of self-esteem—a place to give and get love. Paternal caregiving allows an opportunity for a man to be the father he never had, or to pass on to his own child his own cherished memories.

Often, never having known a reliable and loving father, young men cannot concoct a reliable male persona. Instead, they may do those things that broadly mimic the men they see and know: they can make babies, but not care for them. Perhaps the future can offer more to fathers if they are taught to value their growth-promoting potential as parents of the next generation. But as long as the middle-class men who are the policy makers, politicians, and managers neither know nor comfortably accept their relevance to their children, they will not easily encourage men down the ladder to take family leave or request flexible hours. For real change in the workplace, there must be a generation where managers of both sexes accept and reflexively value "Dad and apple pie."

For many years advancement away from home was denied to women; now it is hard for many women to share the home turf with men. Perhaps as, and if, women reach parity in male domains, they will more respectfully share caregiving with their husbands. As the traditional gatekeepers of the nursery, women can help themselves by reconsidering their perceptions of fathers as caregivers.

Just as corporations and families look different to observers now, so are babies different than we assumed. As a result of recent infant research, our understanding of an infant's vulnerabilities and capabilities has recently been greatly enhanced. But such findings carry a responsibility: it would be both impractical and heartless to know about and yet ignore the impressive and positive impact of *two* caregiving parents on complex newborns—who notice and store early experience in ways we had never imagined possible.

Fathers have memories of mothering, and can reproduce them even with infants. In return for the opportunity, they are loyal to the family and the corporation that allow them to become their best selves: a composite of the love and the lacks of their own two parents. David Whyte (1994) described the conflict and loss confronting family men who are committed to excelling at work: "This split between our work-life and that part of our soul-life forced underground seems to be at the root of much of our current unhappiness. . . . The split between what is nourishing at work and what is agonizing is the very chasm from which our personal destiny emerges" (p. 4).

A generation of managers with working wives and young children is ascending to positions of power. These men will have an opportunity to influence the corporate culture, drawing on their firsthand knowledge of the difficulty of the choice between family and career. It is important that they have validation that men *have* the capacity for deep attachment to their children, and children to their fathers; that fathers can care for children's physical needs as successfully as mothers; that children's lives are enhanced by the influence of two loving, caregiving parents. They can also expect that businesses that give men the opportunity to excel at parenting can expect a payback in loyalty and leadership. It is not an aberration but a fact of inner life that men—in identifications and disidentifications—nurture in ways they learned from their own two parents. The workplace becomes the venue where adult men enact the best and worst parts of their complex selves.

Adult working men can continue to grow: as managers or as the elders of their workplace, they can help younger men be better fathers than they were or had. They can be for the younger generation the mentors they wanted, or the fathers they had. Optimally, fatherhood witnesses the transformation of a man from care-receiver to caregiver. Optimally too, employers will balance what they receive from their employees with what they give. Ideally that will include allowing fathers time with their young children. If attachments are to form between fathers and their new babies, they need access to one another in repeated early demonstrations of reliability and love. When a baby is new, small, and dependent in every way, fathers are most likely to learn how they can fit into that infant's life. By demonstrating that a balance of work and active parenting is an acceptable measure of a man, by giving a man the incentive to be an employee who cares about his job, a manager can simultaneously serve himself and his professional responsibility. Material returns may be longer in coming than the inner knowledge that one is reaching for his best, generative self.

REFERENCES

Abelin, E. (1971). The role of the father in the separation-individuation phase. *Separation-Individuation: Essays in Honor of Margaret S. Mahler*, ed. J. B. McDevitt and C. F. Settlage, pp. 229–252. New York: International Universities Press.

———— (1975). The earliest role of the father. *International Journal of Psycho-Analysis* 56:293–302.

———— (1980). Triangulation, the role of the father and the origins of core gender identity during the rapprochement subphase. In *Rapprochement*, ed. R. Lax, S. Bach, and J. Burland, pp. 151–169. Northvale, NJ: Jason Aronson.

Badinter, E. (1995). *XY: On Masculine Identity*. New York: Columbia University Press.

Benedek, T. (1959). Fatherhood and providing. In *Parenthood*, ed. E. J. Anthony and T. Benedek, pp. 167–183. Boston: Little Brown, 1970.

Biller, H., and Borstelman, L. (1967). Masculine development: an integrative review. *Merrill-Palmer Quarterly* 13(4):253–294.

Blos, P. (1974). The genealogy of the ego ideal. *Psychoanalytic Study of the Child* 29:43–88. New Haven, CT: Yale University Press.

Bowlby, J. (1958). The nature of the child's tie to his mother. *International Journal of Psycho-Analysis* 39:350–373.

Brazelton, B. (1987). *Working and Caring*. Reading, MA: Addison-Wesley.

Burlingham, D. (1973). The preoedipal infant–father relationship. *Psychoanalytic Study of the Child* 28:236. New Haven, CT: International Universities Press.

Catalyst. (1986). The report on a national study of parental leaves. New York: Catalyst.

Fast, I. (1978). Developments in gender identity: the original matrix. *International Review of Psycho-Analysis* 5:265–286.

Filene, P. G. (1974). *Him/Her/Self: Sex Roles in Modern America*, 2nd ed. Baltimore: Johns Hopkins University Press.

Freud, S. (1914). Some reflections on schoolboy psychology. *Standard Edition* 13:241–244. London: Hogarth Press, 1953.

——— (1930). Civilization and its discontents. *Standard Edition* 21:57–145.

——— (1940). An outline of psychoanalysis. *Standard Edition* 23:139–207.

Gerson, K. (1993). *No Man's Land: Men's Changing Commitments to Family and Work*. New York: Basic Books.

Greenberg, M., and Morris, N. (1974). Engrossment: the newborn's impact upon the father. *American Journal of Orthopsychology* 44:4.

Griswold, R. L. (1993). *Fatherhood in America: A History*. New York: Basic Books.

Gunsberg, L. (1982). Selected critical review of psychological investigations of the early father–infant relationship. In *Father and Child: Developmental and Clinical Perspectives*, ed. S. Cath, A. Gurwitt, and J. Ross, pp. 65–86. New York: Basil Blackwell.

Herzog, J. (1980). Sleep disturbance and father hunger. *Psychoanalytic Study of the Child* 35:219–233. New Haven, CT: International Universities Press.

Jacobson, E. (1950). Development of the wish for a child in the boy. *Psychoanalytic Study of the Child* 5:139–152. New York: International Universities Press.

Josselyn, I. (1956). Cultural forces, motherliness and fatherliness. *American Journal of Orthopsychiatry* 26:264–271.

Kestenberg, J. (1956). The development of maternal feelings in early childhood. *Psychoanalytic Study of the Child* 11:279–291. New York: International Universities Press.

Kotelchuck, M. (1972). *The nature of the child's tie to his father*. Unpublished doctoral dissertation, Harvard University, Cambridge, MA.

Kubie, L. (1974). The drive to be both sexes. *Psychoanalytic Quarterly*. 7:349–395.

Lamb, M. (1981). The development of father–infant relationships. In *The Role of the Father in Child Development*, ed. M. Lamb, pp. 459–488. New York: Wiley.

——— (1987). The emergent American fathers. In *The Father's Role: Cross-Cultural Perspectives*, ed. M. Lamb, pp. 1–26. Hillsdale, NJ: Lawrence Erlbaum.

Lansky, M. (1992). *Fathers Who Fail: Shame and Psychopathology in the Family System*. Hillsdale, NJ: The Analytic Press.

Laqueur, T. (1990). *Making Sex: Body and Gender from the Greeks to Freud*. Cambridge, MA: Harvard University Press.

Levine, J. (1991). *Babies and briefcases: creating a family-friendly workplace for fathers*. Testimony before the House of Representatives Committee on Children, Youth, and Families. Washington, DC, June 11, pp. 1–6.

Loewald, H. (1951). Ego and reality. *International Journal of Psycho-Analysis* 10:10–18.

Lynn, D. (1962). Sex-role and parental identification. *Child Development* 33:555–564.

Machlinger, V. (1981). The role of the father in psychoanalytic theory. In *The Role of the Father in Child Development*, ed. M. Lamb, pp. 113–154. New York: Wiley.

Mahler, M. S. (1966). Notes on the development of basic moods: the depressive affect. In *Psychoanalysis—A General Psychology: Essays in Honor of Heinz Hartmann*, ed. R. M. Loewenstein, L. M. Newman, M. Schnur, and A. J. Solnit. New York: International Universities Press.

Mahler, M. S., and Gosliner, B. (1955). On symbiotic child psychosis. *Psychoanalytic Study of the Child* 10:195. New York: International Universities Press.

McAndrews, M. (1992). Companies finding they're not hurt by state's family leave law. *Hartford Courant*, October 27, p. 36.

Noble, B. P. (1995). The bottom line on "people" issues. *New York Times*, February 19, p. 43.

Parke, R., and Sawin, D. (1980). The family in early infancy: social interactional and attitudinal analyses. In *The Father–Infant Relationship: Observational Studies in the Family Setting*, ed. F. A. Pedersen. New York: Praeger Special Publications.

Pedersen, F. (1985). Research and the father: Where do we go from here? In *Dimensions of Fatherhood*, ed. S. Hanson and F. Bozett, pp. 437–450. Beverly Hills, CA: Sage.

Pleck, J. (1993). Are "family-supportive" employer policies relevant to men? In *Men, Work, and Family*, ed. J. Hood, pp. 217–237. Newbury Park, CA: Sage.

Popenoe, D. (1993). Bringing up father. *Time Magazine*, June 28, p. 45.

Pruett, K. (1983). Infants of primary nurturing fathers. *Psychoanalytic Study of the Child* 38:257–277. New Haven, CT: Yale University Press.

——— (1985). Oedipal configurations in young father-raised children. *Psychoanalytic Study of the Child* 40:435–452. New Haven, CT: Yale University Press.

——— (1987). *The Nurturing Father*. New York: Warner.

——— (1991). Fathers and babies in the first six years, In *The Course of Life: Psychoanalytic Contributions Toward Understanding Personality Development*, ed. S. Greenspan and G. Pollock, pp. 73–94, Madison, CT: International Universities Press.

Radin, N. (1976). The role of the father in cognitive, academic, and intellectual development. In *The Role of the Father in Child Development*, ed. M. E. Lamb, pp. 379–422. New York: Wiley.

Ross, J. M. (1974) *The children's children: a psychoanalytic study of generativity and nurturance in boys.* Doctoral dissertation, New York University.

———— (1977). Towards fatherhood: the epigenesis of paternal identity during a boy's first decade. *International Review of Psycho-Analysis* 4:327.

———— (1979). Fathering: a review of some psychoanalytic contributions on paternity. *International Journal of Psychology* 60:317–327.

Schaffer, H., and Emerson, P. (1964). The development of social attachments in infancy. *Monographs of the Society for Research in Child Development* 29(3):5–77.

Spelke, E., Zelazo, P., Kagan, J., and Kotelchuck, M. (1973). Father interaction and separation protest. *Developmental Psychology* 9:83–90.

Tyson, P. (1982). The role of the father in gender identity, urethral erotism and phallic narcissism. In *Father and Child: Developmental and Clinical Perspectives*, ed. S. Cath, A. Gurwitt, and J. Ross, pp. 175–188. New York: Basil Blackwell.

Van Leeuwen, K. (1966). Pregnancy envy in the male. *International Journal of Psycho-Analysis* 47:319–341.

Whyte, D. (1994). *The Heart Aroused: Poetry and Preservation of the Soul in Corporate America.* New York: Doubleday Currency.

Yogman, M. W. (1982). Observations on the father–infant relationship. In *Father and Child: Developmental and Clinical Perspectives*, ed. S. Cath, A. Gurwitt, and J. Ross, pp. 101–122. New York: Basil Blackwell.

Yogman, M. W., Dixon, S., Tronick, E., et al. (1976). The father in separation-individuation. *Bulletin of the Menninger Clinic* 46:231–254, 1982.

PART II

DYSFUNCTIONAL ATTACHMENTS

4

Barriers to Intimacy in Couples

LOUISE CRANDALL

INTRODUCTION

Although poets and philosophers had been trying to unravel the mysteries of love for centuries, it was not until the early twentieth century when Freud (1905) began to formulate his ideas about infant sexuality that he came upon the momentous discovery that in adult love the finding of love is the refinding of the mother of infancy.

Freud grappled with the concept of normal and neurotic love over many years as he struggled to formulate libido theory and tried to explain love in terms of shifting quantities of libido. First, he conceptualized that in love the libido is transferred from the parental objects to new, nonincestuous objects. Second, he thought that libido was being transferred from what we now call the self to the object, and that aspects of the ego ideal are transferred to the object. Last, he thought that libidinal psychosexual development was necessary for mature love. Freud was never satisfied with this theorizing. He knew that libido theory was not adequate to explain all that goes on in loving intimate relationships.

Freud's theories on love were formulated within the topographical model, which postulates that the psyche comprises the conscious, preconscious, and unconscious. It was not until 1923 that Freud introduced the structural point of view that divided the psyche into id, ego, and superego. Although he remained interested in the subject of normal and neurotic love, he did not update his thinking on love from a structural point of view. This was left to later theoreticians.

One of the most important contributions made to psychoanalytic thinking after Freud was put forth in Robert Waelder's (1936) paper on the principle of multiple function. In it he positioned the ego at the center of psychic functioning by saying that it is the ego's function to integrate the diverse aspects of the psyche. First, there is the id, the world of the instincts; second, there is the outside world with its demands on the individual; third, there is the superego with its commands and prohibitions; and fourth, there is the compulsion to repeat. In that same paper, Waelder described his ideas about love. He said that where love has combined the pleasure of sexual intimacy with a satisfying emotional relationship, a near perfect solution has been found to all the contradictory problems of the ego.

This chapter is about the barriers to intimacy in couples. The focus is on the internal barriers that make it difficult for one person to be intimate with another. It is my position that barriers to intimacy are primarily internal. I will be using psychoanalytic theory, as Freud described it in 1923 and as Waelder elaborated it in 1936. It is my hypothesis that problems with intimacy can best be understood as deriving from a series of compromise formations.

I will discuss the participation of libidinal fixations, ego weakness, superego pathology, and the role of the repetition compulsion in problems of intimacy, followed by a presentation of case material describing a patient functioning at the borderline level. In my discussion, I hope to demonstrate the ways in which barriers to intimacy result from internal sources, and the association of intimacy problems with the borderline diagnosis.

THE PARTICIPATION OF THE ID

Freud (1923) used the concept of primary identification to describe the earliest attachment of the infant to the mother at a time when object cathexis and identification are indistinguishable from each other. Whether we use his terms or those of more contemporary writers such as Mahler, this period of the infant's life has great bearing on the individual's later capacity to be intimate.

Mahler (Mahler et al. 1975) has described the development of object relations in the human infant with great detail. She conceptualized a symbiotic period where the mother and child enjoy a dual unity, and where the infant has only a dim awareness of mother as an external object. At about five months, the process of separation and individuation begins to appear. Rapprochement coincides with the toddler's dawning realization that mother is actually a separate person, which brings to a head the conflict between the need for mother and the need for separateness and individuation. The separation-individuation process is thought to culminate with the development of libidinal object constancy, which implies a stable concept of the self and a stable concept of the other. These ideas are essential to our understanding of the problems of intimacy.

An intimate adult relationship requires stable boundaries because it is based on the capacity to partially suspend the boundaries between self and object. If the longings for symbiosis are too strong, emotional and physical intimacy can be experienced as a threat to psychic integrity. If the boundaries between self and other are too weak, sexual intimacy cannot be enjoyed as a kind of regression in the service of the ego. Intimacy involves a limited crossing of boundaries, a temporary return to the stage of dual unity, an identification with the partner. This is one reason why the discovery of similarities plays a crucial role in falling in love. Lovers feel like two bodies with one soul, a sublimated version of symbiosis. Sexual excitement and orgasm can be transformed into an experience of fusion only if boundaries are stable. The boundaries between self and object and the development of a separate self are prerequisites for the adult capacity for intimacy.

Balint (1948) was the first to emphasize the importance of tenderness in romantic love. He suggested that feelings of tenderness are derived from the preoedipal relationship with the maternal object. Where there has been inadequate mothering, and insufficient warmth and tenderness in the daily ministrations to the child, the adult is incapable of tenderness and romantic intimacy. If feeding and bathing were performed by mother without love, the adult may be able to engage in sex but often without tenderness.

For many years following Freud's contribution, psychoanalytic thinking included the notion that only the genitally organized person (a person whose libido has traversed from oral, to anal, to phallic, to oedipal levels, and is then reorganized under the primacy of the genital zone) was capable of genital orgasm and mature love. The concepts of genitality and the genital character grew out of the connection Freud made between libidinal position and character types. Authors such as Abraham (1924), Fenichel (1945), Reich (1933), and Balint (1948) contributed to this way of thinking. It was not until the late 1960s that this view was questioned. We now know that being orgasmic in intercourse is not equivalent to being able to be intimate. Kernberg (1995), for example, has documented that patients with severe borderline and narcissistic pathology, and with little concern for others, are fully able to achieve sexual excitement and orgasm through intercourse.

All that said, most clinicians would agree that where preoedipal issues dominate a love relationship, intimacy can be very difficult to maintain.

ORALITY

Both Freud (1905) and Abraham (1924) were involved in the delineation of the oral phase of libidinal development and the types of symptoms, character traits, and object relationships that develop from it later in life. Patients who have marked oral fixations tend to be dependent, infantile, demanding, greedy. They hunger for narcissistic supplies such as attention, admiration, and love. The ingestion of food is the model of their relationships with others. Cannibalistic trends show up in their wishes to incorporate their objects. They are said to attach themselves to objects as if by suction, or sucking. Intimate relationships are often based on imitation and identification, which makes any individual differences a threat to the relationship.

ANALITY

Freud (1908) and Abraham (1924) were also involved in the delineation of the anal phase of libidinal development and the types of symptoms, character traits, and object relationships that can develop from it later in life. Patients with marked anal fixations are said to be orderly, parsimonious, and obstinate. Treating their love object like feces can be the metaphor for this type of patient. Any disappointment in their intimate partner can lead to a hostile expulsion or rejection. Wishes to control or to dominate the object can be quite prominent. Anally fixated people can be quarrelsome, overbearing, petty, and stingy. They are capable of giving love but also quite capable of withholding love or completely spoiling love. Finding aggression against the object pleasurable is the hallmark of the anal person. Sadism can take the form either of physical harm or psychic torture.

THE OEDIPUS COMPLEX

Oedipal conflict has been traditionally thought of as the hallmark of neurosis. The inability to successfully resolve the Oedipus conflict in childhood causes a vulnerability to neurosis later in life. However, today many acknowledge that oedipal conflict can be pervasive in the more severe pathologies as well (see Abend and colleagues [1983], for example.)

Neurotic levels of functioning are thought to entail libidinal regression from the adult genital level to the oedipal phase and/or to preoedipal positions. For example, Freud characterized hysteria as a regression to the phallic-oedipal stage of development, the obsessional neurosis as one where the regression goes to anal levels, and neurotic depression where the regression goes to oral levels. Associated with all forms of neurosis is unconscious guilt and the need for punishment (Freud 1909, 1924).

Patients functioning at the neurotic level are better able to fall in love and sustain a stable relationship because they have achieved object constancy and therefore they are able to assess and appreciate their partner in depth. However, inasmuch as the neurotic has chosen a partner whom he or she experiences as the incestuous object from childhood, unconscious guilt can interfere with intimacy in a variety of ways. Typically, sexual inhibitions are associated with this type of psychopathology. Various forms of impotence and frigidity are common among this type of patient. Both men and women functioning at the neurotic level appear to have difficulty enjoying sexual intimacy in the context of an emotionally satisfying relationship.

The need to dissociate tender and erotic longings can also lead to a variety of disruptive solutions. Some patients find two love objects and literally separate sex from love. Promiscuity can be the result of oedipal guilt. Neurotic patients embroiled in oedipal conflict often find themselves in relationships where there is a triangle or an injured third person. Feelings of victory, as well as feelings of defeat, often echo the original triangle of childhood. Jealousy and envy can be prominent. The need for punishment can lead the neurotic patient to choose frustrating or unavailable love objects. When the oedipal complex remains strong, any partner is compared to the original love of childhood but never quite equals it. This can result in an incapacity to make a commitment in adulthood.

Much has been written about the differences between the way men love and the way women love and the types of problems both have with intimacy. For both boys and girls it is the early erotic experience with mother in terms of her holding, feeding, washing, and so on that kindles the potential for sexual excitement later in life. It is also in that relationship that intense feelings of ambivalence reside. For girls, this first relationship is a homosexual one, for boys it is heterosexual. This difference has significant consequences. Since men do not switch love objects, their primary love object is the same sex as their oedipal love object. As a result, a man's love for a woman is apt to stir up more preoedipal fears and longings than does a woman's love for a man. Some theorists also feel that this makes men prone to feel more claustrophobic in an intimate relationship with a woman.

It has been suggested that women tend to have less trouble committing to a love relationship; by switching love objects in childhood, the adult woman has already renounced her first love, whereas the man is more likely to be forever looking for the ideal mother (Altman 1977). When women have trouble resolving oedipal conflict and resort to regression, relationships to men that are masochistic and/or very submissive can result. A man's regression to preoedipal levels may make him passive and dependent in his relationship vis-à-vis the woman.

Before leaving the topic of oedipal conflicts as a barrier to intimacy, it is important to note that some authors have made the point that not all oedipal conflict is "bad." Kernberg (1995), for instance, feels that the quality of longing for the unavailable and forbidden oedipal object is a crucial component of sexual passion and love relations, and that, in this regard, the oedipal constellation energizes sexual development and may be considered a permanent feature of all human relations. He feels the challenge is to differentiate neurotic solutions to oedipal conflicts from their normal manifestations.

UNRESOLVED BISEXUAL CONFLICT

Blos (1962) has documented that adolescence proper is the time in normal development for both boys and girls to give up their bisexuality and make an object choice. Those who have not solidified a sexual identity by adulthood have great difficulty in falling in love or sustaining an intimate relationship.

Binstock (1973) echoed this idea in his paper on "Two Forms of Intimacy," where he compares the intimacy between mother and infant with that of the adult couple. He found that where there has been a mature resolution of bisexuality each partner can identify with the opposite sex by identifying with each other in the context of their sexual relationship. When the feminine wishes of a man or the masculine wishes of a woman are too strong, this identification cannot take place successfully. Rather, solutions that interfere with intimacy, such as envy and competitive feelings toward the partner, can result.

Traditional thinking has been that for females where the negative oedipal attachment to the mother has been too strong, a heterosexual object choice will be problematic. Similarly for men, where the negative oedipal attachment to the father has been too strong, a heterosexual object choice will be problematic. While I will not be focusing on the unique characteristics associated with homosexual object choice, I will say that in my clinical experience heterosexual wishes that occur in the homosexual couple appear to be as disruptive to intimacy as homosexual wishes can be in the heterosexual couple.

AGGRESSION

Person (1988) describes the ways in which relationships develop over time. Specifically, she elucidates the idyllic phase of love and the significance of the couple's first quarrel. She says that falling in love frees lovers of ambivalence until the first argument. From that point on, how the couple handles their aggression determines the quality of the relationship. For some couples, resolving the argument symbolically reenacts the expulsion of ambivalence. For others, particularly those with strong streaks of sadism and masochism, passionate anger and even violence are signs of love. As the relationship progresses, the rage triggered by frustrations and disappointment can coalesce with rage from childhood.

Most would agree that there is a delicate balance of love and aggression in all long-standing intimate relationships. The presence of ambivalence can take many forms. It may destroy the capacity for sexual excitement and result in a sexual inhibition. This may manifest as sexual boredom, or it can be put into action via infidelities and other actions that threaten to destroy the fabric of the relationship. Ambivalence can be expressed through withholding of love, withholding of empathy, or withholding of physical affection.

In Stanley Coen's (1992) interesting work on pathological dependency, he describes the way in which certain kinds of patients use relationships with others as a way of avoiding the aggression in their own internal world. Once in a relationship, these patients cannot separate, for to be on their own is too dangerous. At the same time, they use fantasies of merger to protect the love object from destruction. This defensive merger, in turn, impairs the sense of separateness, as it impairs reality testing and the patient's confidence in his ability to manage destructive wishes on his own.

As Kernberg (1992) has suggested, the more primitive the level of aggression, the more massive the projective mechanisms and the more fearful the patient is of depending on others. In these cases, boundaries are weakened and intimacy becomes a threat to psychic integrity. Kernberg has described a hierarchy of hatred. In the most primitive and pathological forms of hatred the aim is to destroy the object, either in fact or fantasy. A less severe degree of hatred is expressed in sadistic tendencies and wishes, where the aim to make the object suffer is experienced with a conscious or unconscious sense of enjoyment. A milder form of hatred centers around the desire to dominate the object; this may include sadistic components, but is self-limited by the degree of the object's submission. Finally, in those with a neurotic level of functioning, hatred may take the form of a rationalized identification with a strict or punitive superego.

The relationship between sex and aggression is a subject that has interested several writers. Stoller (1979), in his book on sexual excitement, has made the point that aggression is an essential component of sexual excitement. Person (1988) reports that too much aggression can lead to sexual inhibition; because the sex act mobilizes aggression, avoiding sex is seen as protecting the partner. Kernberg (1995) agrees that excessive repression of aggression inhibits sexual response, and notes that the integration of libido and aggression is a major component in the capacity for both sexual and emotional intimacy.

NARCISSISM

One of Freud's significant contributions to the topic of love came from his explorations of the subject of narcissism. In his 1914 work, he described the way in which libido, resembling an amoeba, could put its pseudopods out and cathect objects, or be invested in what we would today call the self. In falling in love, the person invests large quantities of libido in his beloved, a process that Freud thought could deplete the reservoir of self-esteem and self-love. This model explained what he sometimes saw clinically, but it did not explain those who were clearly enriched by love. This disparity led him to his idea that the person in love projects his ego ideal onto his lover. When his love is reciprocated, this produces the feeling of bliss that we associate with love.

The relationship between object love and narcissism has been a subject of debate for decades. Kohut (1971), for example, has conceptualized narcissism as having a separate line of development from object love. In any case, for our purpose here, the narcissistic retreat from intimacy into states of self-sufficiency is one of the significant ways that intimacy can be threatened or destroyed. If it is a chronic state, it can make falling in love impossible altogether. If it happens only intermittently, it may not destroy an otherwise stable relationship, but it can interfere with intimacy.

Narcissistic problems can have their etiology in early oral aggression and envy, as Kernberg (1975) suggests, or can be a result of a fixation at the oedipal phase, an inability to resolve the transitory narcissistic phase of adolescence, or some combination of the three.

Narcissistic patients who experience these problems in their most pathological forms do not have the capacity to fall in love or to become intimate with another person. They tend to be fearful of potential love objects because of the massive amounts of aggression they project. They feel anger toward and are resentful of anyone they need. Normal dependency is feared because they fear being exploited. They also cannot tolerate their partners' dependency on them. They experience the ordinary reciprocity of human relations as exploitative and invasive. There is an absence of interest in the personality of a potential love object, and so any connection tends to be at the part-object level. Kernberg (1995) has found that the narcissistic personality has a deep, unconscious hatred and envy of the relationship between his parents, and that this hatred and envy is often turned into destructive wishes against the individual's own functioning as part of a couple.

People who experience narcissistic problems in their milder forms tend to be oversensitive (narcissistic vulnerability), tend to use narcissistic defenses (withdrawal), and also tend to need narcissistic supplies, such as admiration. For example, Edgcumbe and Burgner (1975) describe patients who have narcissistic problems due to a fixation at the

early part of the phallic-oedipal phase, which they have named the
phallic-narcissistic phase. They describe these patients as having difficulties in reciprocal relationships in which the object's real qualities
and characteristics are recognized and valued, and in which the needs
and the demands of the object are accepted. These patients, they say,
have a tendency to use the object as a source of admiration or con-
demnation, as a substitute for internalized approval or sanctions.

Blos (1962) describes the inability to give up the narcissistic
position of adolescence. Blos has documented a narcissistic stage during adolescence that is part of normal development. If all goes well,
the adolescent—temporarily—emotionally withdraws from his parents,
and becomes self-involved and remains defiant of rules that represent
internal and external parental authority until he or she is ready to make
an object choice. A developmental arrest at this position leaves the
individual in a state of prolonged adolescence. Blos feels that although
the individual stuck in adolescence may appear to be capable of intimacy, these patients can be extremely egocentric and demanding in
their relationships. He has found that the object choices of these patients are often used primarily to help them extricate themselves from
their emotional attachments to their families.

THE PARTICIPATION OF THE EGO

It has been suggested that the ego plays a significant role in the capacity for intimacy. The ego is conceptualized as being that part of
the psyche that imparts a sense of duration to love relationships. It is
the function of the ego to bring together the sexual and the tender
currents. It is the ego that synthesizes the pregenital under the primacy
of the genital phase. It is the ego that gives the capacity to tolerate
differences between partners and to endure frustrations.

Bergmann (1987) states that although the ego can lose much of
its power in falling in love, its first task is to observe the real qualities
of the love object and to evaluate the future of the relationship.
Bergmann believes that this task is particularly difficult, since falling
in love is so dominated by displacements and projections. The second
task is that of integration. Because most children have more than one

love object, these object representations need to be integrated and not compete for supremacy later on in life. For example, where there has been disharmony between the mother and father, or if the maternal functions were performed by more than one person, each object can demand its own refinding. The third task of the ego is to counteract the force of the superego that so strenuously objects to the inevitable incestuous aspects of any love relationship. The fourth task of the ego consists of counteracting the extreme demands of the id, which insists on refinding the lost symbiotic state of infancy. The fifth task of the ego is to resist the pressure of the repetition compulsion, both in terms of the object chosen and in the pressure to provoke responses characteristic of the original object. Whereas Freud (1905) spoke about the refinding of a person, Bergmann stresses the aim of love as the refinding of a lost ego state.

THE PARTICIPATION OF THE SUPEREGO

Freud first used the term *superego* in 1923 when he introduced the structural theory. It was then that he made the statement that the superego is heir to the Oedipus complex. He believed that the oedipal child is able to give up his or her oedipal wishes by identifying with the prohibitions of the parents. By introjecting the parents, a new structure is formed. This new structure replaces and helps to repress the sexual and hostile impulses toward the parents. The superego has essentially two sources, the object source, which comes from the objects in the child's environment, and an instinctual source that includes the libidinal and aggressive feelings toward the object that can distort the image of the object. This "introject" frequently gets reprojected in intimate relationships, so that what began as an internalized conflict within one of the partners of the couple now appears to be an interpersonal conflict. It is my opinion that the superego plays a very significant role in problems of intimacy.

For example, Anna Freud (1936) described projected jealousy, in which a husband projects his unfaithful wishes onto his wife and then reproaches her for them. Commenting on her work, Sandler (1985) concludes that it is common, even when the superego is well developed, for people who have very strong guilt feelings to identify with their own superego introjects and to attack others for the very things they feel guilty about themselves.

Kernberg (1995) has written that in normal love relationships the couple activates conscious and unconscious superego functions in each other, resulting in the couple's acquiring, over time, a superego system of its own in addition to that of each partner. The effect of this new superego system depends on the maturity of the superego of each partner. A mature superego protects the couple's relationship. With a mature superego, a person is able to tolerate aggression and ambivalence both in himself and in others. A mature superego is able to tolerate regressive wishes such as dependency longings, wishes for symbiotic merging, and wishes for a good life and for sexual satisfaction and intimacy. The mature superego leads to the capacity to forgive oneself and others.

It has been documented that the more severe the psychopathology, the more primitive the superego (Crandall 1993). For example, the superego of borderline patients tends to be tyrannical, primitive, and cruel. When primitive superego pathology dominates, sadistic superego precursors are enacted and have the potential for destroying the couple. It has been suggested (Altman 1977) that, without adequate superego functioning, hate would dominate the relationship, love would be without compassion and remorse, and that it is only with the participation of superego that it is possible for love to be a source of pleasure and satisfaction even when one's own wishes are not currently being met.

Last, but certainly not least, is the ego ideal. The formation of an ego ideal is a basic prerequisite for the capacity to fall in love. The ego ideal is that part of the superego that contains one's goals and ideals. Freud (1923) stated that the ego ideal is heir to infantile narcissism, and that it is formed as a substitute for the lost narcissism of childhood, when the child was his own ideal. Others have said that the ego ideal also contains ideal images of the parents (see Jacobson [1964], for example). Blos (1962) has said that the ego ideal receives a decisive formative push during the oedipal phase when the love for the parent of the same sex is transformed into wishes to be like the parent. However, in Blos's opinion, the ego ideal does not attain its final organization until adolescence. It is then that the adolescent gives up his love for the parent of the same sex and solidifies his identification with him or her, thus promoting the formation of sexual identity. The superego measures the ego against the ego ideal. When the ego measures up to the ego ideal, the superego responds with love. When the ego does not measure up to the ego ideal, the superego withdraws its love (Freud 1923). In a state of love, it is the ego ideal that is projected onto the partner. This projection is possible because, in childhood, the parents were idealized by the child before the ego was formed. The lover, becoming childish, regresses to this state. When this happens, the beloved will receive the same idealizations as did the parents. When the ego ideal is projected, the tension between the ego and ego ideal is temporarily abolished. When love is reciprocated, it is as if the self were suddenly loved by the ego ideal. This is experienced as the proverbial bliss of love (Bergmann 1987). Pathology of the ego ideal interferes with the couple's capacity to evaluate and value each other and the relationship realistically and to establish ideals and goals for the relationship.

THE REPETITION COMPULSION

Waelder (1936) was the first to consider the compulsion to repeat to be a force so potent that he suggested thinking of it almost on par with the id and superego. Today we think of the repetition compulsion as a compromise formation in which the id, ego, and superego all participate. The concept of differentiating those repetitions that are destructive and prevent change from those that are adaptive and allow for change becomes crucial. In clinical work, we have ample data to support this way of thinking. Patients who have been treated sadistically by a parent often find partners who will treat them sadistically. Sometimes the repetition will include an identification with the aggressor, or turning passive into active, so that the patient who has been treated sadistically by a parent will treat his or her partner in that way. Sometimes the pattern alternates. Wallerstein and Blakeslee (1995), in a recent book on the good marriage, pose the question: How is it that some couples are dedicated to avoiding the tragedies of their childhoods and are able to make a better life for themselves while others cannot?

CASE EXAMPLE—A BORDERLINE PATIENT

Miss A. was a 22-year-old woman who was a freshman in college when she began treatment. She said she wanted to be in therapy because she had concerns about her involvement in a relationship. She had ended a relationship with a man the previous summer when she came to New York to continue her education. Miss A. appeared to be quite confused and still very preoccupied with him. For example, she said that when she began seeing him she wanted sex only and nothing more. After leaving him she was not able to stop thinking about him and this frightened her. This had been her first sexual relationship. She was upset that she had given up control and "handed him the reins."

Miss A. was the middle child born in a sibship of five. Both of her parents were attorneys. Her sisters were one and three years older than she, and her brothers one and two years younger. Her mother was described as a very intelligent, competitive woman who extended herself to others but then resented it. Her father was described as set in his ways. Despite being financially comfortable, the parents did not believe in paying for their children's college education.

Miss A.'s first intimate relationship with a man represented a series of compromise formations. We learned that there were preconditions that made it possible for her to enter into this relationship. The first was that she knew from the outset that the relationship would be time-limited because she was moving to another city, and, second, that she had both herself and the man convinced that it would only be a sexual fling. The reality of the man was barely evident in her awareness, and her capacity for empathy for him was nearly nonexistent. For example, one of her complaints about him was that after she told him she was leaving him, he lost interest in sex. She was hurt and angry and it never dawned on her that he was withdrawing from her as a reaction to her plans to leave him.

After moving to New York, she became involved with a second man with whom she lived for two years. This relationship had the appearance of a passionate love affair. However, on closer inspection we saw that it revealed a great deal about her problems with intimacy. Miss A.'s boyfriend for the next two years was a man she met while working at a part-time job. He was several years older, came from a working-class background, and had few aspirations to improve himself through education. He supported himself by working occasional part-time jobs, and selling street drugs and stolen merchandise. Basically, he had very few demands on his time, a fact that was extremely important to Miss A. because she wanted a boyfriend who could be with her twenty-four hours a day. It was also important to her that he was not a college-educated person and did not particularly value education. This was an enormous relief to the patient because her family had high expectations for her academically. Miss A. had already flunked out of two universities, and she was involved in an intense battle with her parents about whether she would ever complete her education. She used her relationship with her boyfriend to support her rebellious attitude toward her parents and to gain some relief from her very harsh super-ego.

As soon as the relationship began, the two of them began spending most of their days in bed together. She stopped going to her classes and frequently did not come to her session. After about three or four months the symbiotic quality of their relationship began to show signs of strain. Any separation initiated by her boyfriend made her feel unloved, rejected, and enraged. She would report feeling depressed when he left her and would engage in self-destructive acts such as picking at her face, or chewing her nails and cuticles till they bled. It seemed as though she utilized aggression turned against herself as a way to defend against the rage she felt when her symbiotic wishes were frustrated.

At the same time there were wishes to be more separated from this man. She reported that each time she got dressed to leave to go to class, he would entice her back to bed. After we analyzed her own conflicted feelings about attending class and coming to therapy sessions, she reported that to leave him made her feel too guilty. We came to understand that she had made a pathological identification with her mother and thought of him as a child. She felt that the mother who leaves her child should feel guilty.

Miss A. suffered with enormous anxiety and guilt from her oral wishes. She craved food and spent a lot of energy trying to limit her eating. She had a history of binge eating. In her relationship with her boyfriend, she wanted to have sex three times a day. If he faltered on this schedule—one that she experienced like a feeding—she felt murderous rage. Miss A. had a long-standing fear of sex and engaged in sexual behavior in an almost counterphobic way. She had a deep conviction that sex was bad. It was an enormous relief to her that her boyfriend did not share this idea but seemed to enjoy the sexual aspects of their relationship. It was with him that she experienced her first orgasm. She thought that anyone who really enjoyed sex was not normal, and she frequently tried to find ways to make the external environment line up with her internal beliefs. For example, the couple once engaged in sex in a public restroom with the fear (and the wish) that a security officer would find them and put them in jail.

For Miss A., to be in a relationship required total compliance with the other person's real or imagined preferences, demands, and expectations. It appeared that she had extreme longings to be told what to do and projected this onto others. Although she chose her boyfriend in part to escape from the primitive images of her mother, before long her image of him became distorted as well.

Anality was prominent in her relationship with her boyfriend, both in their sexual behavior and in their sadomasochistic interactions. One way this was expressed was by her making him wait for her. If they were to meet after being separated, she would either be an hour or more late, or not show up at all. In trying to understand the meaning of keeping others waiting, she recalled times when, as a school girl, she and her sister would often be the last students to be picked up by her mother after school, and that sometimes the wait was very, very long. This material was understood in terms of her identification with her mother from childhood. Although it was unsubstantiated, I also speculated that in infancy she may have been left waiting in frustration for her mother to feed her, hold her, and comfort her. It seemed that she was using repetition and identification with the aggressor to try to master a trauma that occurred before she had words to express her feelings.

Although heterosexuality had been established in her behavior, Miss A. had an active homosexual fantasy life that was stated in the form of a possibility or a plan, a plan she would discuss with her boyfriend. Consciously, she experienced herself as a liberated woman who thought being bisexual was sophisticated. Unconsciously, her motives were quite complex.

Miss A.'s relationship with her boyfriend became chaotic. She was usually in a rage with him because he had frustrated or disappointed her in some way. She was unaware of what she wanted from him and unaware that she was not getting what she wanted. She dealt with her frustrations by retaliation, which only began a vicious cycle of sadomasochistic interactions. She was in a constant struggle with her own passive and submissive longings, which she perceived as his wish to control her. Consciously, Miss A. felt that she had no power or control over him, yet in reality she appeared to be controlling him and everyone else in her environment.

Miss A. often set up triangular relationships. Her first boyfriend was introduced to her by her sister, and when she began having sex with him she was preoccupied with the idea that her sister was interested in him. But mostly the triangular relationships consisted of her boyfriend and another woman who seemed to be a representation of her externalized superego rather than a true oedipal object.

In the transference, she viewed the therapist as a vicious, vindictive, angry, demanding, and frightening woman who would be pleasant on the surface but seething underneath. We were able to see that her projections were ubiquitous. She was almost always imagining that others wanted to ensnare her, dominate her, and control her. These projections seemed so real to her that she was always fending people off. At the same time she imagined that people were angry with her, and as a consequence she feared rejection and abandonment. She would then counterattack and become even more fearful of being abandoned. Miss A. was not able to observe the real qualities of the love object or to evaluate the future of the relationship. She was unable to integrate the disharmony between primary love objects. She was unable to counteract the force of the superego. She was unable to counteract the extreme demands of the id, which insists on refinding the impossible, the replica of the longed-for symbiosis. She was unable to resist the pressure of the repetition compulsion. Miss A.'s superego was harsh and primitive.

DISCUSSION

It is Kernberg's (1995) view that the borderline patient demonstrates a primitive type of falling in love, one characterized by an unrealistic idealization of the love object, whom they do not perceive at any depth. Kernberg feels that the intense sexual experience is utilized to deny intolerable aggression, and is a sort of primitive reaction formation. This process illustrates what might be called a premature oedipalization of preoedipal conflicts. Intense love affairs can obscure the underlying dynamics related to oral needs and dependency as well as an incapacity to tolerate aggression, and thus can be an attempt to escape from the frightening, frustrating relations with the mother. Kernberg has stated that borderline patients are capable of falling in love only with part objects. But these relationships are fragile and forever at risk of being contaminated by highly distorted images of the mother of infancy. The borderline patient is invested in power because it is an assurance of safety against a total submission to a sadistic object (Kernberg 1995). Miss A.'s relationships seem consistent with this picture.

Before concluding, I would like to say a few words about the relationship between problems with intimacy and the borderline diagnosis. In comparing intimacy problems experienced by patients with borderline levels of functioning with those experienced by persons with less severe psychopathology, several broad generalizations can be made. In both diagnostic categories there seem to be problems associated with libidinal fixation points at both preoedipal and oedipal levels. Miss A.'s conflicts were more at the preoedipal levels, but she too showed signs of oedipal conflict that interfered with intimacy. The conflicts of neurotic patients tend to be more focused at the oedipal level, but it is rare to find a patient free of preoedipal issues. Miss A. seemed to be more frenetic, perhaps desperate, in her search for intimacy, but at the same time was very fearful of it, a dilemma that seems to have its etiology in both inadequate symbiosis and separation and individuation phases.

It is the quality of aggression that separates the two types of patients most dramatically. The aggression found in neurotic patients tends to be limited to the rivalries of the oedipal phase. For example, neurotic patients tend to suffer mostly from guilt over aggressive feelings and tend to have a very punitive superego. In contrast, Miss A.'s aggression was intense and primitive, so that sadomasochistic features dominated her fantasy life and her intimate relationships.

From the side of the ego, Miss A. had far more trouble in choosing a love object that was appropriate for her. She related to her boyfriend largely as a part object and as an escape from her enmeshment with her mother, and did not ever come to know him in depth. Although neurotic patients often have trouble finding a satisfying relationship, they are capable of concern for their partners and capable of knowing them in depth.

TREATMENT IMPLICATIONS

Although patients with intimacy problems are often referred to couples therapists, it is my contention that problems with intimacy are primarily internal, and therefore that a psychoanalytic method will produce the most comprehensive changes in the way the patient relates to significant others. This method thus offers the greatest likelihood of increasing the patient's capacity for intimacy.

I have described the ways in which the libidinal fixations, ego weaknesses, superego pathology, and the compulsion to repeat past object relations contribute to problems of intimacy. The psychoanalytic method, with its use of transference and resistance, is ideally suited to uncovering old ways of relating to love objects. By providing the patient with a setting that is constant and secure, by showing interest, and by encouraging free association, the therapist allows the transference to be elaborated in such a form that it will become possible to demonstrate to the patient how old ways of loving and fears of being intimate are interfering in his or her current life.

In the treatment situation the patient reexperiences early forms of love and their associated intimacies, and a mourning of past object relationships is set in motion that frees up energies for healthier forms of love. As Bergmann (1987) has suggested, every form of falling in love draws upon earlier loves; by systematically uncovering past object relationships, fresh capacities for love are unearthed. The analytic resolution of the transference, with its attendant ambivalence and incestuous nature, permits the sublimation of preoedipal and oedipal love into a normal and reciprocal relationship in real life.

REFERENCES

Abend, S., Porder, M., and Willeck, M. (1983). *Borderline Patients: Psychoanalytic Perspectives.* New York: International Universities Press.

Abraham, K. (1924). A short study of the development of the libido, viewed in the light of mental disorders. In *Selected Papers*, pp. 418–501. London: Hogarth, 1927.

Altman, L. (1977). Some vicissitudes of love. *Journal of the American Psychoanalytic Association* 25:35–52.

Balint, M. (1948). On genital love. *International Journal of Psycho-Analysis* 29:34–40.

Bergmann, M. (1987). *The Anatomy of Loving: The Story of Man's Quest to Know What Love Is.* New York: Columbia University Press.

Binstock, W. (1973). On the two forms of intimacy. *Journal of the American Psychoanalytic Association* 21:93.

Blos, P. (1962). *On Adolescence.* New York: Free Press.

Coen, S. (1992). *The Misuse of Persons: Analyzing Pathological Dependency.* Hillsdale, NJ: Analytic Press.

Crandall, L. (1993). *A comparative study of superego functioning in borderline and neurotic women*: Unpublished doctoral dissertation: New York University, NY.

Edgcumbe, R., and Burgner, M. (1975). Phallic-narcissistic phase: a differentiation. *Psychoanalytic Study of the Child* 30:161–179. New Haven, CT: Yale University Press.

Fenichel, O. (1945). *The Psychoanalytic Theory of Neurosis.* New York: Norton.

Freud, A. (1936). *The Ego and the Mechanisms of Defense.* New York: International Universities Press.

Freud, S. (1905). Three essays on the theory of sexuality. *Standard Edition* 7:125–243.

——— (1908). Character and anal erotism. *Standard Edition* 9:168–175.

——— (1909). Notes upon a case of obsessional neurosis. *Standard Edition* 10:153–318.

——— (1914). On narcissism: an introduction. *Standard Edition* 14:67–102.

——— (1923). The ego and the id. *Standard Edition* 19:3–66.

——— (1924). The economic problem of masochism. *Standard Edition* 19:157–170.

Jacobson, E. (1964). *The Self and the Object World.* New York: International Universities Press.

Kernberg, O. (1975). *Borderline Conditions and Pathological Narcissism.* New York: Jason Aronson.

———— (1992). *Aggression in Personality Disorders and Perversion.* New Haven, CT: Yale University Press.

———— (1995). *Love Relations: Normality and Pathology.* New Haven, CT: Yale University Press.

Kohut, H. (1971). *The Analysis of the Self.* New York: International Universities Press.

Mahler, M., Pine, F., and Bergman, A. (1975). *The Psychological Birth of the Human Infant.* New York: Basic Books

Person, E. (1988). *Dreams of Love and Fateful Encounters: The Power of Romantic Passion.* New York: Norton.

Reich, W. (1933). *Character Analysis.* New York: Farrar, Straus & Giroux.

Sandler, J. (1985). *The Analysis of Defense: The Ego and the Mechanisms of Defense Revisited.* New York: International Universities Press.

Stoller, R. (1979). *Sexual Excitement.* New York: Pantheon.

Waelder, R. (1936). Principle of multiple function: observations on over-determination. *Psychoanalytic Quarterly* 5:45–62.

Wallerstein, J., and Blakeslee, S. (1995). *The Good Marriage: How and Why Love Lasts.* Boston: Houghton Mifflin.

5

Sexual Function and Dysfunction in Intimate Relationships

SILKALY M. WOLCHOK

INTRODUCTION

The concepts of love and attachment imply the attainment of sexual fulfillment. Healthy sexuality is included as a major domain of life within the larger abstract idea of "quality of life," which includes the physical, psychological, social, occupational, and sexual areas. This has been traced by Aaronson (1990) to have originated with the "1947 World Health Organization definition of health as 'a state of complete physical, mental and social well-being, and not merely the absence of disease and infirmity' " (p. 59).

Cella and Cherin (1988) also see the concept of quality of life as reflective of the individual's appraisal of and satisfaction with his or her current level of functioning in comparison with the same person's perception of what is possible or desirable. Thus, not only do love and attachment clearly focus on the nature of sexual function and dysfunction, but satisfactory sexual functioning is an essential aspect of our overall state of subjective well-being. Our quality of life reflects our feelings of satisfaction with life, love, and attachments.

In our contemporary culture, love and sex are closely associated and appear to be "mutually reinforcing" (Byer and Shainberg 1991, p. 78). As a result, sexual function and dysfunction must be recognized as central areas of concern in any discussion of current configurations of "love and attachment."

CURRENT CONCEPTS OF SEXUAL FUNCTION

The current incomplete state of our knowledge makes it almost impossible to define a "normal sexuality" against which to compare "sexual dysfunction." Kaplan (1974, 1975, 1979, 1983, 1987, 1989) has summarized much of what we do know, including "that in the healthy individual, some form of sexual appetite is present throughout life no matter what his cultural origins are" (Kaplan 1979, p. 60). As we find with other human traits, there are wide variations in sex drives, attitudes, practices, and frequency of sexual activity between different individuals.

Kaplan (1979) has extensively described sexual development in general. She has stated that the intensity of sexual appetite is seen to show changes with age and that male and female development take different courses with age.

In detail, she describes how infants are seen to express pleasure when their genitals are stimulated in the process of being bathed or dressed. Currently, sonograms reveal male fetuses' erections in utero. Children show marked curiosity about each other's genitalia and can be observed masturbating and playing sexual games, investigating each other's genitals. Much of this is repressed but, generally, some memory of these activities remains.

At puberty, sexual desire increases markedly. Kaplan (1979) sees this as likely due to the maturing of the cerebral circuits affecting sexual expression at the same time that the gonads are increasing their production of testosterone, which causes these cerebral circuits to become active. Following puberty, male and female sexual desire patterns show marked differences.

Typically, adolescent males show intense sexual interest, have frequent sexual fantasies, become aroused easily, and seek outlets, with a partner or through masturbation, ranging from several times a day to several times a week, in order to avoid experiencing frustration. The male sex drive appears to peak at about age 17 and then slowly diminish. Throughout the male lifetime, sexual desire normally continues and can be aroused, but with increasing age men can go for longer and longer periods of time without sexual expression and not experience frustration.

Female sexual desire, although strongly increasing at puberty, is more easily suppressed, is more variable, seems to require less expression than in adolescent males, and does not diminish after adolescence but increases to a high point at about 40 years before slowly declining.

Spontaneous sexual desire, as well as arousability under exciting conditions or by an attractive partner, continues throughout life in normal persons. However, as the sex drive slowly declines, there is a narrowing range of stimuli that will arouse it and excitation requires increasingly greater psychic and physical stimulation.

Other major factors affecting sexual desire are mood and physical health, again demonstrating the intersection of quality of life and love issues. In normal males and females, love increases sexual desire; stress decreases it. Although fluctuations in desire occur, long absences of sexual activity do not normally occur.

Human sexual response, as based on the 1966 studies of human physiological sexual response by Masters and Johnson and the further treatment advances of Kaplan (1974, 1975, 1979, 1983, 1987, 1989), is now understood to occur and be most effectively studied in three specific phases: desire, excitement, and orgasm. Sexual dysfunction can occur in any of these phases and is diagnosed in relation to the phase affected. Therapy is then based on the specific phase and problem, with definite treatment approaches.

Prior to the development of this simple triphasic model, on which current psychiatric and sexual therapy nomenclature is based, sexual problems were grouped together and called "frigidity" in women and "impotence" in men. In both cases, sexual dysfunctions were seen as manifestations of serious psychopathology. The only treatment was believed to be long-term psychoanalysis, which frequently was ineffective (Fenichel 1945, Freud 1905).

In contrast, nonorganically caused sexual problems in the excitement and orgasm phases have been demonstrated by Kaplan (1979) and others to be successfully treated with short-term therapy. Desire problems resulting from mild sources of anxiety, as seen in simple performance anxiety, anticipated lack of pleasure, or mild residual guilt about sex and pleasure having a cultural origin, are seen to be very responsive to brief sex therapy without patient insight. However, desire problems are more typically the result of deeper and more complex intrapsychic issues and severe relationship problems, which do not generally respond to short-term, cognitive-behavioral sex therapy methods, and require longer-term, insight-based, psychosexual therapy.

THE TRIPHASIC MODEL

Phase I—Desire

In the triphasic model of sexual response, Kaplan (1979) describes libido as having a neural organization similar to the hunger, thirst, and urge to sleep reactions that differ constitutionally in intensity. She sees libido experienced behaviorally as sexual desire, as being a psychosomatic concept, in that desire can be increased or inhibited by numerous internal and external forces.

Included in the internal forces are sex-center responses to hormones. The hormones that produce feelings of desire in women as well as men are the androgens. In men, testosterone, the primary male hormone, is produced mostly by the testicles with smaller amounts produced by the adrenal glands. It controls sexual development, functioning, behavior, and desire, as well as the secondary sexual characteristics. In women, too, desire is produced by small amounts of testosterone, manufactured in the adrenal glands. Although the female hormones, estrogen and progesterone, contribute to a woman's androgen levels, menopause does not diminish sexual desire because women continue to produce testosterone. Desire is seen to vanish when the testosterone hormonal environment is inadequate.

Kaplan (1974) has stated that other internal factors affecting desire result from the sex centers' connections to other parts of the brain; the effects of depression; severe distress states; drugs such as narcotics, sedatives, alcohol, and antihypertensives; and illnesses or treatments that negatively affect the brain's sexual centers (e.g., urological and gynecological disorders that cause sexual activity to be uncomfortable or painful, or renal dialysis treatment).

External factors associated with a lover, such as aroma, sight, sound, and touch, also strongly affect sexual desire. Furthermore, connections of the sex centers to the parts of the brain that store and process experience result in sexual desire being highly sensitive to experiences in the past, so that suppression of sexual desire can be learned in negative or dangerous situations (e.g., past painful relationship problems, or cancer diagnosis and treatment), and desire can blossom in safe contexts.

In addition to age and health, sex centers are also markedly affected by emotion. Negative emotions that serve individual survival and result in avoidance or defense against danger, fear, and anger have priority over sexual desire and reproductive urges. However, inaccurate perceptions of danger are as inhibiting to the sex drive as real danger. Psychological conflict can also be a cause of diminished sexual desire, which Kaplan (1979) sees as the result of active, although unconscious and involuntary, suppression of libido. Phobic avoidance of sex can be the result of conflict-caused anxiety even when desire exists.

Thus, there is a psychophysiologic basis for sexual desire. In actual practice, psychogenic factors are found to be more prevalent than physiologic causes in libidinal disturbance. Fear or anxiety is found by Kaplan (1974) to be the major causal factor in all sexual dysfunctions, but anger at the partner is also a highly prevalent cause for loss of sexual desire. My work (Wolchok 1995) with leukemia survivors, who had no gonadal changes due to their illness or treatment, also revealed that sexual function reports of those adult patients were inversely related to their scores on several self-report measures of psychological distress, especially as seen in the symptom and mood states of anxiety and anger. That is, the greater their scores of psychological distress on standardized measures, the less sexual interest and/or frequency and less sexual satisfaction with their sexual relationships these survivors reported.

Kaplan (1979) emphasizes that anger, like anxiety, can vary in intensity and depth, and that it is a common element by which sexuality can become blocked. She suggests that the most serious sources of anger affecting sexual desire are those derived from infantile transferences, such as feelings of insufficient nurturing or abandonment fears, which may be reevoked by the partner's behavior, illness, or other conditions. In persons free of major psychopathology, anger evokes defenses against openness and erotic feelings and usually serves as an obstacle to sexuality. In contrast, sexual freedom entails a lowering of defenses and may generate profound feelings of vulnerability. Thus, it is safer to block feelings of desire when one feels vulnerable and distrustful.

Sexual dysfunction in the desire phase was originally referred to as Inhibited Sexual Desire (Kaplan 1979), manifested by loss of interest in sex with no, few, or negative thoughts about sex; antisexual attitudes; anxious, panicky feelings about sex; and avoidance of sexual situations.

The *DSM-IV* (1994) includes two Sexual Desire Disorders, described as:

> *Hypoactive Sexual Desire Disorder* (302.71): "Persistently or recurrently deficient (or absent) sexual fantasies and desire for sexual activity" (p. 498), and *Sexual Aversion Disorder* (302.79): "Persistent or recurrent extreme aversion to, and avoidance of, all (or almost all) genital sexual contact with a sexual partner" (p. 500).

Both types of sexual desire disorders can negatively impact interpersonal relationships. Tom, for instance, exemplifies sexual aversion difficulties.

> Tom, a very attractive 48-year-old man, presented with his second wife, Joan, after five years of marriage. Each had been in a sexually active but unhappy first marriage. In their extraordinarily loving and happy current marriage, Tom and Joan shared many interests and activities but were virtually nonsexual except for two or three interactions per year.

Joan's sexual overtures toward Tom were discouraged. However, she interpreted his behavior as demonstrating an innately low desire level at this stage of his life after a urologist had suggested testosterone injections, which Tom had rejected. The crisis that brought them into treatment was Joan's discovery of semen all over the bedclothes upon returning home from work one day. She interpreted this to mean Tom was sexually interested, active, and having an affair with someone else, which was intolerably painful and unacceptable to her.

In reality, Tom had been regularly masturbating but unable to relate with sexual intimacy to his loving, caring spouse. With much work it was learned that Tom's avoidance of almost all genital sexual contact with his wife was a result of his history of growing up in a close and loving relationship with his seductive, alcoholic mother. In that relationship, Tom had to constantly maintain sexual control and deal with his sexually aroused feelings through masturbation. Throughout his life, he had been able to engage in successful sexual interactions only with women he didn't know or whom he did not really care about. The immediate cause of his adult sexual problem was his total avoidance of erotic stimulation and erotic fantasies when in close proximity to Joan. The severe deeper cause was his oedipally related avoidance of sexual intimacy. Long-term, insight-based psychosexual treatment was required to work through these complicated issues.

Phase II—Excitement

The second phase of the triphasic model of sexuality is the excitement phase, characterized by feelings of arousal, penile erection in men, and vaginal lubrication and engorgement in women. Touching and caressing feel much more intense. Sexual fantasies, erotic sights, sounds, scents, and tastes are other factors affecting sexual excitement. Physically, the heartbeat and pulse speed up, blood pressure increases, and breathing becomes heavy. Blood surges into the genital area, resulting in penile erection in males and the lubrication and increase in depth and width of the vagina in women. The skin of the genitals turns a deeper color (Auchincloss 1989, Kaplan 1974).

Sexual dysfunction in this phase is called "Inhibited Sexual Excitement," a term used in the *DSM-IV* (p. 279). It is manifested by difficulty attaining or maintaining an erection in men and by impaired vaginal lubrication and engorgement in women. Dyspareunia, or pain with intercourse, leads to sexual avoidance unless treated promptly. Such dysfunctions require a thorough medical evaluation and treatment of the specific cause, since a physical cause, psychological cause, or a combination of physical and psychological components, even when a physical cause is present, may be responsible.

Vaginismus, vaginal muscle spasm making penetration painful or impossible, is seen as a response to pain or fear of pain. When treated with combined relaxation and sequenced penetration, first by the patient alone and then with her partner, this problem shows good prognosis.

Psychological factors causing excitement-phase dysfunction include anxiety or exaggerated self-focus on performance, dyadic difficulties, and intrapsychic conflict. The nature of the symptom alone will not clarify whether the problem is the result of interpersonally or intrapsychically caused anxiety, so that information regarding partner specificity is essential.

In the excitement phase, a supportive partner is seen to be essential. Treatment relates to the cause of the dysfunction, and extends from counseling and psychotherapy related to anxiety, technique, communication, and self-esteem issues to penile prosthetics, lubricants, and so on.

The *DSM-IV* (1994) includes two Sexual Arousal Disorders, described as *Female Sexual Arousal Disorder* (302.72): "Persistent or recurrent inability to attain, or to maintain until the completion of the sexual activity, an adequate lubrication-swelling response of sexual excitement" (p. 502), and *Male Erectile Disorder* (302.72): "Persistent or recurrent inability to attain, or to maintain until completion of the sexual activity, an adequate erection" (p. 504).

> Albert was a 37-year-old foreign-born man from a culture that prides itself on male sexual prowess. He requested help when he experienced recurring loss of his erections during sexual intercourse with his wife, whom he found attractive and desirable.
>
> For the first nine years of their marriage he had experienced no sexual dysfunction and he and Marianne, his wife, enjoyed a

fulfilled sexual life while becoming parents of four children. However, during the past year of economic business difficulties, simultaneous with growing family responsibilities, Albert's occasional symptoms became pronounced and impossible to ignore.

It was particularly interesting that, in keeping with his cultural background, Albert did not want his wife to be a participant in his sexual therapy. A urological workup revealed no medical cause for the change in his functioning.

Psychosexual evaluation of Albert's problem showed plainly that his mounting career-related stresses were causing him to experience much inner anxiety, feelings of vulnerability, and lowered self-esteem, which manifested themselves in an inability to maintain an adequate erection until the completion of sexual activity. Immediate causes of the dysfunction were his reactions to his first few losses of erection, with ongoing experiences of performance anxiety plus an overconcern with pleasing his partner. They were successfully dealt with by using cognitive-behavioral techniques in brief therapy. The deeper causes were his inability to meet his culturally based expectations as a lover and fear of rejection by Marianne.

The *DSM-IV* (1994) also has a category of Sexual Pain Disorders (Not Due to a General Medical Condition), which includes *Dyspareunia* (302.76): "Recurrent or persistent genital pain associated with sexual intercourse in either a male or a female" (p. 513), and *Vaginismus* (306.51): "Recurrent or persistent involuntary spasm of the musculature of the outer third of the vagina that interferes with sexual intercourse" (p. 515).

Phase III—Orgasm

The third phase in the triphasic model is the orgasm phase, in which genital reflex muscle contractions, associated with intense pleasure, ejaculation, and emission in men, and pleasurable sensation in women, occur, sending waves of feeling through the body. Sexual dysfunction in this phase includes "Inhibited Female Orgasm" (*DSM–III*, p. 279) or anorgasmia in women, and "Inhibited Male Orgasm" (*DSM–III*, p.

280) (i.e., retarded ejaculation), premature ejaculation, or inability to control timing of the orgasm in males.

In females, anorgasmia may indicate the need for longer or more direct stimulation of the clitoris as well as improved communication with the partner, plus the need for more effective methods of relaxation.

This problem was well illustrated by Sarah, age 27, who had been sexually active and under the care of a gynecologist since she was 17, but had never had an orgasm. She was certain that she never would. She and Jim, a man she had originally met in college, had rekindled their friendship and it had blossomed into a meaningful, very loving relationship. They decided to marry, but Jim refused to proceed until they had successfully worked out a means of his giving (and Sarah's experiencing) sexual pleasure from him, as he did from her.

She came into sexual therapy to deal with her problem. In spite of her brightness, education, and years of sexual experience, Sarah appeared not to be very knowledgeable about her own body. Yet she became interested in learning and seemed challenged by the task. Evaluation revealed that she had never actively masturbated as a child, adolescent, or young adult. However, with a partner, she had been regularly experiencing strong sexual desire and arousal, manifested by genital lubrication and vaginal engorgement. Nevertheless, neither manual, oral, nor penile stimulation resulted in her experiencing orgasm.

The immediate psychogenic causes of her dysfunction were revealed to be her inability to "let go" during intercourse, likely insufficient stimulation, and an increasingly obsessive self-observation during sex. Deeper intrapsychic and relationship causes of this condition tended to be mild and were not readily apparent.

While the evaluative process was going on, a friend of Sarah's suggested that Sarah try masturbating with a powerful vibrator. She did and it resulted in her experiencing an orgasm, which helped to nullify her hopelessness about her situation. It also lent weight to the explanation that she needed extensive clitoral stimulation prior to and during intercourse in order to achieve an orgasm (after she has experienced desire and arousal). Relaxation methods, fantasy development, and masturbatory self-awareness leading to extended, more sufficient clitoral stimulation, and not the continued use of a vibrator, were advised to avoid dependence on mechanical stimulation, which would have prevented her from meeting her goal—that she and her partner be successful together.

In males, premature ejaculation is a common concern in the healthy population. Frequently, the cause is the male's not having learned voluntary control over his ejaculatory reflexes. Performance anxiety and lack of awareness of his level of tension often add to the problem. Usually, this syndrome can be treated in brief sexual therapy and has a very good prognosis.

Males have a refractory period, a time following orgasm in which the individual is not physically capable of having another. This time period tends to extend with age, so that men in their seventies and older may require several days between sexual encounters. Women do not have a refractory period and some are capable of having multiple orgasms, one after another.

Orgasmic Disorders included in the *DSM-IV* (1994) are described as *Female Orgasmic Disorder* (302.73) [Formerly labeled Inhibited Female Orgasm]: "Persistent or recurrent delay in, or absence of, orgasm following a normal sexual excitement phase. Women exhibit wide variability in the type or intensity of stimulation that triggers orgasm" (p. 506); *Male Orgasmic Disorder* (302.74) [Formerly labeled Inhibited Male Orgasm]: "Persistent or recurrent delay in, or absence of, orgasm following a normal sexual excitement phase during sexual activity that the clinician, taking into account the person's age, judges to be adequate in focus, intensity, and duration" (p. 509); and *Premature Ejaculation* (302.75): "Persistent or recurrent ejaculation with minimal sexual stimulation before, on, or shortly after penetration and before the person wishes it" (p. 511).

Kaplan (1979) has emphasized that if a problem in the orgasm phase persists over time, problems in the preceding phases of response are likely to be created. Thus, orgasm-phase problems lead to excitement-phase problems, and these to desire problems. Kaplan, who has had extensive clinical experience treating physically healthy persons as well as those with medical problems, has observed that orgasm-phase disorders are often easiest to treat, excitement-phase problems more difficult, and desire-phase problems most difficult. This is because an orgasm-phase problem usually signifies normal desire and a healthy excitement response, with physically or psychologically caused orgasm impairment that is generally not of great magnitude. By contrast, greater psychological limitations in sexual response, more severe physical problems, or both, are likely to be the cause of desire-phase problems and demand more intense long-term treatment for any success.

IMMEDIATE AND DEEPER CAUSES OF SEXUAL DYSFUNCTION

Kaplan (1974) further helped develop sex-therapy methods by distinguishing between the nonorganic psychological causes that are the more superficial and immediate causes of the problem and the deeper causes. Short-term cognitive-behavioral methods of treatment were seen as appropriate for treating the more superficial and immediate causes of sexual dysfunction. Longer-term, less confrontational, and more supportive psychotherapeutic methods are used for more fragile patients or those with problems having deeper causes.

As illustrated in the above case examples of sexual dysfunction, immediate causes are best understood as the patient's current problematic sexual behavior, and the negative emotional reactions he or she experiences immediately prior to the current psychosexual symptom. These include fear and anxiety caused by obsessive self-observation or spectatoring, as well as insufficient stimulation, lack of awareness of sensations premonitory to orgasm, overconcern with pleasing a partner or insensitivity to the needs of a partner, inadequate communication about sex, and mild guilt feelings.

Deeper causes include relationship problems and either partner's intrapsychic causes, such as serious psychiatric disorders, strong sociocultural or religious negative sexual attitudes, or anti-pleasure attitudes. Sometimes the immediate causes serve as defenses or are integral to the deeper psychodysfunctional causes. When this is not so, the sexual symptoms can be treated with brief sexual therapy techniques. When deeper causes are dependent on the immediate causes as defenses or to maintain the psychodynamic homeostasis, more extensive treatment requires that emotional issues be dealt with in treatment.

Neither the diagnosis of the problem nor the content of intrapsychic conflict are accurate indicators of the severity of the underlying sexual anxiety, since the same symptoms may result from either minor or major causes. However, patients with minor anxiety more easily recognize or accept information about the causes of their symptoms in treatment and do not become increasingly anxious as treatment progresses. In contrast, those without insight and who have deeper problems resist recognizing information in relation to the causes of their sexual problems and become more anxious with the improvement of symptoms.

Nor does the symptom indicate if the cause of the problem is intrapsychic or relational. Masters and Johnson (1970) saw the couple as patient and *all* sexual problems as involving *both* partners. Kaplan (1983) did not totally agree and emphasized the requirement that partner specificity be determined, that is, determining whether the same problem occurs with every partner or is specific to one person as partner. She conceptualized that most sexual problems are a combination of intrapsychic and dyadic interactions, with some only intrapsychic, some partner-specific, and some global in effect, occurring with all sexual partners of that patient.

Sexual relationship problems have been described by Kaplan (1974, 1975, 1979, 1983, 1987) as including inadequate information about technique and lack of understanding of one's own and/or one's partner's sexual needs, plus a poor level of communication about these. Additionally, the inability of the partners to meet each other's sexual fantasies because of their basically different needs is a major problem that requires partners to learn how to compromise and to find new methods that meet both of their needs. A partner who really wants sexual compatibility is capable of this.

Deeper relational problems include partner conflict and struggles for control and dominance; partners' unmet conscious or unconscious expectations of each other in relation to their responsibilities; ambivalence or anger; problems with intimacy; strong parental transferences to the partner; psychopathology of either partner; and a history of sexual trauma (e.g., rape or incest).

EFFECTS OF ILLNESS

Another event that will affect sexual function in most intimate relationships, whether of recent or long-term duration, is serious illness. For example, persons newly diagnosed with an illness who undergo subsequent treatment, such as surgery, radiation, or chemotherapy regimens for various forms of cancer, have been observed to experience a noticeable loss or diminution of sexual function following amputation, hormonal disruption, nerve damage, appearance concerns, emotional responses, and so on. Treatment frequently results in problems of infertility, sterility, inhibited desire, erectile difficulties, impotence, symptoms of premature menopause, dyspareunia, impaired orgasm, depression, anger, poor body image, diminished sexual self-esteem, sexual identity issues, continuing somatic distress, embarrassment, feelings of mutilation, and other concerns (Schover 1988a,b).

Other serious illnesses with sexual side-effects caused by the illness itself, or by patients' treatment or medications, include diabetes, endocrine disorders, cardiovascular problems, painful disorders (e.g., severe lower back pain), and substance abuse. Therefore, assessment of medical status is essential in the evaluation of sexual function/dysfunction.

The major standard used to differentiate between organically and nonorganically caused dysfunction is whether the impairment is global, that is, occurring at all times (which is likely to be organic), or fluctuating and situational (likely to be not organic). As a result, Kaplan and Sadock (1988) emphasize the need for the clinician to get a pre-symptom baseline of the impairment, in addition to the current complaint.

In keeping with the recognition of the effects of illness on sexual function, *DSM-IV* (1994) includes the following in a large category of Sexual Dysfunction Due to a General Medical Condition in which the diagnostic criteria are:

> Clinically significant sexual dysfunction that results in marked
> distress or interpersonal difficulty predominates in the clinical pic-

ture. There is evidence from the history, physical examination, or laboratory findings that the sexual dysfunction is fully explained by the direct physiological effects of a general medical condition. The disturbance is not better accounted for by another mental disorder (e.g., Major Depressive Disorder). [p. 518]

The code and term are then based on the predominant sexual dysfunction:

Female Hypoactive Sexual Desire Disorder Due to (Indicate) the General Medical Condition (625.38) "if deficient or absent sexual desire is the predominant feature" (p. 518).

Male Hypoactive Sexual Desire Disorder Due to (Indicate) the General Medical Condition (608.89) "if deficient or absent sexual desire is the predominant feature" (p. 518).

Male Erectile Disorder Due to (Indicate) the General Medical Condition (607.84) "if male erectile dysfunction is the predominant feature" (p. 518).

Female Dyspareunia Due to (Indicate) the General Medical Condition (625.0) "if pain associated with intercourse is the predominant feature" (p. 518).

Male Dyspareunia Due to (Indicate) the General Medical Condition (608.89) "if pain associated with intercourse is the predominant feature" (p. 518).

Other Female Sexual Dysfunction Due to (Indicate) the General Medical Condition (625.8) "if some other feature is predominant (e.g., Orgasmic Disorder) or no feature predominates" (p. 518).

Other Male Sexual Dysfunction Due to (Indicate) the General Medical Condition (608.89) "if some other feature is predominant (e.g., Orgasmic Disorder) or no feature predominates" (p. 518).

Substance-Induced Sexual Dysfunction is also included in detail in the *DSM-IV*.

This resulting multiple symptomatology illustrates Greenberg's (1983, 1984) statement about cancer patients: "Sexual behavior is always simultaneously somatic, psychological, and interpersonal"

(p. 2281). Lower levels of sexual interest and activity and feelings of lessened physical attractiveness are frequently reported by these patients, and are significantly associated with their increasing psychological distress. Such findings again point to the need to focus on both physical and psychological factors and their interaction when dealing with sexual concerns.

Even with cancer survivors of illnesses having no effect upon sexually related body parts or gonadal functioning, frequency of, or satisfaction with, sexual activity, body image, gender role identity, and adjustment in sexual relations are found to be impaired (Lesko et al. 1987). Such results indicate that there are psychosexual sequelae in survivors whose illnesses have caused no physical impairment to gonads or sexually related organs that are indistinguishable from those suffered by patients in whom gonads and organs have been impaired. This can also apply to patients with cardiovascular problems such as heart disease or stroke, as well as other illnesses. Further intensive investigation seems required to identify and understand the specific causes of such results and to develop timely, appropriate, and successful psychosocial interventions.

The triphasic model of sexual response is a valuable format against which to view the psychosexual effects of illness, or crises and their methods of treatment. Inherent in this theory is the concept that sexual desire is normally diminished in mammals, including humans, when physical or psychological stress is experienced. The diagnosis and treatment of serious illnesses constitute major life stresses in both of these domains even when no sexually related organ is involved (Auchincloss 1989). Following a diagnosis of illness, sexual desire is frequently lessened or lost early on, and returns as health is regained. Schover (1988a,b) and Auchincloss (1989) have both stated that inhibited sexual desire and loss of interest in sex is not unusual during the time that the patient is in active treatment and concerns about health issues and treatment predominate. The treatment itself may cause disruption in the patient's hormonal system, affecting desire. Treatments extended over time, as well as those with long-lasting side effects, often cause diminution of desire that may be related to changes in appearance to which either the patient or the partner, although loving, may initially react with anxiety, avoidance, or depression. With help, both the patient and the partner can learn to accept the change without either ignoring or obsessing about it.

Patients are often concerned about the effect of sexual deprivation on their partners and its likely impact on their short-term and long-term relationship. However, the result may be that both the patient and the partner lose interest in sex, as avoidance of sexual situations by one partner is frequently associated with prolonged loss of sexual desire in both (Leiber et al. 1976).

Experiences both of patients and of healthy persons in the general population indicate that problems in the orgasm phase may be related to fatigue, depression, stress, pain, drugs, medication, or anxiety. However, Auchincloss (1989) has stated that current research has found orgasm problems *alone* are not frequently reported by cancer patients. In males, premature ejaculation is found to be a rare complaint in these patients unless it preexisted the illness.

However, in most illnesses and treatments, pleasure continues to be experienced from touching. Shover (1988) states that although some types of surgery or treatment can prevent a man's ability to have erections or manufacture semen and may leave a woman with a painfully dry or tight vagina, few treatments damage nerves and muscles involved in the sensation of orgasm, so that pleasure and satisfaction can be experienced from sexual touching even when major changes in sexuality have taken place.

PSYCHOSEXUAL TREATMENT NEEDS OF THE PHYSICALLY ILL PATIENT

In general, psychosexual treatment involves diminishing anxiety and preventing the return of these anxiety patterns, rebuilding confidence based on successful sexual experiences via use of stimulating positive factors, and diminishing negative, anxiety-related factors. Specific treatment techniques are utilized toward this end.

Although problems can arise in the desire, excitement, or orgasm phases of sexual response in healthy persons as well as physically ill patients, the situation of patients is complicated by medical influences in addition to factors of psychological response to treatment. Patients may have special problems with pain, fatigue, and medications, as well as communication, all of which affect sexuality and require special attention that frequently is not forthcoming.

Auchincloss (1989) states that although every adolescent, adult, or elderly patient realistically should be considered to have sexual concerns, and that patients' needs for sexual information and counseling are obvious, medical care has not routinely dealt with this area. She notes that this situation appears to have resulted from health care teams' embarrassment about the subject, the belief that nothing can be done, incorrect preconceptions about sexual functioning, and limited time to deal with patients. She goes on to comment that patients often do not know what to say or to whom to speak about new sexual problems or exacerbated old ones. They may feel it is inappropriate or uncomfortable to initiate such discussion. As a result, avoidance of sexual concerns and issues by both staff and patient is common.

Depending on the individual's developmental stage, the impact of the illness and treatment may arouse very different sexual concerns (Auchincloss 1989). Single persons of all ages with histories of serious illness, including divorced or widowed individuals, are seen to be at markedly increased risk for sexual dysfunction (Bullard et al. 1980). Often they feel doubtful that anyone will ever find them desirable. They may have experienced changes in appearance important to self-esteem, and may require time and help to work through these issues. It is not unusual for single patients to confront concerns about sexual functioning well after treatment ends, when their contact with medical staff is minimal, says Auchincloss (1989). Many patients receiving treatment have been shown to desire more information about sex, although most of those studied have said they would not broach the subject themselves. Thus, there is growing awareness of the treatment team's need to introduce discussion of these matters, obtain information, and provide appropriate support and useful knowledge about the possible impact of treatment on sexual functioning at diagnosis, during treatment, and after treatment. Such discussion would also convey to the patient that sex is an appropriate topic to bring up at any future time, especially since concerns about the illness and the risk of dying are usually primary at the time of diagnosis. Worry about the effects of treatment on one's sex life can soon follow, however, and is frequently associated with fear of abandonment or becoming a burden to one's partner (Holland and Rowland 1989).

There is clearly a value in recognizing the need for appropriate interventions and remedying the current situation. There is also an urgency, for, as early as 1983, Kaplan had developed and described procedures for prevention, early identification, and treatment of sexual problems associated with medical illness that are still not in general usage.

CONCLUSION

In summary, satisfying sexual functioning is a healthy, realistic goal and contributes to a desirable quality of life for both partners in an intimate relationship. When problems prevent this fulfillment, many medical and psychotherapeutic methods are now available to effectively treat the causes.

Essential to good sexual function is a basic understanding of one's own and one's partners sexual needs and changes during the various ages and stages of life. When necessary, psychosexual therapy affords an opportunity for a couple to work together to deal with their problem and not feel hopeless about a major aspect of their intimate life.

REFERENCES

Aaronson, N. K. (1990). Quality of life research in cancer clinical trials: a need for common rules and language. *Oncology* 4(5):59–66.

American Psychiatric Association (1980). *Diagnostic and Statistical Manual of Mental Disorders,* 3rd ed. Washington, DC: Author.

——— (1994). *Diagnostic and Statistical Manual of Mental Disorders,* 4th ed. Washington, DC: Author.

Auchincloss, S. S. (1989). Sexual dysfunction in cancer patients: issues in evaluation and treatment. In *Handbook of Psychooncology,* ed. J. C. Holland and J. H. Rowland, pp. 383–413. New York: Oxford University Press.

Bullard, D. G., Causey, G. G., Newman, A. B., et al. (1980). Sexual health care and cancer: a needs assessment. *Frontiers of Radiation Therapy and Oncology* 14:55–58.

Byer, C. O., and Shainberg, L. W. (1991). *Dimensions of Human Sexuality*. Dubuque, IA: Wm. C. Brown.

Cella, D. F., and Cherin, E. (1988). Quality of life during and after cancer treatment. *Comprehensive Therapy* 14(5):9–75.

Fenichel, O. (1945). *The Psychoanalytic Theory of Neurosis*. New York: Norton.

Freud, S. (1905). Three essays on the theory of sexuality. *Standard Edition* 7:125–243.

Greenberg, D. B. (1983). *Methodology in behavioral and psychosocial research paper*. Paper presented at the American Cancer Society workshop conference, St. Petersburg, FL, April 21–23.

———— (1984). The measurement of sexual dysfunction in cancer patients. *Cancer* May 15 (Suppl.):2281–2285.

Holland, J. C., and Rowland, J. M., eds. (1989). *Handbook of Psychooncology*. New York: Oxford University Press.

Kaplan, H. S. (1974). *The New Sex Therapy: Active Treatment of Sexual Dysfunctions*. New York: Brunner/Mazel.

———— (1975). *The Illustrated Manual of Sex Therapy*. New York: Brunner/Mazel.

———— (1979). *Problems of Sexual Desire*. New York: Brunner/Mazel.

———— (1983). *The Evaluation of Sexual Disorders*. New York: Brunner/Mazel.

———— (1987). *Sexual Aversion, Sexual Phobias, and Panic Disorder*. New York: Brunner/Mazel.

———— (1989). *How to Overcome Premature Ejaculation*. New York: Brunner/Mazel.

Kaplan, H. S., and Sadock, B. J. (1988). *Synopsis of Psychiatry, Behavioral Sciences, Clinical Psychiatry*, 5th ed. Baltimore: Williams & Wilkins.

Leiber, L., Plumb, M., Gerstenzang, M. L., and Holland, J. C. (1976). The communication of affection between cancer patients and their spouses. *Psychosomatic Medicine* 38:379–389.

Lesko, L. M., Mumma, G., and Mashberg, D. (1987). Psychosocial functioning of adult leukemia survivors treated with bone marrow transplantation (BMT) or standard chemotherapy (SC). (Abstract), *Proceedings of the American Society of Clinical Oncology* 6:255. (Abstract No. 1002).

Masters, W. H., and Johnson, V. (1966). *Human Sexual Response*. Boston: Little, Brown.

———— (1970). *Human Sexual Inadequacy*. Boston: Little, Brown.

Schover, L. (1988a). *Sexuality and Cancer for the Woman Who Has Cancer and Her Partner*. New York: American Cancer Society.

———— (1988b). *Sexuality and Cancer for the Man Who Has Cancer and His Partner.* New York: American Cancer Society.

Wolchok, S. M. (1995). *Psychosexual function in survivors of adult acute leukemia.* Unpublished doctoral dissertation: New York University, NY, Shirley M. Ehrenkranz School of Social Work.

6

Trauma's Influence on Love and Attachment

LISA GILMAN

Attachment behaviour . . . is a characteristic of human nature throughout our lives—from the cradle to the grave.

—John Bowlby

Traumatic disruption in early child–parent attachment formation has been documented by numerous theorists as having profound effects on the development of self representation and ego functioning (Ainsworth 1973, Bowlby 1969, 1988, Mahler et al. 1975). This chapter addresses the impact of sexual trauma on one's ability to develop love relationships and to form emotional attachments. The focus is practice-oriented, and is informed by ego psychology and object relations theories.

I will begin with a definition of sexual trauma, followed by a discussion of the symptomatology and clinical manifestations of trauma, the ego structure of the trauma survivor, including the constellation of defenses, and a discussion of common responses to trauma such as eating disorders, promiscuity, self-mutilation, chemical dependency, and their relationship to attachment formation. Distinctive features of treatment and the therapeutic relationship will be examined, while the prominent themes of trauma—shame, humiliation, safety, self-deprecation, power, and control will be addressed throughout the text. An underlying assumption is made that the therapeutic relationship is a primary corrective love relationship for the traumatized client. Finally, a case example will be used as an illustration of these topics.

SEXUAL TRAUMA DEFINED

Sexual trauma has been defined in formal and informal ways within different disciplines to include varying degrees and types of sexual abuse (Courtois 1988). Sgroi and colleagues (1982) delineate a range of sexually abusive behaviors, some of which do not involve physical contact with the child, but which may include sexual comments, flirtations, and intrusive and sometimes overstimulating observations of the child. The range of behavior may include nudity, disrobing, genital exposure, observation of the child, kissing, fondling, masturbation, fellatio, cunnilingus, digital penetration of the anus or rectal opening, penile penetration of the vagina, and dry intercourse. They note that authority and power enable the perpetrator, implicitly or directly, to coerce the child into sexual compliance (Sgroi et al. 1982, p. 9).

Sexual trauma will be defined in this chapter using the above-mentioned continuum of behaviors, but limited to intrafamilial sexual abuse of female children by their parents. The abuse may have occurred in childhood or adolescence and may include physical violence and emotional neglect.

CLINICAL SYMPTOMATOLOGY AND BEHAVIORAL MANIFESTATIONS OF SEXUAL TRAUMA

Traumatic disruption in child–parent attachment due to sexual abuse results in the development of an array of psychological and physiological symptoms and behavioral manifestations. In order to provide accurate and comprehensive treatment for the trauma survivor, it is crucial that psychodynamic psychotherapists combine their comprehension of the impact of sexual trauma on the organization of the self with an understanding of the neurobiological sequelae of trauma and the various psychopharmacological interventions (Davies and Frawley 1994, van der Kolk and Greenberg 1987). Specific medical explanations and a review of medical research addressing the physiological impact of trauma on the autonomic nervous system (Davies and Frawley 1994, van der Kolk and Greenberg 1987, van der Kolk et al. 1996), on select neurotransmitters and the endogenous opioid and endocrine system (Davies and Frawley 1994, van der Kolk 1987b), and on hippocampal functioning and the taxon system (Davies and Frawley 1994), while useful, are beyond the scope of this chapter.

Cognitive impairment, affective responses, behavioral manifestations, sexual problems, and other somatizations may occur in the trauma survivor. Cognitive impairment as a response to sexual trauma includes intrusive and/or obsessive thoughts, thought blocking, fugue states, amnestic periods, difficulty with word retrieval, an inability to pay attention to nonthreatening stimuli (van der Kolk et al. 1996), and hypervigilance (Davies and Frawley 1994). Affective responses include mood lability marked by swings between states of hyperarousal and affective numbing (van der Kolk and Greenberg 1987), depression, anxiety, depersonalization, derealization, isolation of affect, and affective constriction. Behavioral manifestations are represented by social isolation, promiscuity, eating disorders, forms of self-mutilation such as cutting and trichotillomania, addictions, startle reactions, compulsive or ritualistic behavior, and painful body memories of the trauma in the form of flashbacks (Courtois 1988, Davies and Frawley 1994, Herman 1992). Heightened sensory perceptions may alternate with numbness. Sexual problems such as pain or numbness in the genitalia (Courtois 1988) are common. Other somatizations may include nausea, gastrointestinal problems, migraine headaches, and sleep disorders (Courtois 1988, Davies and Frawley 1994).

EGO STRUCTURE

Borderline ego structure and its relationship to trauma has been studied by numerous researchers (Davies and Frawley 1994, Herman and van der Kolk 1987). Research for more accurate diagnostic clarification is needed (Davies and Frawley 1994). However, a beginning diagnostic picture for the trauma survivor includes the psychoanalytic criteria for borderline ego structure (Kernberg 1984) and the *DSM-IV* (1994) criteria for Post Traumatic Stress Disorder.

Borderline ego structures include split self and object representations with diffuse ego identity and the use of primitive defense mechanisms (Goldstein 1990, Kernberg 1984, Masterson 1976). Trauma survivors often exist in a state of undifferentiation from abusive parents, commonly coping by vacillating between rigid and diffuse ego boundaries. The internalized bad object representations of the abuser function as internal persecutors, attacking the client's ability to utilize her own ego functions accurately. Moreover, the introjected bad object results in a looming fear of rage or aggression, which may be either self rage or internalized parental aggression.

In addition, because trauma survivors were not related to by the abuser as whole people, but rather as part objects, they may believe that their value lies in the self-representation that also holds feelings of shame and humiliation. The trauma survivor spends time trying to figure out what others want from her. Often a "false self" as described by Winnicott (1960b) emerges as a result.

It is extremely damaging to one's development when parents fail to provide a secure base (Bowlby 1988), and are concomitantly the sources of physical and psychological danger (van der Kolk 1987a). Van der Kolk (1987a) observes that trauma occurs when one loses the sense of having a safe place in which to retreat to deal with frightening emotions or experiences. This results in a state of helplessness, a feeling that one's actions have no bearing on the outcome of one's life.

The Constellation of Defenses

The primitive defense mechanisms of splitting, dissociation, projective identification, denial, compulsive repetitions, hypervigilence, and projection predominate in trauma survivors (Courtois 1988, van der Kolk 1987). Additional defensive responses to trauma include faulty reality-testing under stress, an inability to sublimate, and poor regulation of impulses (Courtois 1988, Davies and Frawley 1994, Herman and van der Kolk 1987).

Splitting functions as a denial of a psychic truth. The reality of the horrendous treatment the trauma survivor has endured is too much to integrate with the need to see the parents as all-good, loving, protective caretakers. Thus, the internalization of the object as bad is split off from consciousness and kept separate so as not to "contaminate" the image of the good object.

Dissociation provides a similar protective function. Affective and emotional attachments to the traumatic events and their cognitive significance are fragmented, split off, and function independently from each other (Courtois 1988, Davies and Frawley 1994). The ability to dissociate develops in response to overwhelmingly terrifying events that are too painful to acknowledge. This differs from repression as a defensive response to coping with information too difficult to process. Dissociated memories of the traumatic events often reemerge in fragments and present in an intrusive manner, with visual images, unexplainable somatic sensations that can be extremely painful, changing physiological states, and night terrors (Davies and Frawley 1994, McCann and Pearlman 1990, van der Kolk and Greenberg 1987).

Projective identification functions as a linkage or connection with the object (Bion 1959) and occurs when split-off self-representations of the trauma survivor are projected onto others, who then identify with this split-off projected aspect of the self. The development of the capacity to attach to another, or the belief that another will feel the impact of the trauma survivor's feelings, is damaged by earlier attachment to an abusive, unresponsive, or nonempathic parent. As noted by Bowlby (1988), the pattern of attachment that an individual develops during the years of immaturity—infancy, childhood, and adolescence—is profoundly influenced by the way his parents or other parent figures treat him (p. 123). This defensive response may foster a replication and emotional reenactment of the trauma survivor's experience of earlier attachment relationships, and preserves the trauma survivor's self-representation as bad and unlovable.

Denial of the abuse and/or the parent's responsibility for it is the ego's acknowledgment that the abuse was too difficult to cope with at that time, and is also the ego's attempt to protect itself. Denial can enhance the attachment to the illusion that the parents were loving caretakers.

Early traumatic disturbance in interpersonal relationships leads to subsequent vulnerability to trauma. *Repetition compulsion* ensures attachment to the bad object. When the parent–child attachment bond is disrupted by sexual trauma, the child is left with feelings of shame, humiliation, self-loathing, and fear of abandonment. These feelings are barriers to the development of loving attachments. As a defense, the trauma survivor may develop attachments to (or perceive others as) inconsistent, unavailable, rejecting, and abusive people who are unable to achieve reciprocity or mutuality in their relationships; the predominant feature of this relationship is self-blame. The trauma survivor often feels unlovable and deserving of the partner's abusive behavior. The attachment to the internalized destructive early object is replicated in order to keep the attachment to the parent.

Trauma survivors may feel excited or more "alive" if they feel persecuted or sought after by abusive people. For many survivors, attachment to the notion that bad things will happen has a protective function. Love has been understood as having some inherent connection to abuse and the potential for persecution. Abuse was the basis for attachment to the parent. Thus, the incorporation of the need for abuse can be understood as a way to ensure the receipt of love. It is the love and abuse that are fused. The trauma survivor may defensively respond to the abusive behavior by understanding herself as important enough to pursue. A false sense of self-worth and a feeling of being alive is defensively created in response to the persecution.

The compulsion to repeat the trauma may also be the survivor's desperate attempt to understand the abuse as something that could have been prevented or controlled, or could be mastered. One trauma survivor described the following: "If only I could have figured it out, or done something different. Maybe if I was smaller, or prettier, or quieter. Maybe then it [the abuse] would have never happened. It was my fault. I caused it. My parents couldn't have." If this illusion is destroyed, then the ability to see the parent as good and herself as bad can no longer be maintained.

An attachment to the abuser is also upheld through identification. The survivor needs to identify with the aggressor in order to ward off the terror of her own self-representation as a helpless victim. By keeping the recognition of the self as victimized split-off, the trauma survivor can hold onto a depiction of herself as powerful (Davies and Frawley 1994).

The Moral Defense

The moral defense is the internalization and identification of the self as bad and the parents as good. This manifests itself in a defensive attempt to preserve the parent–child relationship. Fairbairn (1943) describes the key feature of this defense as "the conversion of an original situation in which the child is surrounded by bad objects into a new situation in which his objects are good and he himself is bad" p. 68). The nature of the attachment to the parent is of extreme significance—without the bad object, there is no object, and this important relationship loses its meaning. Regardless of how badly the parent treats the child, the child's need for her parents compels her to internalize bad objects. Since the need for them is so great, the bad objects remain in the unconscious, enabling the child to continue to be attached to the parents. It is the strong need for parents that assigns power to the parent over the child (Fairbairn 1943).

COMMON RESPONSES TO TRAUMA

The trauma survivor often engages in chemical dependency, self-mutilation, bingeing and/or starvation, and promiscuity in a desperate attempt to ward off anxiety in response to the absence of a secure base. These coping mechanisms are external ways of controlling and self-modulating feelings. They are enacted in an attempt to replicate the parent's function as the container of emotions. These concrete ways of distracting the self enable the trauma survivor to put energy into some activity as an avoidance of pain that is too overwhelming for the ego to manage. Additionally, they may serve as a disruption or a way of incorporating chaos into daily life.

Chemical Dependency

Chemical dependency provides a false sense of control over feelings, and temporary relief from painful memories (Bass and Davis 1988). The relationship to the drug becomes one that the trauma survivor believes she can self-regulate and rely on. In addition, strong attachments develop to the rituals that accompany drug and alcohol use, because they are predictable and self-managed.

Self-Mutilation

For the trauma survivor, self-mutilation, including trichotillomania, excessive body-piercing, carving of the skin, scraping the body with sharp objects, and cigarette burns, can provide an overwhelming feeling of relief and control, a way to punish oneself, proof of self-existence, an angry gesture, and/or self-punishment (Bass and Davis 1988). The scars from self-mutilation, the compulsive quality of the behavior, and the secrecy of the act provide a barrier to intimacy and love relationships, enabling attachment to the bad object to remain.

Eating Disorders

Eating disorders are a manifestation of the client's ability to separate or split the perception of the self. Bodily representations are "kept separate" from psychic representations of identity. Bingeing, starvation, and other types of eating disorders provide familiarity and predictability. Like other addictions, eating disorders act as a means of organization and provide a false sense of autonomy and control. Since there was no way to control the abuse during childhood, it is imperative for the adult trauma survivor to have a sense of control and self-regulation (Miller 1983).

Eating patterns represent how the trauma survivor has internalized relations to others as well as her sense of self. When food functions as a replacement of parental love, the trauma survivor feels some sense of control over its regulation, amount, and quality. In these instances, the eating behavior and type of food mask feelings of helplessness and enable the trauma survivor to self-soothe. Uncontrollable incorporation of food can be understood as a means of coping with the loss of the ideal of a safe and loving attachment to the parent, as a representation of either oral aggression or feelings of deprivation, or as a fear of being consumed. The physical repercussions of starvation can be an attempt at removal of sexuality by regaining a child's physique, a concrete display of feelings of loss and the deprivation of safe and consistent love, or the manifestation of the desire to disavow any needs—even the most basic needs—in order to maintain some sense of power. The need for anything has been experienced by the trauma survivor as dangerous.

Promiscuity

Like eating disorders, promiscuous behavior indicates the survivor's ability to keep separate bodily and psychic representations of identity. Promiscuity may represent the trauma survivor's denial of need for love relationships. Sexual partners are viewed as expendable, and promiscuity enables the trauma survivor to identify with her abuser. "I get great pleasure in using others. Why not?" For others, sex and love remain undifferentiated. Promiscuous trauma-survivors may feel some sense of control over their need for another person by determining how much connection can develop in the relationship. It is a way of preserving self-identity and remaining attached to the self-representation; this self-representation permits one to act as if one were without emotional needs, powerful, and self-sustaining, and provides a false sense of autonomy.

The promiscuity may also serve as a means to connect with another. For the trauma survivor, love, power, sex, and affection may have been undifferentiated. Maltz and Holman (1987) note that, "given the coercive dynamics of incest, many survivors have assumed that in order to get love they must have sex. Sex becomes the key to obtaining closeness, attention, touching, and intimacy" (p. 57). Sexual behavior and sensual gratification may substitute for the lack of and quest for love from the primary love object (Balint 1979).

TREATMENT

The Therapeutic Relationship

van der Kolk (1987b) maintains that "the most powerful influence in overcoming the impact of psychological trauma seems to be the availability of a caregiver who can be blindly trusted when one's own resources are inadequate" (p. 32). It is often the therapeutic relationship that becomes the first corrective love attachment. Ideally, the treating clinician creates a holding environment (Winnicott 1960b) for the client where the therapist safely becomes a container for all of the client's projections (Bion 1959). Acceptance of feelings including shame, fear, rage, destructive impulses, and fantasies enables the client to begin to develop some sense of self. The therapist acts in a caretaking role by consistently holding, soothing, and containing the client's feelings as needed. Secrets can be broken safely and without harmful repercussions. The purpose of treatment is to help survivors integrate the traumatic memory in order to make room for the present. The therapist will help translate the horrific internal experience of the trauma survivor into communicable language (van der Kolk 1987a).

Work with the traumatized client should be ego supportive in order to bolster ego functions so the client can tolerate an analysis of the resistances and the lifting of that which has been repressed and split off through dissociation. Fairbairn (1943) contends that "the deepest source of resistance is fear of the release of bad objects from the unconscious; for, when such bad objects are released, the world around the patient becomes peopled with devils which are too terrifying for him to face" (p. 69). With a secure base, the trauma may eventually become conscious (van der Kolk 1987b). Split self–object representations can become fused, following which a true sense of self is attained and object constancy is achieved. Winnicott (1971) states:

> Psychotherapy is not making clever and apt interpretations; by and large it is a long-term giving the patient back what the patient brings. I like to think of my work this way, and to think that if I do this well enough the patient will find his or her own self, and will be able to exist and feel real. Feeling real is more than existing, it is finding a way to exist as oneself, and to relate to objects as oneself, and to have a self into which to retreat for relaxation. [p. 117]

Transference and Countertransference

The enactment and interpretation of transference and countertransference will facilitate the integration of split-off elements of self and object representations (Davies and Frawley 1994). The treatment relationship between the trauma survivor and therapist can foster a deep emotional tie that may evoke intense visceral and behavioral countertransferential and transferential reactions, encompassing unexplained terror, intrusive images of a violent or sexual nature, pain or lack of sensation in any area of the body including the genitals, inability to focus, heart tremors, sexual arousal, numbness, stomach cramps or nausea, distorted self-perception of body size, flooding of emotions, chest tightness, dizziness, amnesia, loving feelings, fantasies of merger, anger or rage, fantasies and fear of retaliation, impaired concentration or judgment, and the wish to be aggressive (Davies and Frawley 1994).

Transference

Issues of secrecy, power, control, deprivation, shame, and/or humiliation make the desire for trusting and safe relationships both highly attractive and terrifying for the client (Courtois 1988, McCann and Pearlman 1990). Primitive idealizations and devaluation predominate in the treatment relationship. Eroticization of the transference is also common.

The trauma survivor may attempt to maintain attachment to the abuser by defending against connection to the therapist. Often this is manifested by the client's acting out, forgetting what has been contracted with the therapist, and/or self-destructive acts. The client defends against cognitively and affectively integrating the abusive experience as a way of denying the horror of the trauma. The more fragile the ego, the more difficult is the acknowledgment of truth. Denial of the need for attachment to the therapist can serve as a way to preserve the bad object.

Identification with the aggressor may result in attempts to demoralize the therapist. Since parents would often react to children's feelings of anger by shaming them with violence or sexual abuse, clients may fear their own aggression will result in retaliation by the therapist. Projection of anger and persecutory fantasies in the transference may lead to the client's feeling terrified and result in her ego fragmentation.

Because of very early disruptions in the trauma survivor's development of self, the client sees herself as merged with the bad object, and thus may think, "If they are bad, so must I be." Feelings of low self-esteem and self-deprecation may be projected onto the therapist, and the client often believes that the therapist hates her (Courtois 1988). One client asked for three years, "Do you think I am a loser?"

Many times the survivor responds to the therapist's holding and containing the patient by sexualizing the relationship. The trauma survivor may overtly attempt to seductively engage the therapist through

dress or verbal interchange. Quite often these flirtations or sexual overtures appear desperate, or are accompanied by an aggressiveness or
shameful presentation (Davies and Frawley 1994). For the trauma survivor, love, sex, affection, shame, and aggression have been merged,
and, for many, seductive behavior is the only way to relate to others
(Courtois 1988).

The client functions in a state of consciousness that is experienced
as if she were being traumatized again (van der Kolk et al. 1996). The
client's recognition of her sense of dependency on the therapist may
result in a terrifying fear of abandonment. Helpfulness by the therapist
may be perceived as an attempt to control or to foster the client's dependence on the clinician, which can be frightening for the client. As a
result, the client may be solicitous of and superficially compliant with
the therapist (Davies and Frawley 1994). The trauma survivor's pervasive feelings of shame and humiliation predominate, and it often seems
unimaginable for the client to believe that the therapist could care about
her without hurting, abandoning, sexually abusing, or shaming her.
Spiegel (1986) describes this as a traumatic transference, whereby the
client unconsciously expects to be used or abused in the way that the
parent abused her.

In treatment, if an awareness and understanding emerges that it is
possible to be loved and cared for in a safe, consistent, nonabusive way,
it can feel extremely painful, disappointing, devastating, enraging, and/
or terrifying. Acknowledgment of the absence of this type of relationship with the parent can either result in further fragmentation, or initiate the onset of ego reparation and integration.

Themes of merger with a good object in the therapeutic alliance
may also arise in the transference material. There are often intense
strivings by the client to regressive roles in response to a desperate
yearning for closeness (Davies and Frawley 1994). If the client regresses
and the desire for symbiosis results in a weakening of the client's ego
boundaries, the client may become terrified. Alternatively, she may feel
safe in this regressive symbiotic position. Consistency, the interpretation of transference, supportive interventions, and the development of
trust and safety may enable the client to use the therapeutic relationship as a corrective one and to safely rework her ability to feel and

receive love. When the object of attachment is available and responsive, a pervasive feeling of security and a desire to continue the relationship results (Bowlby 1988).

Transferential Treatment Binds

Consider the following binds presented in treatment by trauma survivors:

- I need to get help. / I need help to trust.
- I need to be invisible for self-protection. / I want to be noticed to be protected by others.
- I'm supposed to feel to benefit from therapy. / I can't feel, or I dissociate even when I don't want to.
- I must be alone to survive. / I need relationships to survive.
- I want you to believe me. / Acknowledgment of the trauma makes it real.
- It feels good to be cared about in a safe way. / Why wasn't I cared about by my parents? Now I have to deal with the acknowledgment of the absence of their caring.
- I want to be able to make an impact in the world. If it's possible to make an impact, why didn't my parents respond to my needs?

Courtois (1988) notes that "the therapist is faced with the challenge of a client who does not trust or feel she deserves a good relationship and who attempts to sabotage one as it develops, and yet needs exactly those things she fears and feels she doesn't deserve" (p. 219). The clinician can help create a holding environment where the patient is soothed and helped to understand that these disorganizing and confusing feelings have meaning, will be made sense of together, and can be addressed at the trauma survivor's own pace.

Countertransference

Several authors have written about countertransferential reactions to working with the trauma survivor (Courtois 1988, Davies and Frawley 1994, Herman 1992, Kroll 1993). The trauma survivor's use of projective identification, primitive defense mechanisms and dissociation, self-destructive behavior, diffuse ego boundaries, discussions of unthink-able acts of sexual abuse and violence, primitive idealizations and devaluations, traumatic and eroticized transferences, and the need for consistent relatedness and presence of feelings may evoke numerous countertransferential responses in the treating clinician.

Therapists treating trauma survivors often have visceral reactions that are unfamiliar and disorganizing, arising in response to split-off parts of the client that are projected or dissociated, or in response to the clinician's own unresolved issues. Common countertransferential re-sponses may appear very similar to the clinical symptomatology and behavioral manifestations of the trauma survivor. The therapist should receive clinical and emotional support to help contain and process the strong countertransferential feelings that arise in treatment of the trauma survivor.

The therapist may feel the following:

disconnected	unimportant	inadequate
enraged	depreciated	a strong pull to regress
deprived	disapproving	disbelieving
sexually aroused	ashamed and	hatred of the client's
devoted and	humiliated	parents
loyal	valued	secretive about
devalued	unable to concentrate	intervention
demoralized	helpless	frightened
		despairing

In addition to the above-mentioned reactions, the therapist may experience the world as dangerous and people as bad, have nightmares, encounter intrusive thoughts or images of abuse, and may even feel a strong pull to enact the role of the abuser. Weakening of ego bound-aries, loss of attachment to self-representations, and/or muted cognitive and affective responses are common countertransferential responses to the disturbing content of the patient's abuse (Davies and Frawley 1994).

Use of the Transitional Object

Transitional objects serve as important tools to enhance the sense of secure attachment. Since most trauma survivors lack a stable inner representation of a comforting person and have not yet achieved object constancy, these concrete objects can foster a sense of safety and security by acting as reminders and representations of the protective and caring relationship that exists as a result of treatment, and the hope that it embodies. One trauma survivor described her experience of a transitional object:

> *I take it around with me everywhere. It helps me to protect myself when I don't feel able to. It reminds me that someone thinks I'm going to be okay. That there's hope. I keep it in my knapsack. Nobody knows it's there, but it gives me strength, and makes me feel that I'm not alone. Sometimes I just look at it, and all the colors. Green, blue, black . . . safe and angry. The texture is nice, too. It's rough, and feels like it's never going to break.*

AN ANALYSIS OF CARA: SEXUAL TRAUMA, ATTACHMENT, AND LOVE

The following section includes verbatim journal entries written by a client, and an analysis of Cara. The samples of journal entries were written by Cara prior to, during, and subsequent to my two-month maternity leave. The discussion will illustrate the clinical profile of the trauma survivor, as well as the disorganizing impact that the disruption in parental attachment has on the daily functioning of the survivor, and on ego functioning and structure. Manifestations of transference and countertransference; themes of power and control; displays of rage, shame, humiliation, and fear of abandonment; the client's use of denial, projection, splitting, and dissociation as defense mechanisms; examples of self-destructive behavior, the use of transitional objects, and the experience of the therapeutic relationship as a corrective love relationship are all discussed in analysis of the case material.

Cara's Initial Presentation

Cara, a young adult client, had been in treatment with me three times weekly for three years prior to my giving birth. She survived intrafamilial sexual abuse, experienced intermittent threats of parental abandonment alternating with love and affection, and was a witness to and recipient of familial violence during her childhood preschool and elementary school years.

Traumatic disruption in Cara's attachment to her parents negatively influenced her ability to function and to form healthy, emotional love relationships. She initially presented with a combination of a borderline ego structure and some common behavioral, cognitive, and physical manifestations of trauma, which included the following: an eating disorder, social isolation, a false-self presentation, mood lability with depression predominating, ritualistic behavior, alternating states of heightened sexual arousal accompanied by feelings of shame and humiliation with complete disinterest in sex and lack of sensation during sexual activity, intrusive thoughts and thought blocking, sleep disturbances, feelings of depersonalization, and use of the defense mechanisms of dissociation, denial, projection, the manic defense, repetition compulsion, and splitting.

Pre-Maternity Leave

A few months prior to my maternity leave, Cara expressed feeling terrified that I was going to have the baby and stop caring for her. She felt that suddenly I would "change" and either leave her or hurt her in some way. Thoughts of my maternity leave evoked feelings of terror, horror, sexual feelings toward me alternating with rageful and aggressive fantasies, and prevailing fears of abandonment and annihilation of herself or the baby. Cara needed to carry two transitional objects with her: a crystal rock, which she found on my bookshelf at the onset of treatment and she named "the purple thing," and a business card on which she had me write that I was coming back. She felt extreme anxiety that she would lose the rock, or that it would disintegrate. She spent numerous sessions telling me that nothing could replace "the purple thing" and cried over the fear of its potential loss.

Although she referred to the baby as bad and dangerous and discussed her persecutory fantasies, some observing ego existed and she was able to cognitively understand her anger and fear of losing me as a transferential manifestation of her feelings toward her parents. However, her rage toward her parents was split off and dissociated. She began to voice her concerns and begged me not to change, explaining that when her brother was born "everything changed"; she referred to his birth as "ruining everything." Anger toward her parents was too dangerous. Her brother and now my baby had become the bad, threatening object. She said that she would never be as little and cute as the baby and so she wanted it to die, because if it didn't I would never be able to continue loving her. While she disclosed these feelings to me, she admittedly knew that this was a displacement and seemed to participate in the regression by allowing her visceral reactions to supersede her cognitive awareness of the reality of the treatment dynamics.

She referred to the time that her mother was pregnant and after the pregnancy with despair. She discussed how her expression of feeling after the birth of her brother was responded to with aggression, punishment, humiliation, shame, threats of abandonment, or long periods of isolation. She was flooded with intrusive memories of things she didn't want to remember and describes dissociative coping mechanisms such as "going into the patterns of wallpaper, rugs, or tiles, or leaving my body and observing the situation," both in the present and as a child. During childhood she felt so "out of control" she would remind herself that she could always "go into a pattern" to ward off feelings of helplessness. She wrote the following:

> *Today is a day where everything sucks, or is about to, where my bloated body disgusts me yet fascinates me, where I have the same moral turpitude as t.v. talk shows, where genuine laughter is an alien concept. Everyone is leading productive & purposeful lives except me, everyone is where they are supposed to be except me, happy couples stroll by arm in arm, and I float past, phantom-like, with my feet 3 inches off the ground.*
>
> *Sexxxy girls walk by, each marketing her own brand of sexuality and allure, strutting and posing. I wonder how they do it, how they maintain their hairdos & nails w/o cracking apart like hard boiled eggs, how they keep the animal nature at bay. I cannot do this. No, today I want to squat and pee in the tub, shit in the corner on the floor & leave it overnight, eat until I explode it out, bleed it out. My body's odors will accumulate like building blocks stacked atop each other, my gums bleeding when I see them in the bathroom mirror.*

*I am sweating profusely in my sleep. I wake up, and it's in
the crook of my arms, under my breasts, on pillow, on sheets.*

Lisa [therapist] *seems very far away. I both want & don't
want to hear her voice. I am nervous about her upcoming maternity leave. MA-TER-NIT-Y LEAVE. leave leave leave leave. I hate
her for it, hate her for having a life, a baby, a partner. How can
she leave me, huh? Maybe she'll go away and never come back—
cute helpless baby, ugly baby, I hate it, I imagine it being born
& coming out w/ all the guck on it, & Lisa will still be happy &
love it, the rodent thing all pink & hairless, I hate it. Why does it
have to come out your vagina—pleasure center, secret, taboo,
forbidden, a liability, can't say anything, silenced, feels good &
bad. Why can't the baby be born through your ear instead?*

The traumatic disruption in parental attachment is exhibited by
Cara's depression, isolation, desire for loving relationships, and in her
confusion about sexuality and the relationship between love and sex,
secrets and safety. She describes dissociative states—her focus on the
sound of maternity leave or floating three inches off the ground, and
sweating—as examples of cognitive and physiological responses to
trauma.

Cara feared that her attachment to me as a good object and acknowledgment of me as a sexual person would contaminate our relationship and endanger her. Her belief that my baby would be loved un-
conditionally and safely was a painful contrast to her experience of being
loved by her parents. She expected to be abandoned, and felt angry and
fearful about the disruption in our relationship.

Cara's identification of and disgust with others' false-self images
was representative of her own experience of being valued as a part
object, a role she could no longer maintain. Her aversion to and fascination with her body as bloated and others' bodies as sexy signified
the internal struggle between her own and her parents' ego ideal. If
Cara admitted to wanting to be valued as a whole object, she had to
contend with the split-off representation of her parents as placing value
in her as a part object.

Her preoccupation with and attachment to her own bodily prod-
ucts, such as blood, urine, and feces, were representative of her need to

bind herself—to maintain some part of herself that had not been contaminated by others' desires of her. They were concrete symbols that parts of her still existed—her most primitive and basic functions. It signified all that she held in and maintained control over. She wanted to explode and leave it out as proof of the abuse that was internalized, converted to poison, meant to be kept a secret, and silenced. She was desperately trying to keep herself from fragmenting.

The Maternity Leave

The threat that my maternity leave presented Cara with was great. Representations of self and objects became split again and ego boundaries became more diffuse. As time elapsed, Cara regressed. Once I began my leave, the manic defense returned, and Cara began to have increased difficulty remembering that she was not bad. She spent more time at her parents' home, felt unable to concentrate, and began to question her memories of their parenting techniques. She feared that she would not be able to forget her anger toward her parents, and felt fearful that I would not return and that she would be left "with nothing." She further questioned if the meaning of our relationship was real. The traumatic transference surfaced as internalized bad objects resurfaced, and was illustrated in her overwhelming feelings of fear, rage, aggression, fear of annihilation and abandonment, and persecutory fantasies. She wrote the following text and headings during my maternity leave:

BEGINNING: ANGER

I'll start by saying how difficult these past two months have been—how much it has sucked, how much it still sucks. I hate you, your stupid rules, the pacts we've made, the pinch-hitter therapist in Brooklyn. I hate the work we have done, I hate you for leaving. I hate the rodent gerbil baby you have. I hope it's ugly and cries all the time, ha.

I hate going out to see the pinch-hitter. I get on the stupid subway at rush hour, crammed into a metal car with gaggles of civil servant workers, and when I get out of the subway station I have to walk past this place that sells artificial limbs. They have a display of plastic arms and legs in the windows, and I feel like that—missing a vital appendage and the prosthetic ones don't even come close. I hate you. You seem very very far away, on Pluto maybe, if anywhere at all. I've wanted to take the baby and put it on top of a garbage heap in a dumpster. With the baby lying on the trash, I'd say, "Ooops! Sorry! I didn't know!" I want to make you forget about the baby, forget about ever having it, ever wanting it, erase the whole thing from memory. I am taking your business cards and tearing them up and giving them back to you. They don't work. And, I'm giving back also the little rocks you gave me, they don't work either. They don't protect me, they don't shelter me. All they do is sit there and look at me dumbly. A big fucking help they are. All your ideas are dumb. This one included.

I want to make you say you'll never pull this shit again. That's it, no more babies or baby-related problems. The baby will have to take care of itself. I hope it has an elephant trunk growing straight out of its forehead, and it'll have to join a freak show to make a measly living.

MIDDLE: ANXIETY

Lisa, I don't want to fix things, I don't want to do well especially when you're not here. I don't want to figure things out with you or without you either . I'm very alone in my hermit hole apartment. I let my days pass away without my knowledge—the city still pulses, traffic lites change, phones ring.

Please don't love the baby. I hope you don't, can't you just let your partner love it and you don't have to pay attention to it, it could be an invisible roommate or something like that. Maybe you could give it away or kill it or maybe it'll die all by itself. But I wouldn't want you to be sad about it for long, just long enough so you feel badly about leaving me by myself for so long. Then you can forget that you ever had the baby and you wouldn't want another one O.K.?

Lisa please make all this go away wrap it up in a brown package with string and mail to a black hole O.K. will you please? Please? I don't know if I can make it through the next few weeks.

BEGINNING OF THE END: A LIGHT SEEN, MAYBE

I am breathing easier now that there's only one week to go. Still sleeping lots, dreaming disturbing dreams. But there is a feeling of relief somehow, that you're coming back, and we'll work things out.

I told a friend of how I don't want to figure things out right now by myself. I don't want to sort out being angry with you/your pregnancy vs. other issues it stirred up, fact vs. fiction, present vs. past. Not interested in it at all, would rather hide, pretend, bury, dilute, delude.

A word of caution: When you come back next week I'll still be pissed, stubborn, juvenile disinterested uncooperative ugly sneering. I'm gonna give you a hard time I hope all your clients do, I hope you have a seething mass of pissed-off clients that you have to deal with. I hope you pay for your absence. I'm sorry to be so mean and vengeful Lisa, but this is how I feel.

I've wanted to do all sorts of crazy stuff—run off to London, get married in the Middle East—something. Something to make you see how traumatized I am from your absence. I have to show you how upset I am.

Well that's it. I am tired I am haggard. I want to be ugly yet I'm sick of it. I am sick of me, of your absence of expecting your stupid return, of not feeling good. I am tired of plumbing the depths and spiraling deeper into my own head. I'd like my brain and soul to go on a long vacation without me and leave me in peace.

Transferential manifestations of the desperation for parental love, sibling rivalry, rage, and the fear of disruption of attachment to her parents are illustrated in the content of Cara's writing. When there is a threat of loss of a valued relationship, anxiety and angry behavior are common responses (Bowlby 1988). Cara's angry and fearful reaction to my maternity leave represents both her strong attachment to me and a transferential manifestation of the earlier traumatic response to her brother's being born.

Illustrated in her writing is Cara's strong desire to deny the reality of her abuse and emotional deprivation, the limited supply of love her parents were able to provide for her and her brother, her self-experience as incomplete, her desire for symbiosis, and her desire to have her brother be "the deprived one." Intrusive transferential memories resulted in Cara's feeling disorganized, and unable to process her experience. Internal attacks on ego functions made the ability to think rationally nearly impossible. The function of the transitional objects diminished as my absence grew longer, and the internalized representation of me as the good object was split off and hard to reach.

Post-Maternity Leave

When I returned from maternity leave, Cara's need to identify with the aggressor to ward off her feeling of being out of control, her compulsion to repeat, and her self-identification as helpless began to diminish. Split-off self-representations alternated from powerful to victimized. She was able to begin to safely experience the original rage, anger, fear, and helplessness that she felt as a young child. She wrote:

> *END: ALL POINTS CONVERGE*
>
> *Lisa, you've come back, baby gone from your belly still hate you am so shocked that you're back I'm in disbelief that you're here felt like I was going to faint so sick with worry dread anxiety could barely walk to our appointment head hurt faint dry throat When you opened the office door, I felt so happy and relieved and scared, I started crying like a lottery winner. All I needed was fat fake Ed McMahon and his stupid prize patrol.*
>
> *Just because you're back, though, it doesn't mean the four year old voice inside me is going to shut up. I simultaneously want to silence her and broadcast her, forget her and reclaim her. I still hate you for getting me into this mess, for showing me another fucking way. Still, I honestly can't believe you're back, that you haven't disappeared permanently to Baby Land. I've wanted to go to every retail outlet in the five boroughs and empty them all of baby paraphernalia—no diapers, rattles, teething toys, bottles. "I'm sorry Ms. Gilman, but we're out of everything your baby needs, and we're not expecting another shipment soon."*

> *Christ, I am glad this is all over—my headache's gone, up-*
> *set stomach gone, skin less itchy, not sweating anymore. It eases*
> *my mind to know you're not dead, that you exist. For a while*
> *during your absence, I felt unsure of your existence, thought*
> *maybe I made you up. I'm so relieved.*

POST: WATER SHED

> *Today after first session back with Lisa. It had come round*
> *full circle. I had an accident. I actually shit in my pants. I'm in*
> *shock it happened. I'm scared I've regressed, although there is*
> *something comforting in being so helpless.*
>
> *Doing errands. While in a store I realized I went in my pants.*
> *Total shock. No idea what happened.*
>
> *Waddled gingerly out of store, found a nearby bathroom.*
> *Genuinely confused as to what happened. Why, how. I am a mess.*
> *Body took over, independent of free will, of control. My waste*
> *everywhere. Mortified. Relieved, literally and figuratively. Washed*
> *myself. Wanted to go home, near familiar things and surround-*
> *ings. Things are getting hysterically funny, tragic. Took a sponge*
> *bath, like you'd give a baby, got into comfy clothes and just sat—*
> *lights on, t.v. on, mindless magazines in reach. I'd hit a new high*
> *or a new low—unsure of which.*

The journal entries illustrate Cara's use of an observing ego, and her desire to disavow this newly acquired ability. The self-acknowledgment of her regression, fear of replicating her relationship with her parents, and a wish for the ability to erase her traumatic past is coupled with the hope and desire for a corrective experience within the therapeutic relationship.

The secure base and loving attachment developed through the therapeutic alliance enabled her to experience her original feelings of shame, humiliation, fear of abandonment, deprivation, and sibling rivalry in response to limited displays of parental love and loss of control. Splitting, denial, and projection no longer predominated. She was able to miss me and feel love and anger simultaneously. Cara was able to express her rage and loss of control without fear of my retaliation or that I would shame her. Our treatment relationship served as the first corrective love relationship where a safe and secure attachment could be formed. Safety and love replaced abuse, inconsistent love, and threats of abandonment and humiliation, and formed the basis for a healthy attachment. Over the next year, Cara continued to be able to tolerate the analysis of repressed and dissociated material.

The treatment relationship became a vehicle for the client to develop a strong attachment to a good object. The use of transitional objects in treatment proved to be a successful tool to aid in the development of object constancy (Mahler et al. 1975) by helping the client remember that she is able to feel soothed, protected, and cared for. Treatment combined consistency, the development of trust and its meaning, predictability, and safety. A secure base was created in which the analysis and interpretation of transference and countertransference occurred. The therapeutic alliance enabled the client to begin to have a corrective emotional experience.

CONCLUSION

Sexual trauma profoundly influences the development of self-representation and ego functioning, and one's ability to develop love relationships and to form emotional attachments. Trauma survivors often develop borderline ego structures, which include split self and object representations with diffuse ego identity and the use of primitive defense mechanisms. This ego structure, in combination with the array of psychological and physiological symptoms and behavioral manifestations that may result from sexual trauma, can be debilitating. Chemical dependency, self-mutilation, eating disorders, promiscuity, feelings of shame, self-deprecation and humiliation, and issues of power and control make the development of healthy attachment formation near impossible.

The therapeutic alliance can be a primary corrective love relationship. It incorporates the timely interpretation and understanding of transferential and countertransferential responses to trauma, the creation of a holding environment, and the use of the transitional object to enhance the sense of secure attachment. Treatment will provide the trauma survivor with the opportunity for healthy love and attachment.

REFERENCES

Ainsworth, M. D. S. (1969). Object relations, dependency, and attachment: a theoretical review of the infant–mother relationship. *Child Development* 40:969–1025.

―――― (1973). The development of infant–mother attachment. In *Child Development and Social Policy (review of child development research)*, ed. B. M. Caldwell and H. N. Ricciuti, vol. 3, pp. 1–94. Chicago: University of Chicago Press.

American Psychiatric Association (1994). *Diagnostic and Statistical Manual of Mental Disorders*, 4th ed. Washington, DC, author.

Balint, M. (1979). *The Basic Fault.* New York: Brunner/Mazel.

Bass, E., and Davis, L. (1988). *The Courage to Heal: A Guide for Women Survivors of Child Sexual Abuse.* Santa Cruz, CA: HarperCollins.

Bion, W. R. (1959). Attacks on linking. In *Second Thoughts: Selected Papers on Psycho-Analysis,* (pp. 93–109). Northvale, NJ: Jason Aronson, 1967.

Bowlby, J. (1969). *Attachment and Loss. Vol. 1: Attachment.* New York: Basic Books.

―――― (1988). *A Secure Base: Parent–Child Attachment and Healthy Human Development.* New York: Basic Books.

Courtois, C. A. (1988). *Healing the Incest Wound.* New York: Norton.

Davies, J. M., and Frawley, M. G. (1994). *Treating the Adult Survivor of Childhood Sexual Abuse.* New York: Basic Books.

Fairbairn, W. R. D. (1943). The repression and return of bad objects. In *Psychoanalytic Studies of the Personality*, pp. 59–81. London: Tavistock/Routledge and Kegan Paul, 1981.

Goldstein, E. (1990). *Borderline Disorders: Clinical Models and Techniques.* New York: Guilford.

Herman, J. L. (1992). *Trauma and Recovery.* New York: Basic Books.

Herman, J. L., and van der Kolk, B. A. (1987). Traumatic antecedents of borderline personality disorder. In *Psychological Trauma*, ed. B. A. van der Kolk, pp. 111–126. Washington, DC: American Psychiatric Press.

Kernberg, O. (1984). *Severe Personality Disorders.* New Haven, CT: Yale University Press.

Kroll, J. (1993). *PTSD/Borderlines in Therapy: Finding the Balance.* New York: Norton.

Mahler, M. S., Pine, F., and Bergman, A. (1975). *The Psychological Birth of the Human Infant—Symbiosis and Individuation.* New York: Basic Books.

Maltz, W., and Holman, B. (1987). *Incest and Sexuality.* Lexington, MA: Lexington Books.

Masterson, J. F. (1976). *Psychotherapy of the Borderline Adult: A Developmental Approach.* New York: Brunner/Mazel.

McCann, I. L., and Pearlman, L. A. (1990). *Psychological Trauma and the Adult Survivor.* New York: Brunner/Mazel.

Miller, A. (1983). *For Your Own Good.* New York: Farrar, Straus & Giroux.

Sgroi, S. M., Blick, L. C., and Porter, F. S. (1982). A conceptual framework for child sexual abuse. In *Handbook of Clinical Intervention in Child Sexual Abuse,* ed. S. M. Sgroi, pp. 9–38. Lexington, MA: D. C. Heath.

Spiegel, D. (1986). Dissociation, double binds, and post-traumatic stress in multiple personality disorder. In *Treatment of Multiple Personality Disorder,* ed. G. G. Braun, pp. 63–77. Washington, DC: American Psychiatric Press.

van der Kolk, B. A. (1987a). The psychological consequences of overwhelming life experiences. In *Psychological Trauma,* ed. B. A. van der Kolk, pp. 1–30. Washington, DC: American Psychiatric Press.

——— (1987b). The separation cry and the trauma response: developmental issues in the psychobiology of attachment and separation. In *Psychological Trauma,* ed. B. A. van der Kolk, pp. 31–62. Washington, DC: American Psychiatric Press.

van der Kolk, B. A., and Greenberg, M. S. (1987). Psychobiology of the trauma response: hyperarousal, constriction, and addiction to trauma reexposure. In *Psychological Trauma,* ed. B. A. van der Kolk, pp. 173–190. Washington, DC: American Psychiatric Press.

van der Kolk, B. A., McFarlane, A. C., and Weisath, L., eds. (1996). *Traumatic Stress: The Effects of Overwhelming Experience on Mind, Body and Society.* New York: Guilford.

Winnicott, D. W. (1960a). Ego distortion in terms of true and false self. In *The Maturational Processes and the Facilitating Environment,* pp. 140–152. Madison, CT: International Universities Press, 1965.

——— (1960b). The theory of the parent–infant relationship. In *The Maturational Processes and the Facilitating Environment,* pp. 37–55. Madison, CT: International Universities Press, 1965.

——— (1971). *Playing and Reality.* New York: Tavistock.

7

Intimacy Problems in Addiction

ELLEN GRACE FRIEDMAN

Throughout history, writers, poets, and artists have portrayed the difficulties of developing close, loving relationships with others. Intimacy or mature love may be conceptualized as a highly developed achievement, with its first beginnings in simple infantile needs (Guntrip 1989). The ability to develop interpersonal intimacy is the result of the individual's mastery of complex interrelated tasks and requires the resolution of early-life developmental conflicts that inform adult relatedness. While infantile love seeks to "get," mature love fuels reciprocal dependence and willing sacrifice to others. Mature love welcomes emotional vulnerability and values tenderness, responsibility, and responsiveness. It is this love that is so tragically absent in the lives of many patients who seek treatment for addiction.

In my discussion of intimacy and addiction, I will briefly review the epidemiology and definition of addiction, describe the way psychoanalytic theories view addiction, and discuss the ways that different methods of addiction treatment create venues for recovering addicts to work through their resistances to creating intimate relationships with others.

EPIDEMIOLOGY OF ADDICTION

Drugs and alcohol have been used throughout history for a variety of religious and therapeutic purposes. Both psychoanalytic and nonanalytic paradigms have been developed to organize the many theories that explain addiction. Current models of addiction include the moral, social learning, genetic, biochemical, and psychoanalytic models, which provide the basis for respective treatments.

Only a small percentage of the people who use drugs or alcohol become addicted (Doweiko 1996). It is estimated that 2 percent of the American population is addicted to illegal drugs (Holloway 1991) and that 10 percent of the population is addicted to alcohol (Gazzaniga 1988). However, for those people, the use of drugs and alcohol creates serious, often life-threatening consequences. Substance abuse plays a role in the lives of between one-third and one-half of those individuals seen for psychiatric emergencies (Doweiko 1996) and is also linked with the spread of HIV/AIDS. Studies of the co-morbidity of addiction and mental health problems show that most substance abusers have either lifetime or current psychiatric disorders (Rounsaville et al. 1982), lending credence to the belief that addiction is often a symptom of preexisting psychological distress and also a cause of psychiatric problems.

In this chapter the term *addiction* is used to refer to the range of substance abuse disorders, which demonstrate "the cognitive, behavioral, and physiological symptoms that indicate that the individual continues use of the substance despite significant substance-related problems" (*DSM-IV* 1994, p. 176). Included in this definition is the compulsive misuse of both legal and illegal drugs and alcohol. It does not include other compulsive behaviors that are popularly termed "addictions," such as gambling, sex, and work.

THE RELATIONSHIP BETWEEN PSYCHOANALYTIC THEORY, ADDICTION, AND INTIMACY.

Most psychoanalytic theories of addiction are extensions of larger theories of psychosexual development. Numerous theorists have used addiction to "exemplify the principle of whatever broad psychoanalytic

model they were proposing" (Morgenstern and Leeds 1993, p. 194).
Two of these models, drive theory and object relations theory, are discussed below.

Drive Theory

Drive theorists believe that the love of others is not present at birth but
evolves through the stages of psychosexual development. Their theories describe love's beginnings in the personal and non-object-related
world of the child's own aggressive and libidinal strivings. Freud and
later drive theorists believed that addiction substitutes for libidinal
strivings. In a letter to Fliess, Freud (1897) wrote that masturbation was
the primal addiction and that the later addictions are substitutes for
masturbation. Drive theorists believe that addicts do not adhere to the
"reality principle." Freud explained that the use of intoxicants permits
the pleasure principle to succeed in the face of adversity (Yorke 1970).
Attempting to link Freud's earlier work based on his understanding of
alcoholics with a broader understanding of addiction, Rado (1933) created the term *pharmacothymia* to unite all the addictions into one term.
In 1945, Fenichel wrote that addicts are "fixated to a passive-narcissistic aim and are interested solely in getting their gratification, never in
satisfying their partners nor, for that matter, in the specific personalities of their partners. Objects are nothing for them but deliverers of
supplies" (p. 377).

These theories created the basis for later understandings that view
the addict in terms of fixation to an oral stage of psychosexual development. They explain that unresolved needs for pleasure, self-esteem,
and satisfaction set the stage for later addiction. Proponents of drive
theory view the inability to maintain sobriety or abstinence in terms of
the repetition compulsion and as a wish to return to the state of omnipotence and bliss that the addict cannot achieve in reality. They explain the deteriorating course of the addict as an attempt to avoid the
alternatives—among which Rado suggests are suicide or psychosis.

Drive theory asserts that addicts have difficulty achieving intimacy
for several reasons. They remain fixated at the level of primary narcissism. Addicted patients, fixated at primary narcissism, have not developed the capacity to experience love toward others as separate individu-

als, but instead look to others only for self-reflection, admiration, and to enhance their own self-regard. Self-love fails to become object love, hampering the addict's ability to experience and relate to other people.

To love others requires the ability to reconcile inner needs with outer reality. Freud postulated that in the process of human psychic development the pleasure principle that dominates early psychic life progresses to a stage where pleasure is sought in the context of external reality. Reality is not always pleasurable and requires that the pursuit of pleasure might "have to be postponed or substitutive outlets [be] sought" (Giovacchini 1982, p. 153). The body as the sole or primary source of pleasure is gradually replaced by achievement, interpersonal relatedness, and mature sexuality, as the person achieves harmony by joining with and relating to others. To care about others and to achieve intimacy require the ability to accept delay in gratification and to tolerate disappointment, while appropriately sublimating sexuality and aggression.

Mature loving requires relating to a world and to people whom the individual cannot omnipotently control. For addicts, drugs and alcohol induce temporary states of pleasure and the illusion of omnipotent control, at great cost to self and others. The physiological craving and lifestyle of the addict's compulsive drug-seeking behavior create a downward spiral as he or she withdraws further and further from reality and relatedness with others.

The development from autoeroticism to primary narcissism to later secondary narcissism is marked by the progression through the psychosexual stages of psychic development. Classical theory links psychic development to movement originating in the oral stage to the later phallic-genital stages. Within this frame, the ability to create a mature sexual relationship is a marker of successful libidinal development. Many addicts suffer from profound sexual difficulties and sexual dysfunction. The mature expression of sexuality through genital relatedness is markedly absent from the lives of many addicted patients, depriving them of the rewards of enhanced self-regard achieved through mature sexuality. Instead, addicts appear to love the drug and alcohol that gratify them in an "oral" or "perverse" manner, whereby pleasure and comfort are derived from the substance rather than achieved via object love.

Using psychoanalytic understandings, Wurmser (1978) evolved an addiction-specific theory whereby drug and alcohol use is motivated by psychic conflict. Unlike many other theorists, Wurmser believes that addicts do not suffer from a deficiency of ability or developmental arrest but instead suffer from intense intrapsychic conflict. Addiction is a symptom of this conflict. The conflict is between the psychic agencies, causing a narcissistic crisis in which the value of the self is called into question and causes a profound disappointment in self and others. Wurmser believes that addicts fear a return of the repressed narcissistic crisis that motivated the drug use.

In Wurmser's (1978) view, the superego of the addict is harsh and punitive rather than weak. Substances are used to obliterate the power of the superego and to banish reality (Wurmser 1984). As a result of the superego conflict, addicts fear being controlled or closed in. Wurmser believes that rather than being selfish pleasure-seekers, addicts have many fears and doubts about their self-worth. He posits that addicts are phobic and have strong fears of commitment, pleasure, or success. According to Wurmser, addicts live in constricted worlds where relationships are frightening. Consonant with other drive theorists, Wurmser believes that drug users get from chemical manipulation of their feelings the experiences that others get from actual achievement and interaction.

Wurmser (1984) believes addiction results from actual "overwhelmingly traumatizing outer reality" and "unusually severe real exposure to violence, sexual seduction, and brutal abandonment, and/or of real unreliability, mendacity, betrayal, and abandonment, and/or real parental intrusiveness or secretiveness" (p. 253). The results of these experiences make addicts hostile, rebellious, defiant, and aggressive toward authority.

Following Wurmser's theory, addicts have problems in achieving intimacy because they feel profoundly worthless. Their sense of worthlessness was created by childhood trauma that caused intrapsychic conflict. As adults, addicts shield themselves from experiences that they fear will be humiliating and avoid experiences that they believe may expose their worthlessness. In treatment, this inner struggle becomes apparent as patients express self-hatred and aggressive self-contempt and denigrate the possibility of anything positive or valuable existing within themselves. Their unrelenting blame of themselves for past errors or mistakes is often unduly cruel, judgmental, and unforgiving.

Frequently they project their self-hatred onto others or the environment. Describing their personality structure, Meissner (1986) cites addicts' tendency to blame others for their problems, their guardedness and paranoid traits, and their "compulsion to put and keep themselves in a weak, vulnerable, and helpless position" (p. 353).

Following Wurmser's formulations, we can recognize the etiology and significance of the addict's many interpersonal problems. Patients suffering with addiction problems live in conflict. They fear the love they need. Addicts fear intimacy because they are fearful of being overwhelmed by their affects, most notably, but not only, fear and rage. Because of their inability to tolerate both pleasant and unpleasant affects, addicts avoid any experience where they might lose control, which is experienced as potentially damaging to their self-esteem. This dynamic constellation precludes the creation of intimate relationships in which vulnerability to intense feelings of love, sexuality, anger, and disappointment are expressed.

Early histories of abuse and trauma provide addicts with little basis upon which to trust others. Trauma and abuse destroy trust. Without this, there is little basis for intimacy. Additionally, the need for continued drug use during adolescence and adult life hampers addicts' ability to commit to others or to act responsibly to fulfill their commitments.

Wurmser believes that classical psychoanalytic treatment is the cure, but stresses that the analyst must be kind and flexible (1985). As noted by Kaufman (1994), "the therapist who provides a great deal of structure, teaches self-preservation, and provides reality testing may be experienced as overly punitive or guilt inducing" (p. 9). Wurmser also recognizes the value of ancillary measures, advocating a deeply grounded treatment in which he includes self-help groups, pharmacological intervention, education, psychotherapy, and family counseling.

Miguel

Miguel is a 35-year-old Latino male and recovering polydrug abuser. He was raised in poverty in Detroit, Michigan. Both parents were addicted to narcotics. Because of his parents' addictions, Miguel's family was isolated from their relatives. His early history was notable for maternal neglect and a father who was violent and inconsistent. As a teenager, Miguel married for one year. The marriage was difficult. Miguel used heroin and had frequent liaisons with other women. He was arrested several times for drug-related offenses. His wife left him when she learned she was pregnant. At the same time the marriage ended, Miguel learned that his father had died of AIDS-related illnesses. After the marriage ended, Miguel became despondent and his drug use escalated into polysubstance abuse, including the use of heroin, cocaine, and alcohol. When he learned that he was HIV-positive, Miguel decided that he "didn't want to die like my father, like a dog," detoxified from drugs and alcohol, and entered therapy.

After a year of weekly individual supportive therapy sessions, Miguel began to remember his childhood and feel the pain that motivated his heroin use. In a therapy session he began to weep. With his body shaking and eyes fixed on the floor he said, "Now that I don't use drugs I remember. I remember what I don't want to know. When I was 12 years old my father broke my arm. I asked my mother 'why did he do that?' She said, 'What did you do to get him angry?' When she said that I wanted to die. When I remember this I want to use drugs again or kill myself. It's better than remembering."

As a child Miguel suffered profound trauma. His self-esteem was battered by his father's violence toward him and by the neglect and cruelty of his mother. He believed his mother; he believed that he deserved the treatment he received from his father, and he believed his mother when she accused him of causing his father's violence. Deprived of security, warmth, and positive reflection of his "self," his sense of worthlessness and rage at himself and life was unbearable. Heroin temporarily soothed his rage and helped him to avoid contact with people by refocusing his energy on drug-seeking behaviors. Compulsive drug use helped him avoid remembering, feeling hurt, and feeling vulnerable.

Although he married, Miguel was unable to commit to the marriage. Continued drug use, immersion in the drug world, and frequent sexual liaisons with other women buffered him from emotional vulnerability and supported the illusion that he did not need to depend on others. His lack of commitment to the marriage was defensive; it was his attempt to avoid being controlled. His defensive shield was shattered when he lost his wife, and the ending of the marriage provided Miguel with additional proof of his worthlessness.

Having only a limited repertoire of coping skills and few options for real achievement, his downward trajectory into substance abuse escalated. Miguel's substance abuse was multidetermined. He used drugs to avoid overwhelming feelings of self-contempt and despair. His continued drug use helped him to repress the traumas of childhood and the failures of adult life and to avoid vulnerability in his relationships with others.

Khantzian (1980, Khantzian et al. 1990) believes that addicts suffer from both structural and functional deficits. Addicts, in Khantzian's view, are neither pleasure-seeking nor death-seeking, but instead are trying to make up for a deficient ability to care for themselves. Khantzian and colleagues (1990) are credited with developing the "self-medication hypothesis" in which they state that individuals gravitate toward a certain drug that will fill that person's psychological "hole" (p. 10). According to Khantzian and colleagues, the drug of choice is specific to the psychological need of the person.

Khantzian and colleagues (1990) developed Modified Dynamic Group Therapy (MDGT) to treat the characterological issues of patients with addictive problems. They state, ". . . while abstinence and relapse prevention are fundamental to an effective MDGT approach, characterological insight and change are its ultimate goals" (p. 23). Woody (McLellan et al. 1990) frames the goals of Khantzian's groups as affect tolerance, the building of self-esteem, the discussion and improvement of interpersonal relationships, and the development of appropriate self-care strategies among the substance abusers (Khantzian et al. 1990). Consonant with other theorists, Khantzian believes that Alcoholics Anonymous and other treatments can be useful adjuncts.

Following Khantzian's theory, addicts suffer from intimacy problems because they cannot accurately recognize their feelings toward situations and others. Structural deficits create an inability to evaluate and respond correctly to internal cues and in the interpersonal realm. Addicts make poor object choices and frequently misinterpret the feelings and motivations of others.

Since addicts are unable to care for themselves, they demand that others provide for them. The difficulties that addicts experience in caring for their feelings and needs seriously affect their interpersonal relationships. To compensate for their inability to care for themselves, they make excessive demands on others. In so doing, other people's needs do not exist for them. Since they require that other people be continuously sacrificial and giving, emotional reciprocity cannot occur. Relationships with others remain shallow, exploitive, or nonexistent.

Object Relations

Current understandings of the development of intimacy and its relationship to addiction have been formulated by object relations theorists. These theorists believe that from birth infants experience themselves as living in an interpersonal world. They believe that "the key psychological formula is the relationship of the person to the environment. The significance of human living lies in object-relationships, and only in such terms can our life be said to have a meaning . . . "(Guntrip 1989, pp. 19–20). When infantile needs are not met, then childhood love may become love made hungry or love made angry (Fairbairn 1941). The failure of early relationships causes a schizoid condition whereby addictions serve as substitutes for human relationships. Drug and alcohol use become substitutes and act as an "exciting object" (Seinfeld 1991, p. 101) in an otherwise barren life.

According to object relations theory, addicts are starving, angry, and fearful people who suffered great disappointment and fear of others in their early lives. They have developed "false selves" and do not allow themselves to experience emotional vulnerability in their relationships with others. The childhood failure to have experienced a "good enough mother" (Winnicott 1956), an "average expectable environment," and unconditional regard and love leads them to replace human objects outside of their control for drugs . Drug use serves several purposes for patients suffering from schizoid conditions: it replaces the I–thou relationship with an "I–it" relationship (Buber 1958), it both excites and satisfies, and it enables them (addicts) not to need people for themselves (Seinfeld 1991).

Sharon

Sharon was a 45-year-old woman who was abusing alcohol when she began psychotherapy. Initially, she was very unstable and acted out in the clinic by screaming at and devaluing the psychiatrist, while idealizing her therapist. Sharon was unable to tolerate waiting for sessions, and despite considerable intellect and many years of prior therapy, presented with little ability to understand her emotions. Detoxification was followed by individual psychotherapy and enrollment in a day treatment program.

Sharon's early history was notable in that she was the only child of a wealthy California family. Until age 7 she lived with both parents. Her mother was an alcoholic. Her father was a veterinarian who made the young girl watch while he performed surgery on animals, and had her accompany him when he went to meet his mistress. She would wait in the car for hours during her father's trysts. He told her that his affair was "their special secret." When her mother learned of the father's affair, she blamed Sharon for not telling her and told Sharon that it was her fault that the marriage failed. When the marriage ended, her father abandoned the family and her mother withdrew the little affection that she had previously given to Sharon.

After beginning therapy, Sharon continued to abuse alcohol intermittently for one year. When she was abusing alcohol she was rageful and self-destructive. When she wasn't abusing alcohol Sharon presented as depressed, lonely, empty, and walled off from others and from her feelings. Her relationships with men, whom she initially idealized and later devalued, were intense and short-lived. When she experienced disappointment, criticism, or neglect, Sharon became enraged and withdrew. She became infuriated when other people would not provide attention or praise. When this was explored, Sharon explained that she was entitled to preferential treatment.

Sharon remained free of alcohol for many years. She was able to accept the death of a beloved grandmother and the loss of a breast to cancer. Several years after beginning treatment, Sharon revealed that she had an illegitimate daughter whom she had given up for adoption at birth. She wanted to see her daughter and to apologize for abandoning her. She dedicated herself to achieving this reparation, located the daughter (then in her twenties), and met with her. Their reconciliation lifted Sharon's despair and sense of utter isolation.

Sharon's early childhood experience left her starving for her mother's acceptance and love. Her father, whom she idealized, made her believe she was "special" through their shared secret, yet betrayed and neglected her. She suffered severe disappointment when her father left and her mother blamed her for the end of her parents' marriage. Sharon was able to integrate neither the "good" and "bad" aspects of her parents, nor those within herself. She created a "false self" to survive; that self was independent, special, and entitled. She renounced her authentic needs and withdrew from people. Alcohol allowed Sharon to identify with her alcoholic mother, while it served to assuage her anxiety and rage and additionally allowed her to act out her grandiosity and entitlement.

Krystal (Krystal and Raskin 1970, Krystal 1978) focused his understanding of addiction on two areas: the affective function and the severe pathology in object relations of the addict. He wrote that addicts suffer from an inability to recognize, name, and verbalize emotions. To Krystal (1978) it is this inability that prevents addicts from knowing the correct responses to their feelings and to other people. Krystal posited that the basic problem of the substance abuser lies in his or her disturbed object relations and the effect this has on the structuring of the self. He notes that substance abusers hold great ambivalence toward others. Addicts act as if they must rely on something external, either on others or drugs, to provide for or take care of them. When others do not provide for them they feel "attacked and devalued" (Morganstern and Leeds 1993, p. 200). However, Krystal believes that addicts' lack of self-care is not a deficit but an attempt to enslave others to take care of them.

Krystal (1977), like other theorists, believes that substance abuse is a variant of borderline personality organization. He recognizes the strength of the addict's rage, and states that "the intensity of the narcissistic rage, the persistence of the aggressive impulses makes one wonder if all addiction is a hate addiction" (p. 235).

An important aspect of Krystal's formulations is his understanding of the motivation for substance abuse. He believes that drugs assume symbolic meaning as a "primary maternal object." The symbolic drama enacted in drug use involves craving union with the ideal object while dreading it. To Krystal, compulsive drug use is motivated by the symbolic introjection during intoxication followed by separation during withdrawal.

Following Krystal's (1977) formulations, addicts' obstacles to achieving intimacy result from their intense rage and ambivalence toward others. Their rage destroys the ability to recognize their feelings, needs, and reactions, which then get acted out without awareness. Addicts demand to be taken care of by others and experience intense rage when others do not protect them or care for them. People in the addict's personal life often describe feeling both seduced and devalued by the addict. It is common for families or partners of substance abusers to say that their addicted relatives love the drug more than anything or anyone.

Krystal (1977) believes that the severe pathology of addicts precludes the use of traditional psychoanalytic treatment for most patients. Because of the addict's lack of awareness of feeling states and use of projective identification, transference interpretations will not be useful. Instead, he recommends that therapy begin with assistance in dealing with the issues of the addict's affect tolerance and alexithymic condition. Because of the intense borderline transferences of addict patients, he suggests that several therapists be involved. Krystal sees value in providing a quasi-didactic therapy emphasizing self-care, and recommends that psychotherapy begin with a preliminary stage that is educative, followed by a period where patients are taught to manage their emotions.

Roger

Roger was a handsome, 35-year-old lawyer, the fourth of six children, all of whom had severe emotional problems. His father was a prominent politician. His mother was a homemaker who demanded that everything and everyone be pretty and neat. The facade that the family presented to the community was very different from Roger's experience at home. At home, his father was withdrawn and distant. He capitulated to his wife's demands for a luxurious life and gave up contact with his own family because his wife didn't like them. Roger's mother was also sadistic. When she visited Roger in the hospital after Roger had a serious accident, she told him that she had put his beloved dog to sleep because it had urinated on her new rug. Since early adolescence, Roger had been addicted to alcohol and heroin, causing embarrassment to his family.

Despite his addiction, Roger achieved in his career and was able to attract women. His first romance ended when his girlfriend told Roger that he "didn't feel." He experienced feeling "terrible" about losing her and using drugs to cope with the loss, but he didn't know what she meant. After completing law school he moved to Los Angeles, where he detoxified from drugs and lived for a year. But he felt lost, moved back to Boston and his family, and began abusing alcohol again. One night another patron in a bar suggested he go to therapy.

Roger adamantly refused to go to Alcoholics Anonymous or any group program for support, declaring that he would stop on his own, and he did. He landed a job at an impressive law firm where he was very competitive with other lawyers and insisted that he constantly be the best and most esteemed. Roger had no use for his fellow lawyers, regarding them as obstacles to his personal success and recognition. He had no close friends, and felt uncomfortable in unstructured social situations. His judgment was poor. He did not seek medical treatment when he was ill, preferring to "cure" himself. After the bombing of the World Trade Center, he carried a camcorder into the building despite clear rules that this not be done. He stated he did this because a reporter whom he never met before asked him to. He did not understand why this request might have appropriately caused him anxiety. He began a relationship with an actress who came from an emotionally expressive family. Roger enjoyed her family and the attention and concern they gave to him. During the time he and his girlfriend lived together, Roger visited his own family several times. Whenever he visited, he provoked heated arguments with his mother.

After several years in treatment, Roger learned that his father had lost his money. He became fearful that his father would be unable to pay Roger's debts, and he blamed his mother's selfishness and demands for his father's financial failure. He became severely depressed. After three years of living together, his girlfriend insisted that they marry or end the relationship. Unsure whether he loved her but fearful of living alone, he married her. After the marriage, Roger became impotent, felt repulsed by his wife's touch, found himself increasingly interested in pursuing other women, and was infuriated by his wife's demands that he tell her what he was feeling. He agreed to enter marital counseling but ended the treatment when the therapist did not agree with his demeaning view of his wife. Shortly after that he prematurely ended individual therapy, announcing that he was too busy and knew the answers. Shortly after ending therapy, Roger separated from his wife and reimmersed himself in drugs and alcohol. When he left, his wife discovered personal journals he had written during the marriage saying how much he hated her. Sadly, Roger was killed soon thereafter when he fell from a building rooftop while inebriated.

The tragedy of Roger's existence can be understood in terms of Krystal's formulations. Because Roger suffered from alexithymia, he was ill-prepared to deal with his feelings or reactions. He did not know what he was feeling and often guessed at his emotions. His inability to recognize anxiety caused his judgments of people and situations to be very poor. He took risks without reasonable fear or regard to his safety. He selected women based on how they looked and how they treated him. Initially, he attempted to take from his wife and her family feelings and emotions that he was unable to feel for himself. He was jealous of her friendships and artistic achievements and anything that she had or did that did not involve him. Roger was ungenerous to his wife. He was infuriated by her separate existence, and by her appropriate demands for relatedness and sexual contact. Any sign of separation from his mother or symbolic mother caused him great anxiety, and he created arguments and dramatic self-destructive activities to force his mother to react to him.

Roger's veneer of self-sufficiency was easily shattered. In fact, he remained very much connected to his mother or to "symbolic mothers" whom he both needed and hated. Alcohol and heroin provided venues where Roger could symbolically re-create his fantasy of union and separation.

THE ROLE OF PSYCHOTHERAPY IN THE DEVELOPMENT OF INTIMACY

Irrespective of theoretical orientation, individual psychotherapy permits the creation of a stable, nonjudgmental, nonexploitative relationship. The therapist's neutrality creates a safe situation in which the addict's rage, fear, distortions, and judgments of self and others can be explored and where authentic needs to give and receive love are supported. The consistent positive regard given to patients by the therapist offers them an opportunity to recognize and disavow their resistances to involvement with others by learning to recognize and respect their own feelings. The understanding and compassion that patients receive from their therapist serve to restore their belief in themselves as people whose feelings can be understood, people capable of intimacy. The stability of the therapeutic relationship, the consistency and nonjudgmental attitude of the therapist, and the therapist's belief in the patient's essential goodness and ability to grow and change create a strong therapeutic alliance.

Thomas

When Thomas began treatment at age 34, he drank large amounts of alcohol daily and was without friends. He presented as rageful, delusional, and barely functioning in his work as a messenger. His early history was gleaned through fragments that he presented during the four years I worked with him. His mother was cold and sadistic, his father was incompetent, and his older brother was a homeless schizophrenic. His childhood was notable for long-standing vision problems, sexual abuse by his brother, and the absence of love. He was saved by a strong intellect, talent in sports, and the ability to create a compensatory fantasy relationship that preserved his tenuous connection to life.

Thomas imagined that he had a horselike creature named Hapless. He explained that Hapless meant hopeless and helpless. Hapless, who was half-man, half-horse, lived in the forbidden forest where women, money, and prestige were available whenever needed. Hapless told Thomas not to give up on life, that Hapless would never leave him, and accompanied Thomas through his isolated life and chaotic existence. When I explained to Thomas that I could not see or hear Hapless, that Hapless was his creation, Thomas reported on Hapless's ideas, observations, and feelings. In session, Thomas would say that Hapless was bored or didn't understand what I was saying. I would respond by saying that perhaps Thomas felt that way also.

After four sessions, when I was certain that Thomas recognized that at least some of his problems were alcohol-related, I approached the issue of his addiction to alcohol. I explained the issue simply. I told Thomas that I couldn't be useful to him if he continued to drink and that I didn't want to waste his money or time or to disappoint him. He thought about what I said over a two-week period and announced that he would stop drinking.

When I recommended a detoxification program or Alcoholics Anonymous, Thomas initially became upset, believing that I was rejecting him and that I didn't want to help him myself. I told Thomas that the alcohol had affected his body and I wanted him to detoxify safely and that we could continue the work once he was safe. Thomas detoxified at a crisis center for alcoholics, and remained edgy and uncomfortable. Shortly after detoxifying he told me that I was correct about the benefits of AA and that he was leaving therapy because two treatments were too much. Thomas returned to therapy about six months later. He said that there were things he didn't want to talk about in AA.

Unlike an alcohol-induced hallucination that disappears once the effects of alcohol are gone, Hapless remained as the primary relationship in Thomas's life. When Thomas returned to treatment he described Hapless in far more human terms—Hapless was dapper, strong, and similar to the man who played Rocky's manager (the prizefighter popularized in the movies by Sylvester Stallone). Hapless's phantasmagoric qualities were replaced with the strong yet benign qualities of a good father. Hapless's role in Thomas's life had changed. Hapless was there to support Thomas in fighting the Powerful Thing that was alcohol. Hapless encouraged Thomas to volunteer to help at AA meetings, eat well, and talk to me. Hapless was there when Thomas tried to fix a ceiling fan and cried from frustration and rage because his father had never taught him to do anything well.

Thomas's movement into nonalcoholic life brought with it a growing curiosity about others and about relationships. Initially Thomas expressed this through Hapless in the transference. In session, he reported that Hapless wanted him to buy Florsheim shoes to wear to marry me in, that Hapless was looking up my skirt, and that Hapless wanted to know if I had relationships. Thomas became curious about his low treatment fee (I had kept his fee low despite the fact that he had a new job with a higher salary because of his profound deprivation and mistrust of others' motives). Thomas asked to see the fee scale of the clinic to see what "normal people pay." When he located his fee, he volunteered to pay $1 more than necessary, saying that it was "good karma" to give.

Two years into treatment, Thomas began to develop friendships with others at AA. An AA member got him a job as a doorman. Hapless became old and frail. He advised Thomas on how to live without alcohol and gave him faith in his own abilities. He told Thomas that he could make it in the human world now. In sessions, Thomas discussed his fear that Hapless would die. Uncharacteristically, one night Thomas phoned me in tears. He told me that Hapless had died. He was bereft. The death of Hapless represented a turning point from the half-human, nonrelated world of the alcoholic to the human world where relationships matter and loss is painful.

Thomas relapsed when I went on vacation. He admitted himself to a hospital detoxification center and was discharged the day before his session. We discussed the idea that he used alcohol because he felt a loss, and I was empathic and compassionate in helping him to avoid feeling hopeless about his relapse. He continued in therapy for two more years, and the therapy focused on helping him identify his feelings and reactions to the people who lived in the building where he worked and to friendships with Alcoholics Anonymous members. His rage when he felt misunderstood, his disillusionment with the lives of the wealthy apartment dwellers, his delight at taking his first vacation "sober," and his growing recognition of his value to his friends were all surprise revelations to him. He suffered a disappointing relationship with a woman without relapsing and briefly retreated into the fantasy of Hapless.

After four years of treatment Thomas decided it was time to leave therapy. He told me that his new insurance didn't cover my care. He terminated over a six-month period designed by him, reducing his weekly sessions to biweekly ones and, for the last two months, monthly sessions. Thomas told me in leaving that I was like a good grandmother to him—present, yet unintrusive. He said that he felt sure that his satisfying work, friendships in AA, and new therapist would be able to provide the support he needed.

Thomas was psychotic when he entered treatment. Addressing his physiological addiction to alcohol was a priority, since no therapy could occur until he had achieved freedom from alcohol. This was a process that occurred initially via detoxification and later by support from both Alcoholics Anonymous and individual therapy. He needed to learn that he was human, he needed to find ways of relating to others in nondestructive ways, and he needed to believe that he was not alone in his struggle.

Thomas needed support from a therapist who was nonjudgmental and kind. He needed a safe place to talk about his delusional horse without fear. Hapless represented the initially grandiose, omnipotent self that Thomas wished himself to be, as well as the half-human form he feared he was. Hapless was a stable object under his control. He was a good-enough mother and a good-enough father who was constant, supportive, and available at will. He gave voice to Thomas's wishes, and assuaged his terrors. He voiced Thomas's feelings before Thomas could identify them as his own. Hapless kept Thomas from being completely alone.

As the alcohol left Thomas's system with the support of AA and therapy, he was able to create a life offering satisfying relationships with others, productive work, and a sense of personal competence. As he was able to achieve a life with others, the need for a phantasmagoric companion dissipated, and Thomas was able to mourn his loss while maintaining abstinence. In restoring his development, he was able to become curious, generous, and realistic.

Thomas never discussed his anger toward me, although I am sure it was there. We never fully analyzed his reasons for ending treatment, although I have my ideas. I believe that Thomas identified me with a painful, difficult time in his life. In his mind, when he left treatment, Thomas wasn't the same person he was when he began to work with me. I believe that he was ready to work in a different way and chose to do it in a different setting.

THE LIMITS OF PSYCHOANALYTIC THEORY

Psychoanalytic theory, based on understanding the etiological underpinnings of addiction and looking retrospectively at the person, often fails to appreciate the effect of the addiction itself on the functioning of the patient, and may overstate the addict's liabilities. Successful assessment of clients with addiction problems must consider that some of the patient's symptoms may be transient feeling states induced by the substance. It is critical that psychotherapists understand that the extended use of substances over a protracted period in and of itself creates for the addict a situation that is both regressive and isolating. As noted by Kaufman (1994), many behaviors of addicts are secondary patterns that result from their substance-abusing lifestyle. Behaviors such as impulsivity, low frustration tolerance, and using others, which have been seen by analysts as proof of the addict's oral character, may be the result of the lifestyle that develops once a person becomes addicted. Kaufman (1994) notes that in order to maintain their drug habits, "addicts do not give human relationships priority above their need to find money and drugs to maintain their habits. They are unable to make any personal commitment" (p. 17).

By and large, psychoanalytic theories have not integrated understandings of the physiology of addiction, and have yet to incorporate an understanding of the way drugs and alcohol affect the emotional and cognitive functioning of patients. The depression of an addict in early recovery may be a temporary state caused by drug withdrawal and exhaustion, and some of the floridly psychotic features of active cocaine abusers dissipate quickly after detoxification. All too often, psychoanalytic psychotherapists decide that the client's presenting problems reflect characterological issues and do not understand or explore the physiological and psychological chaos brought on by the drugs or by withdrawal.

Additionally, it is necessary to understand the way compulsive drug use over protracted periods of adolescent or adult life has changed our patients' lives. Drug use changes people—if only by removing them from ordinary opportunities to interact with others and from chances to grow and learn through these interactions. Psychoanalytic formulations of addiction must recognize the profound deleterious effect that criminalizing and stigmatizing has on the addict's lifestyle and social options, and how this affects addicts' self-esteem. Recognition of these factors is critically important for the therapist, in order to avoid immediately pathologizing patients' low self-regard and fearfulness, feelings that may accurately reflect the manner in which our society judges and treats people who suffer with addiction.

USE OF ADJUNCTIVE TREATMENTS

For clinicians, the traditional schism between psychotherapy and addiction treatments that are medical, moral, or behavioral has created difficulties in the accurate diagnosis and treatment of patients with substance-abuse issues. Psychoanalytic therapy has character change as its goal while addiction treatments accept abstinence as primary. This dichotomy of perspectives has caused both a lack of respect for and poor integration of these services. Adjunctive treatments that provide pharmacologic help (methadone maintenance), social rehabilitation (therapeutic communities), and recovery programs such as Alcoholics Anonymous can help recovering addicts to develop or recover a sense of self by providing concrete help as well as contexts for constructive interactions with others. It is important for psychotherapists to appreciate their reparative value.

Methadone Maintenance

Methadone maintenance programs assert that chronic addiction is a disease that is treated with methadone, a synthetic narcotic. Methadone programs offer health and social rehabilitation counseling. Since methadone maintenance is a medical treatment, patients are neither stigmatized nor expected to "develop their characters" to become abstinent. Some methadone maintenance programs conduct group programs teaching self-care, offering peer support, and providing educational and vocational rehabilitation.

Twelve-Step Programs

Twelve-step programs (Alcoholics Anonymous, Narcotics Anonymous, and others) create a safe place where recovering substance abusers are welcomed. Twelve-step programs stress belonging. The most important word is the first word in the steps: "we." These groups assure recovering addicts that they are not alone, and that, despite the fact that they may feel unlovable and worthless, there is a benevolent Higher Power. The twelve-step programs teach members how to relate to others while caring for their own needs, and offer concrete ways to become responsible in relationships with others. Recovering addicts learn how to forgive themselves and how to make amends to others.

Twelve-step programs help members give language to their feelings and learn to hear the feelings of others. Through ritual, the program teaches addicts ways of recognizing and dealing with their feelings rather than impulsively acting upon them. The acronym "HALT" teaches members to recognize hunger, anger, loneliness, and tiredness, and provides nonaddictive ways of dealing with them.

Therapeutic communities resocialize addicts to live without mood-altering substances. The community is a "family," and the twelve-step principles are cornerstones of care. These groups provide safety, belonging, order, and for the channeling of aggression through productive labor and mutual responsibility.

CONCLUSION

Addiction can be seen as a solution that causes problems, and as a symptom of distress that creates life-threatening consequences. The myriad problems caused by addiction in areas of health, law, and social and occupational arenas must be addressed if clinicians are to help addicted patients to develop lives of interpersonal relatedness and intimacy. Whatever the etiology and diagnosis of a particular patient, the addiction is a symptom of narcissistic disorder and may mask psychosis, character disorder, or neurosis. For some patients, addiction may be a compromise, for others an attempt to compensate for a deficit.

The intimacy issues of addicted patients have evolved from early histories of neglect, instability, and lack of love. The therapist needs to assist the patient in developing healthy self-regard before the patient can develop interpersonal intimacy. Each treatment must be informed by an empathic understanding of the person and the meaning of substituting drugs or alcohol for interpersonal relationships in the patient's life. Issues such as gender, class, and ethnicity are currently receiving attention and this research is assisting in the development of psychotherapeutic understandings of the etiology of addiction among subpopulations of substance abusers. A paradigm is still needed that can integrate physiological, contextual, social, and affiliation needs into our psychodynamic understanding of addiction.

Successful psychotherapy of addicted clients must offer unconditional personal regard and also establish parameters in which the client can succeed. Relapse should not be seen as a failure of the person or of the treatment: it usually takes several attempts to stop using drugs or alcohol before gains are maintained.

Mature love will develop from the claiming or reclaiming of the client's emotional life, at first trapped behind the false identity of the addict. The personal self of the client will evolve as his or her stability is supported by the therapist and the client is able to experience abstinence through interpersonal and intrapsychic crises. The role of the psychotherapist with addicted clients is essential in providing this support.

REFERENCES

American Psychiatric Association (1994). *Diagnostic and Statistical Manual of Mental Disorders,* 4th ed. Washington, DC: American Psychiatric Association.

Buber, M. (1958). *I and Thou.* New York: Scribner's.

Doweiko, H. E. (1996). *Concepts of Chemical Dependency.* Pacific Grove, CA: Brooks/Coles.

Fairbairn, W. R. D. (1941). A revised psychopathology of psychosis and psychoneurosis. *International Journal of Psycho-Analysis* 22:28–58.

Fenichel, O. (1945). *The Psychoanalytic Theory of Neurosis.* New York: Norton.

Freud, S. (1897). Letter no. 79. In *The Origins of Psychoanalysis: Letters to Fliess,* ed. M. Bonaparte, A. Freud, and W. Kris, pp. 238–240. New York: Basic Books.

Gazzaniga, M. S. (1988). *Mind Matters.* Boston: Houghton-Mifflin.

Giovacchini, P. (1982). *A Clinician's Guide to Reading Freud.* New York: Jason Aronson.

Guntrip, H. (1989). *Schizoid Phenonema, Object Relations and the Self.* Madison, CT: International Universities Press.

Holloway, M. (1991). Rx for addiction. *Scientific American* 264(3):94–103.

Kaufman, E. (1994). *Psychotherapy of Addicted Persons.* New York: Guilford.

Khantzian, E. J. (1980). An ego–self theory of substance dependence. In *Theories of Addiction*, ed. D. J. Lettieri, M. Sayers, and H. W. Wallerstein, p. 967. NIDA Research Monograph 30. DHHS Publication No. ADM 80. Washington, DC: U.S. Government Printing Office.

Khantzian, E. J., Halliday, K. S., and McAuliffe, W. E. (1990). *Addiction and the Vulnerable Self.* New York: Guilford.

Krystal, H. (1977). Aspects of affect theory. *Bulletin of the Menninger Clinic* 41:1–26.

——— (1978). Self representation and the capacity for self care. *Annual of Psychoanalysis* 6:209–245.

Krystal, H., and Raskin, H. (1970). *Drug Dependent: Aspects of Ego Functions.* Detroit, MI: Wayne State University Press.

McLellan A. T., Woody, G. E., Luborsky, L., and O'Brien, C. P. (1990). Preface. In *Addiction and the Vulnerable Self,* ed. E. J. Khantzian, K. S. Halliday, and W. E. McAuliffe, pp. ix–xii. New York: Guilford.

Meissner, W. W. (1986). *Psychotherapy and the Paranoid Process.* Northvale, NJ: Jason Aronson.

Morgenstern, J., and Leeds, J. (1993). Contemporary psychoanalytic theories of substance abuse: a disorder in search of a paradigm. *Psychotherapy* 30:194–206.

Rado, S. (1933). The psychoanalysis of pharmacothymia. *Psychoanalytic Quarterly* 2:1–23.

Rounsaville, B. J., Weissman, M. M., Kleber, H., and Wilber, C. (1982). Heterogeneity of psychiatric diagnosis in treated opiate addicts. *Archives of General Psychiatry* 39:161–166.

Seinfeld, J. (1991). *The Empty Core.* Northvale, NJ: Jason Aronson.

Winnicott, D. W. (1956). The anti-social tendency. In *Through Paediatrics to Psycho-Analysis*, pp. 306–315. London: Hogarth.

Wurmser, L. (1978). *The Hidden Dimension.* New York: Jason Aronson.

——— (1984). The role of superego conflicts in substance abuse and their treatment. *International Journal of Psychoanalytic Psychotherapy* 10:227–258.

——— (1985). Denial and split identity: timely issues in the psychoanalytic psychotherapy of compulsive drug users. *Journal of Substance Abuse Treatment* 2:89–96.

Yorke, C. (1970). A critical review of some psychoanalytic literature on drug addiction. *British Journal of Medical Psychology* 43:141–159.

PART III

ATTACHMENT IN THE THERAPEUTIC PROCESS

8

The Significance of Infant Attachment for Later Life and Adult Treatment

All of us, from the cradle to the grave, are happiest when life is organized as a series of excursions, long or short, from the secure base provided by our attachment figure(s).

—John Bowlby

John related that he spent the first three months of life in an incubator. Fifty-year-old John's understanding is that his mother received a post-card from the hospital telling her to come and get him. John believes that as a result of this early separation he and his mother missed their opportunity to bond. He tells his therapist that he and his mother, and, unfortunately, also he and his father, never got along very well. He reports sadly that he is unable to connect with people, does not know how to relate. For a short time, as a young adult, John lived on a farm. He often tells the story about a gosling there who imprinted to a duck. The goose was betwixt and between, always with ducks but never fitting in, and never with his own family of geese. John feels as he imagines the gosling felt, unable to properly connect to another human being. He sees himself always disconnected, an oddity among the universe of humans, able to relate superficially, but never able to feel deeply attached. It was clear in the first session that John would have difficulty attaching to me as well.

INTRODUCTION

When attachments are problematic, a person's whole view of the world is affected. Both theoretical and experimental researchers have turned their attention to the nature of early attachments, to the way they get represented, their patterns, and to what happens when attachments are disrupted. Bowlby, a psychoanalyst and ecologist, was an early pioneer and the father of attachment theory. Contributions to developmental theory, both by infant researchers and by followers of Bowlby, have relevance to psychoanalysis.

Attachment theory and infant research literature proved useful in my understanding of John's attachment pattern, his longing to form an attachment, and his fear of allowing himself to do so. His attachment dilemma was a central organizing principle in the treatment. In this chapter, I discuss the relationship between attachment theory and infant research in both general and case-specific terms.

Bowlby (1988) believed the infant to be programmed to form an attachment with its significant caretakers. Attachment behavior, according to Bowlby, is "any form of behavior that results in a person attaining or maintaining proximity to some other clearly identified individual who is conceived of as better able to cope with the world. It is most obvious whenever the person is frightened, fatigued or sick, and is assuaged by comforting and caregiving" (pp. 26–27).

If the attachment to the caretaker is secure and the infant feels safe, the attachment system recedes and the infant is free to go out and explore. In his separation, loss, and mourning studies Bowlby (1958, 1969, 1973, 1980) observed the strength of the early attachment tie and what happened when this tie was disrupted. In these studies, Bowlby drew attention to the importance of real-life events that impacted development and resulted in psychopathology (Osofsky 1995). Bowlby believed that attachment is a lifelong need.

Another ecological theorist augmented these theories of attachment. Ainsworth and her colleagues (1978) conducted an observational study of 1-year-old children interacting with their mothers both before and after a brief separation. They identified the following attachment patterns: *secure attachment* (B baby), *insecure avoidant* (A baby), *in-*

secure-ambivalent (insecure-resistant) (C babies), and *insecure-disor-ganized* (D babies).

When the B (secure) baby is distressed by separation, she will move toward mother, indicating that she wants to be picked up and held. The B baby wants to establish visual or vocal as well as tactile contact (Holmes 1993, Stern 1995). Once this has been accomplished, the securely attached baby can return to excited or contented play. The insecure avoidant (A baby) ignores mother on reunion and will show few overt signs of distress on separation. Here, mother may not make an effort to reunite with her baby. Interestingly, Stern (1995) notes that

> it is not that he [the infant] really didn't notice. Current thinking suggests that he notices it very well, that he is vigilant and under considerable stress (as measured by hormonal responses [Grossman and Grossman 1991] or by physiological responses [Sroufe and Walters 1977]) and, in fact, is acting to avoid placing an attachment demand upon a parent who would not tolerate it and who might react by creating greater distance between them or with aversive behavior. [p. 106]

C babies (insecure-ambivalent) are highly distressed by separation and not easily pacified on reunion. They seek contact, but then resist by kicking, turning away, squirming, or batting away offered toys. They continue to alternate between anger and clinging to the mother, and their exploratory play is inhibited. The D baby (insecure-disorganized) demonstrates confused behaviors. The baby may "freeze" or make stereotyped movements when reunited with its parent. Bowlby (1973) expanded Ainsworth's classifications, equating the patterns of insecure attachment to an overall pattern of anxious attachment (Sable 1994). John, referred to above, demonstrates behavior consistent with the insecure attachment pattern (the A baby).

Attachment behavior evolves during the first year of life in interaction with a significant other. The bidirectionality of influences in this dyadic system of infant and mother has been documented by many infant researchers (Beebe and Lachmann 1988, Beebe et al. 1992, Cohn and Tronick 1988, Gianino and Tronick 1988, Sander 1977, 1985, Zeanah et al. 1990). In recent years there has been a growing interest in the mother–infant dyad as a system focusing on the innate capacities the infant brings to the interactive exchange, how these capacities affect the ways the infant interacts with the caregiver, and, reciprocally, how the caregiver acknowledges these capacities, reads the signals and responds to them. Interactions that affect bonding, for example, include face-to-face exchanges, verbalizations, synchrony of responses, and mutuality of interchanges (Silverman 1992). The reciprocal, mutually interactive process between the infant and the caregiver is never-ending. Infant researchers seem to agree that the inherent capacities referred to above are shaped by interactions with the primary caregiver. The infant born with the capacity for relatedness under optimal circumstances will form early social relations and attachment (Silverman 1992).

Bowlby (1969) suggested that early patterns of attachment get internalized in what he called *working models*. A working model contains both conscious and unconscious representations that people use to appraise and respond to situations they find themselves in (Sable 1994). The attachment patterns identified by Ainsworth and colleagues (1978) and cited above (ABCD) can be understood in terms of Bowlby's concept of working models. They can also be understood in terms of Representations of Interactions that become Generalized (RIGS) (Stern 1985), and interaction structures (Beebe and Lachmann 1988, Beebe and Stern 1977). Patterns of expectation become represented. For example, the anxiously attached babies expect their mothers to be inconsistently responsive. Since they have no confidence in mother's availability, they protest, are angry, and fear disappointment. Stern (1994) described attachment schemas as "Schemas-of being-with-another-in-a-certain-way," which he shortened for utility's sake to "Schemas-of-being-with" (p. 12). Baby's mother is depressed. Baby wants and expects mother to be animated, but is not able to make it happen. Mother breaks eye contact, and is not responsive contingent to baby's wish for connection. Mother is limp, not animated, flat in affect, inactive. Baby responds in kind and loses body tonus, becoming quiet and deflated. Both baby and mother experience a micro-depression. This interaction sequence may become part of what was referred to above as a "working model" of engagement. This working model of relationship colors subsequent relationships until and unless it is transformed by subsequent experience. Different ways of organizing attachment behavior reflect differences in the mental representation of the self in relation to attachment (Slade and Aber 1992).

Evidence is now accumulating that documents substantial continuing association of attachment patterns throughout development. Attachment, or the "quality of relatedness" (Stern 1985, p. 186) that develops in childhood, is active in peer relationships, and in fact remains active throughout the life span. There is increasing evidence that later relationships are based on the formation of these early relational experiences (Osofsky 1995, Parkes et al. 1991). Main (1995) suggests that the nature of the child's early tie to the mother predicts attachment status in adolescence and young adulthood. A study by Dozier (1990) found that patients who had secure attachment relationships at the beginning of treatment were more compliant with therapy. Patients who had avoidant tendencies were less receptive to treatment (Cicchetti and Toth 1995). Sable (1989) reported that a study of eighty-one widows whose spouses had died one to three years earlier confirmed the lifelong significance of early attachment patterns. The anxiously attached women exhibited more anxiety and depression than women who had not had such relationships, and the anxiety and depression they experienced in the bereavement process were heightened by childhood experiences of separation, loss, and threats of abandonment.

ATTACHMENT AND PSYCHOTHERAPY

Bowlby understands attachment to be fundamental in human relationships. When one's core attachments are problematic, one's view of the world is powerfully influenced. When one operates from a secure base, one's sense of efficacy is enhanced. In the absence of a secure base, defensive strategies emerge (Holmes 1993). The two primary strategic defensive strategies, as Holmes formulates them, are: "I need to be near to my attachment figures in order to feel safe, but they may reject my advances, so I will suppress my needs both from myself and them, and remain on the emotional periphery of relationships," or, "I need to be near to my attachment figures but they may fail to respond to me or intrude on me in a way I can't control, so I will cling to them and insist on their responding to and caring for me" (p. 150).

Holmes (1993) states that there are five key themes that determine an individual's core state of attachment and suggests how psychotherapy can help in developing secure attachments. These states are "the need for a secure therapeutic base; the role of real trauma in the origins of neurosis; affective processing, especially of loss and separation; the place of cognition in therapy; and the part played by companionable interaction between therapist and patient" (p. 151).

Attachment theory fits well with a systems perspective of treatment. While my theoretical stance in working with John was self-psychological, I have a special interest in the effect of the earliest interactions and attachment patterns on the analyst–patient dyad. In the case description that follows, emphasis is placed on attachment themes.

John

John has been in analysis three years. A brilliant, disorganized man, John's affairs are always in disorder. He finds it difficult to regulate himself either in his business or personal life. He does not know when he is hot or cold, does not experience hunger, and therefore misses many meals. He believes that life will begin for him when he gets "rich and can afford to have a relationship." John lives on the edge. He goes from rags to riches to rags with rapidity. He claims an addiction to poverty. He is unable to sustain any sense of prosperity either in relationships or life. His many failed relationships and inability to regulate himself propelled him to seek treatment.

John told me often that as a child he wouldn't attend to his mother when called. He would continue his play, minimizing contact with a mother he felt was rejecting. His reports of his school years are rife with contradictions. Always in trouble at home for noncompliance with the family rules, he was president of his class, started a school newspaper, and rallied enough enthusiasm and pressure on the school to get a new baseball field. At the same time he had few friends, never did his schoolwork, was always in trouble with the administration, and was told over and over again that he was recalcitrant and that he would be expelled if he did not conform. Indeed, expulsion was his fate, and though extraordinarily intelligent and well read, he never completed his formal education. Throughout his life, this deficiency has been a source of poor self-esteem. Despite John's lack of education, he found a way to utilize his impressive talents in the business arena, becoming economically successful in the process. Poor relational skills, however, were his undoing, and he would continually lose jobs and financial security.

Early in the treatment John regaled me with his accomplishments. He observed me carefully, waiting to see how I would react. My initial understanding and interpretive activity reflected my awareness that it was vitally important to John that I appreciate and admire his prodigious talents. Later I came to understand that the barrage of articles, tales of accomplishments, and so on served defensive purposes. These covered over his insecurity about his own talents and skills but also served to keep him at a distance from me. Over the years of treatment John repeatedly complained that he was friendless and didn't know how to keep a friend. For thirty years his pattern had been to walk the city late at night, alone and lonely. Oddly enough, this lonely man knew hundreds of people, though he felt connected to none. He had indeed even been married for several years. His memories of courtship do not include getting to know his wife. They met, rushed into an ardent sexual relationship, married, and cohabited until she ended the marriage, stating that he could not or did not know how to have a relationship. John said, "I don't wait to find out whether or not I actually like the woman. If there is chemistry, we have sex and then we start living together. Only later do I discover I don't know anything about feeling intimate." He found it helpful when I speculated that his ambivalence and discomfort motivated him to rush through the preliminary "getting to know you" stage in a relationship. The way he did it helped him to avoid difficulties along the pathway to intimacy. I thought it interesting that Shaver and Hazan (1992) found that subjects rated as ambivalent on an attachment questionnaire reported greater sexual attraction toward the opposite sex and a shorter period of engagement prior to getting married.

In an abortive effort to feel attached, John began to attend twelve-step meetings. Attendance did not lead to attachment. He *did* find that people admired him for his storytelling ability. For moments his precarious self-esteem was bolstered. However, unable to feel comfortable in any "home group," he wandered from meeting to meeting getting to know the names of more and more people, but maintaining his tragic sense of disconnection. A prodigious reader, John reported that years ago he had encountered one of Bowlby's books dealing with separation and loss. He has never forgotten the thrill and horror of recognizing in it his own attachment dilemma. He said he lived his life as if he were still in the incubator all alone and struggling to breathe. He felt he was doomed to a life without intimacy or connection. These themes emerged when once again I had offered an interpretation that his perpetual movement from meeting to meeting, his pattern of calling people and leaving messages but never being home to receive the return calls—as well as many missed therapy sessions—might be a way to avoid the possibility of attachment.

With a great deal of embarrassment and a painfully apparent shyness, John met my eyes one day. There were several moments of a shared gaze and a very warm feeling between us. Breaking the gaze, John turned quickly to see if his briefcase was in place. He made his own interpretation. He said he felt almost giddy. The connection he felt at that moment meant to him that he might possibly be able to have a "real" attachment to someone. His impulse, he said, was to back away and begin to talk about his business ventures. This would reestablish his sense of himself as connected only to his quest to make money in order that he might *someday* be able to afford a relationship. Then, and only then, could he feel himself entitled to be attached to anyone. Our moment of connection challenged that expectation. John was elated and I was too. He said he felt as if he experienced a thaw. I, myself, for the first time, experienced John as fully in the room with me. With a more secure attachment and less dread of feeling close to me, he was able to explore and attempt to put together a narrative of his life. At that point his experience of his father emerged in the treatment.

John's father, a minor league baseball official, had a violent temper. As a child, John lived in terror of his father's temper. He grew up with the absolute belief in the validity of his father's warnings, "three strikes and you're out." His interpretation of that was that if he struck out he would be evicted from his home. This schema—"fear of striking out"—organized his experience of others. He lived in fear of "being found to be inadequate" and therefore did not allow himself to get close to anyone. Hypervigilant, his sensitivity to any sign of rejection was acute. Behaviorally it was manifest in what he termed his "procrastination." By not finishing a job, he would not have to find out that he had "struck out." Completion of assignments was inevitably followed by deflation and depression. We began to speculate that the predictability of John's forward movements, followed by deflation and depression, might have to do with expectations set in place early in his life. Momentary success or financial reward was in diametric opposition to a persistent belief that his parents expected him to "strike out." The following dream serves as an illustration.

> *He was sitting on a chair with a friend. It felt as if the seat was part of an atrium elevator at New York's World Trade Center. Atrium elevators are open and you can look out of them as you are ascending. When they reached the top, they looked over the edge of the elevator, and below them was the inside of the World Financial Center, filled with life, people having a good time, eating, doing financial trades. His buddy said to him, "All you have to do is put your leg over the edge and you will be on the inside." John was terrified, experiencing extreme anxiety, even in the dream. He began to put his leg over the edge, and then had the experience of the elevator seat with him on it falling away from the building into black desolation, nothingness. He awoke terrified.*

Our understanding of the dream was that should he enter the world of people, obtain financial success, or plentifulness of any kind, he believed he would lose the only relationships he had known: those with his parents, who had no expectations of John's becoming a success. He would be totally alone in the world.

As John came closer to achieving financial security, his self-disparaging comments became more relentless. These moments of forward movement, as well as any elation about the beginnings of a relationship, led to feelings of increased anxiety, depression, and disorganization. He would then rail against himself. "Why are you so lazy? Why don't you act instead of procrastinating? How can you expect to be a success when you're just a high-school dropout?" He would then point to some external evidence of his failures. I drew attention to the pattern, noting that my experience of him differed from his. I asked him to reflect on his own experience. He began to make the connection between his own relentless self-denigration and his mother's repeated statements that he would never amount to anything. His punitive, self-critical attitude seemed to restore a tie to his doubting mother. He told me repeatedly that he was a hopeless case. He now understood that his ambivalence about becoming financially secure was connected to his fear of attachment.

Currently, John is involved in a mighty struggle. He comes into the office, tries to engage with me, struggles to keep his eyes open, actually disengages by falling off to sleep for a few seconds, wakes and looks toward me. Following a mutually held gaze, John feels energized, reengaged, and is totally amazed by the shift he experiences in his state. John has forgotten our first experience of this gaze experience. I have not. The beginning of a new attachment experience is taking place.

DISCUSSION

Benjamin (1988) reflects that "As she cradles her newborn child and looks into its eyes, the first-time mother says, 'I believe she knows me. You do know me, don't you? Yes, you do' " (p. 13). She goes on to suggest that this mother "would not be surprised to hear that rigorous experiments show that her baby can already distinguish her from other people, that newborns already prefer the sight, sound, and smell of their mothers" (p. 13). This important early experience was missing for John and his mother. The human environment of sounds, smells, and responsiveness that infants require to experience their sameness with other humans (Kohut 1980) was cut short by his first ninety days, which had been spent in a preemie ward. We cannot ever know what those first three months were like for John. What we do know is that early care for John was not provided by a constant caretaker and that his mother was absent for those three months. She entered his life only upon receipt of the postcard from the hospital mentioned earlier. John's recalled experience was that the two were never comfortable with one another.

The importance of the infant–caretaker dyad has been memorialized by Winnicott's (1960) famous statement "there is no such thing as a baby" (p. 39). This dyad was disrupted from the beginning. There is increasing evidence from the field of neurobiology (Schore 1996) of the importance of attuned responses in forming attachments. Vision is one important ingredient in the establishment of the primary attachment to the mother (Bowlby 1969). Mutual gaze interactions between mother and infant play a crucial role in the developing infant from both a neurobiological and social standpoint. Mother's attuned matching and contingent responses to the infant's internal state are critical in the infant's formation of self-regulatory procedures (Beebe 1986, Beebe and Lachmann, 1988, Schore 1996). John's difficulty with self-regulation (temperature, hunger, and so on) had been a cue to me that he had experienced faulty interactive attachment experiences as an infant. Koulomzin and colleagues (1993) reported a self-regulatory disturbance at four months in those infants who would be classified at one year as having an insecure-avoidant attachment to their mothers. When studied at four months, in comparison to the secure infants, the avoidant infants look at the mother less. "Such facial matching experiences contribute to feeling known, attuned to, and on the same wavelength, and provide each with a behavior basis for entering into the other's feeling state (Koulomzin et al. 1993, p. 446).

John's terror of contact thawed somewhat as he and I engaged in mutual gaze. I was encouraged that, for that moment, we really were "on the same wavelength." We both understood those experiences as a first step in a less avoidant, if as yet ambivalent attachment.

John's attachment schema could be classified as insecure-avoidant. This working model was the basis of John's resistance to forming an attachment to me. Often in this treatment, I felt discouraged. It became a challenge to me to maintain hope in the face of John's early traumatic life experiences. John began treatment with the hope of someday being able to form an attachment. His hope kept alive my hope that this was a possibility. I looked for cues that in some way John was experiencing me as a "secure base" from which to explore his inner as well as his outer world. The gaze experiences were very helpful to both of us in that regard. It was helpful to me to understand his many missed sessions as ways to protect himself from forming an attachment to me. John's sense of himself as "bad" for "forgetting" slowly became transformed with our understanding of his attachment dilemma as an important metaphor for describing his avoidant behavior.

The attachment literature informed me that for someone who might be considered anxiously-avoidant, close contact is fraught with fears of pain and rejection. Infant research provided me with acute sensitivity to the nonverbal dimension in this treatment. Attachment theory and infant research provided *me* with a "secure base" from which to do my work.

REFERENCES

Ainsworth, M., Blehar, M., Waters, E., and Wall, S. (1978). *Patterns of Attachment: Assessed in the Strange Situation and at Home.* Hillsdale, NJ: Lawrence Erlbaum.

Beebe, B. (1986). Mother–infant mutual influence and precursors of self- and object representations. In *Empirical Studies of Psychoanalytic Theories*, vol. 2, ed. J. Masling, pp. 27–48. Hillsdale, NJ: Analytic Press.

Beebee, B., Jaffee, J., and Lachmann, F. M. (1992). A dyadic systems view of communication. In *Relational Views of Psychoanalysis*, ed. N. Skolnick and S. Warshaw, pp. 61–81. Hillsdale, NJ; Analytic Press.

Beebe, B., and Lachmann, F. M. (1988). The contribution of mother–infant mutual influence to the origins of self and object representations. *Psychoanalytic Psychology* 5:305–357.

———— (1990). The organization of representations in infancy: three principles of salience. Paper presented at the American Psychological Association Tenth Annual Spring meeting, Division of Psychoanalysis, New York, April.

Beebe, B., and Stern, D. (1977). Engagement–disengagement and early object experiences. In *Communicative Structures and Psychic Structures*, ed. N. Freedman and S. Grand, pp. 137–154. New York: Plenum.

Benjamin, J. (1988). *The Bonds of Love.* New York: Pantheon.

Bowlby, J. (1958). The nature of the child's tie to his mother. *International Journal of Psycho-Analysis* 39:350–373.

———— (1969). *Attachment and Loss*, vol. 1. New York: Basic Books.

——— (1973). *Attachment and Loss*, vol. 2, *Separation-Anxiety and Anger*. New York: Basic Books.

——— (1980). *Attachment and Loss*, vol. 3: *Loss, Sadness and Depression*. New York: Basic Books.

——— (1988). *A Secure Base*. New York: Basic Books.

Cicchetti, D., and Toth, S. L. (1995). Child maltreatment and attachment organization: implications for intervention. In *Attachment Theory: Social, Developmental, and Clinical Perspectives*, ed. S. Goldberg, R. Muir, and J. Kerr, pp. 279–308. Hillsdale, NJ: Analytic Press.

Cohn, J., and Tronick, E. (1988). Mother–infant face-to-face interaction: influence is bidirectional and unrelated to periodic cycles in either partner's behavior. *Developmental Psychology* 24:386–392.

Dozier, M. (1990). Attachment organization and treatment use for adults with serious psychopathological disorders. *Developmental Psychopathology* 2:47–60.

Eagle, M. (1995). The developmental perspectives of attachment and psychoanalytic theory. In *Attachment Theory: Social, Developmental, and Clinical Perspectives*, ed. S. Goldberg, R. Muir, and J. Kerr, pp. 123–152. Hillsdale, NJ: Analytic Press.

Gianino, A., and Tronick, E. (1988). The mutual regulatory model: the infant's self and interactive regulation and coping with defense capacities. In *Stress and Coping*, ed. T. Field and P. Schneidermann, pp. 1–37. Hillsdale, NJ: Lawrence Erlbaum.

Grossman, K., and Grossman, K. (1991). Attachment quality as an organizer of emotional and behavioural responses in a longitudinal perspective. In *Attachment Across the Life Cycle*, ed. C. M. Parkes, J. Stevenson-Hinde, and P. Marris, pp. 93–114. London: Routledge.

Holmes, J. (1993). *John Bowlby and Attachment Theory*. London: Routledge.

Kohut, H. (1980). Reflections on advances in self psychology. In *Advances in Self Psychology*, ed. A. Goldberg, pp. 473–554. New York: International Universities Press.

Koulomzin, M., Beebe, B., Jaffee, J., and Feldstein, T. (1993). Infant self comfort, disorganized scanning, facial distress and bodily approach in face-to-face play at four months discriminate A versus B attachment at one year. *Abstract Issue*, p. 446. New Orleans: Society for Research and Child Development.

Main, M. (1995). Recent studies in attachment: overview with selected implications for clinical work. In *Attachment Theory: Social, Developmental, and Clinical Perspectives*, ed. S. Goldberg, R. Muir, and J. Kerr, Hillsdale, NJ: Analytic Press.

Osofsky, J. D. (1995). Perspectives on attachment and psychoanalysis. *Psychoanalytic Psychology* 12(3):347–362.

Parkes, C. M., Stevenson-Hinde, J., and Marris, P., eds. (1991). *Attachment Across the Life Cycle*. London: Routledge.

Sable, P. (1989) Attachment, anxiety and loss of a husband. *Women and Therapy* 11(2):55–69.

———— (1994). Anxious attachment in adulthood: therapeutic implications. *Journal of Analytic Social Work* 2(1):5–24.

Sander, L. W. (1977). The regulation of exchange in the infant caretaker system and some aspects of the context-content relationship. In *Interaction, Conversation and the Development of Language*, ed. M. Lewis and L. Rosenblum, pp. 133-156. New York: Wiley.

———— (1985). Toward a logic of organization in psychobiological development. In *Biologic Response Styles*, ed. K. Klar and L. Siever, pp. 20–36. Washington, DC: American Psychiatric Press.

Schore, A. N. (1996). The experience-dependent maturation of a regulatory system in the orbital prefrontal cortex and the origin of developmental psychopathology. *Development and Psychopathology* 8:59–87.

Shaver, P., and Hazan, C. (1992). Adult romantic attachment: theory and evidence. In *Advances in Personal Relations*, ed. D. Perlman and W. Jones, pp. 29–70. London: Kingley.

Silverman, D. (1992). Attachment research: an approach to a developmental relational perspective. In *Relational Perspectives in Psychoanalysis*, ed. S. Warshaw and N. Skolnick, pp. 195–216. Hillsdale, NJ: Analytic Press.

Slade, A., and Aber, J. L. (1992). Attachments, drives, and development: conflicts and convergences in theory. In *Interface of Psychoanalysis and Psychology*, ed. J. Barron, M. Eagle, and D. Wolitzky, pp. 154-185. Washington, DC: American Psychological Association.

Sroufe, L. A., and Walters, E. (1977). Attachment as an organizational construct. *Child Development* 48:1184–1199.

Stern, D. N. (1985). *The Interpersonal World of the Infant*. New York: Basic Books.

———— (1994). One way to build a clinically relevant baby. *Infant Mental Health Journal* 15(1):9–25.

———— (1995). *The Motherhood Constellation*. New York: Basic Books.

Winnicott, D. W. (1960). The theory of the parent–infant relationship. In *The Maturational Processes and the Facilitating Environment*, pp. 37–55. Madison, CT: International Universities Press.

Zeanah, C., Anders, T., Seifer, R., and Stern, D. (1990). Implications of research on infant development for psychodynamic theory and practice. *Journal of the American Academy of Child Psychiatry* 28:657–668.

9

Maternal Love and Its Manifestations in the Therapeutic Process

JUDITH RAPPAPORT

The concept of motherhood in Western culture has shifted from the image of an idealized good figure or a dangerously powerful representation to one of a mother who has her own complicated subjectivity. This shift has consequences in terms of therapeutic work. In this chapter, using popular literature, object relations theories, and current feminist literature, I describe this evolving concept, while briefly looking at Daniel Stern's motherhood constellation and Winnicott's maternal paradigm. Case examples and treatment implications follow.

There are three major requirements of the mothering role: (1) to protect and preserve the child's life, (2) to nurture the child's emotional and intellectual growth, and (3) to help the child adjust to cultural mores and gain social acceptance. It is important to note that the third expectation is often overlooked in the professional literature. That may be so because that literature is based on and created by middle-class whites. Economic and social conditions profoundly shape how women mother. For example, physical survival, the first requirement of motherhood, cannot be assumed among poor children. In some countries government intervention prevents the mother from fulfilling any or all of these functions.

THE GOOD MOTHER

These expectations for motherhood still prevail and are generally accepted. However, many cultural and temporal influences affect the idea of what constitutes motherhood. Before a large percentage of mothers entered the workforce, it was society's expectation that they serve as full-time mothers. Mothers were expected to be seamlessly suited to the needs of their infants, selfless and all-loving in feeling as well as behavior. Therefore, if anything went wrong with the children mothers took the blame. Even today, when so many women are working outside of the home, a well-known pediatrician, Penelope Leach (1990), writes that women who work are breaking their children's hearts. This requirement for perfect accommodation has been echoed in the jargon of everyday life as well as in the professional literature.

Classical analytic theoreticians promulgated a narrow view of the mother's role. Their primary focus was on the satisfaction of instinctual aims; lesser importance was given to the mother's emotional availability. However, object relations theory focused on key aspects of motherhood and applied them to technique. It described the holding, containing, attuned mother who became the holding environment (Winnicott 1960, 1969a), the containing vessel (Bion 1977), and the selfobject (Kohut 1977). Winnicott explored the many facets of mothering, creating the analogue of the nursing couple in the therapeutic situation. While emphasizing the importance of the mother–child dyad, object relations theorists describe the mother as an object who is required to be responsive to her child's emotional needs. This mother was to be self-effacing, nurturing, and facilitating. I believe this describes a fantasy of an ideal mother, the answer to all our wishes. The fantasy involves a wonderful woman who cares for us, sees to our needs, and repairs all. It is inevitable that mothers cannot fulfill this ideal, for these expectations are impossible to achieve. Paradoxically, this theory inadvertently disempowers women by creating expectations that are impossible to fulfill, and so result in failure and therefore guilt.

PATHOLOGIES OF MOTHERING

A powerful image of the bad mother has been developed in literature, in our public imagination, and in professional papers concerned with pathologies of mothering. Analytic literature, with its emphasis on the unconscious, shows how the mother is viewed as both a loved and hated object. From Deutsch (1945) through Langer (1992) there has been acknowledgment that mothers may be seen as devouring and deadly. In Melanie Klein's (1937) theory of development, an infant moves from the paranoid-schizoid position through a depressive position. A healthy result is the infant's development of a capacity for concern for the mother. Klein described how the infant's projections create a good but also a bad and destructive breast. These projections of the bad breast (bad mother), when excessive, can interfere with progress through the depressive period. Adrienne Rich (1976) described, as only a poet can, how monstrous she considered herself when ambivalent and hateful feelings toward her children surfaced. The therapist frequently listens as a patient describes her experience of her devouring mother. Rich described her experience of herself as a bad mother. Thus, both poet and patient describe the bad mother from very different vantage points.

As early as Euripides, the mother (Medea) is depicted as a woman whose intense passions of lust and revenge toward her husband drive her to kill their children. In fairy tales such as "Snow White" and "Hansel and Gretel," stepmothers want to kill their children. In Toni Morrison's *Beloved* (1994), a mother kills her daughter to save her from slavery. This is an extraordinary description of a slave mother's subjectivity. To this mother, in that historical frame, the motivation for killing was utmost love. The book illustrates the necessity of understanding motherhood from within its social context. In another recent book, *The Ladder of Years* (1995), Anne Tyler writes of a less violent act. She depicts a woman who left her home and children. Society would have no difficulty in labeling her a "bad mother." For her, leaving her family seemed the only route to self-delineation. It is difficult to comprehend what could be bad enough to motivate a mother to abandon her children. A patient was infuriated when the mother in the movie *Reckless* (1994) abandoned her children. It was many sessions later when she recalled that the movie mother left her family, having discovered her husband planned to murder her. Several years ago a considerable amount of attention was focused on the case of Susan Smith whose horrific murder of her children belied all we consider good about motherhood.

THE ABUSING MOTHER

The abusing mother either performs actively, or passively allows abuse to occur. In the Oedipus myth, for example, the father leaves his child to die. The mother passively accepts this heinous act. Many abusing mothers are repeating past traumas by enacting what was done to them. It is interesting to note that Ireland (1993) hypothesizes that abusive mothers have perversions specific to women. She sees abuse as a compulsive act charged with hostility. The motive for the abuse is the mother's fantasy of revenge or retaliation against her own mother. In Ireland's view, abuse involves dehumanizing the infant, who is viewed as an extension of the mother. Child abuse, therefore, is ultimately an act against the mother's own body. Welldon, in *Mother, Madonna, Whore* (1988), states, "Odd though it may sound, motherhood provides an excellent vehicle for some women to exercise perverse and perverting attitudes toward their offspring and to retaliate against their own mothers" (p. 63). The babies who are experienced as part-object extensions by their mothers bear the brunt of their mothers' past humiliation. A mother's hatred or ambivalence toward her child does not in itself create an abusive mother. Dissociative processes and/or repressive measures may lead to repetition of the past, thus contributing to abusive relationships. Mothers of newborns frequently reveal in therapy their hatred for their babies. Often these mothers unconsciously identify with their own abusive mothers. Even the decision to have a child has multiple determinants. This decision is often impeded by old maternal representations as well as past trauma. In a recent article I have written of the impact of sibling suicide on the desire for a child (Rappaport 1994a).

FEMINIST OBJECT RELATIONS

Feminist object-relations writers challenge the validity of the representation of the all-good or all-bad mother. They highlight the rich subjectivity of mothers. Specifically, they move away from seeing mothers as objects. Significant is the recognition that the mother has a subjectivity that includes sexual and aggressive impulses toward her children. The mother's subjectivity significantly impacts her child.

Simone de Beauvoir focused attention on motherhood. In her 1952 book, *The Second Sex*, she indicated that society devalued women largely because of their role as mothers. No doubt she influenced Chodorow's (1978) extensive investigation of the effect of women's mothering on social relations. Chodorow believes that the societal structure contributes to difficulties of mothering by seeing it as women's work only.

Currently, Kristeva (1986), Cixous (1985), and Irigary (1985) are the French forerunners for a body of feminist literature that delineates the uniqueness of the female experience in motherhood. I will mention a few American counterparts. Ruddick (1989) describes the specific disciplined thinking state required for motherhood, one filled with tensions and conflict requiring constant judgment. She believes that what is important is the way a mother navigates all her conflictual thinking. This reflective quality of thought, specific to and characteristic of maternal thinking, includes nurturance and binding connections. Domash (1988) describes the necessity for the mother to continually juggle wishes to unite with her infant and child, but also to be separate from him or her. Kraemer (1996) states that maternal love consists of tensions between the mother's desire to provide a holding environment and her desire to recognize her own needs. Kraemer warns that idealization of motherhood ignores the existence of unacceptable feelings as well as the constant struggle and juggling of feelings required in mothering. Problems arise when the mother cannot handle her unacceptable feelings. She might become self-reproachful, attempt to lose herself in her baby, retaliate, or even collapse. The challenge for the mother is twofold: to tolerate and not deny her unpleasant feelings, such as envy or aggression, and to keep hopefulness and reparative desires alive. Reparative desires are crucial factors in a mother's ability to withstand unpleasant feelings.

Benjamin (1994) recast the metaphor of the nursing dyad to a model based on intersubjective relatedness and mutual recognition. In her view, both mother and infant must recognize each other as independent, autonomous subjects. A major task of motherhood is to navigate the inherent tensions between the mother's sense of herself and the child's sense of its own agency. Constant tensions between recognizing the other and asserting the self are always present. Additionally, Benjamin writes about the deeply ingrained, unconscious, omnipotent representations of mothers. She disagrees with Chasseguet-Smirgel (1985), who attributes the persistence of omnipotent fantasies to the infant's dependency. Benjamin considers the fantasy of an all-powerful mother a paranoid reaction. She believes that infant research corroborates that mutual recognition between mother and child and the existence of a shared reality may mitigate the fantasy of omnipotence. Benjamin is suggesting that commonly held unconscious representations can change with awareness of the richness of maternal subjectivity.

We have run the gamut. After Freud's lack of interest in motherhood, the mother was considered entirely responsible and usually idealized or hated. Currently, the mother is viewed as holding her complicated subjectivity in reciprocal engagement with her child.

THE THERAPIST'S SUBJECTIVITY

Parallel with the growing acknowledgment and investigation of a mother's subjectivity, there has been a similar focus on the subjectivity of the therapist. For example, Wrye and Welles (1994) describe a basic and normal maternal erotic transference and countertransference, referring to the early mother–infant relationship in all its tactile aspects, including its fluids—milk, drool, urine, and so on. This transference–countertransference situation recreates a primal, preverbal, sensuous relationship that is both libidinal and aggressive, with many somatic aspects. Contrary to the classical idea of an eroticized transference that is defensive, this transference is seen as a rich source for analytic work—though it is often feared by both patient and therapist. I might add that my work has been enriched by acknowledging and encouraging this sensuous base. I believe that early maternal sensuality has not been sufficiently recognized in therapeutic work. Likewise, I think more therapeutic attention could be paid to the sensual experiences of motherhood that have to do with nursing. Therapists are loathe to consider nursing mothers as having sexual feelings, and therefore neglect an important part of early sensual-sexual feelings that might emerge in the transference.

WINNICOTT

It was Winnicott (1960) who most clearly utilized the analogue of the infant and maternal care, the nursing couple, for the therapeutic situation. His work is an elegant investigation of emotional development and the maternal care it requires. According to him (1962), the maternal function is not mainly to satisfy drives but to hold emotionally. By providing a nurturing milieu the mother protects the baby from impingements, allowing the baby a temporary omnipotence that fosters a feeling of agency and creativity. From a near total devotion, the mother gradually adapts to the child's developing needs (1956). The mother seems to intuit what is required and though she may waiver, if she's not too distorted in her own development, she'll find a way to provide enough for her child.

Similarly, the therapist provides a holding environment, a necessary backdrop to treatment in which the real aspects of maternal care are symbolically represented through the therapist's reliable and empathic presence. Often, with the severely disturbed patient, holding replaces interpretative work. The therapist, like the idealized mother, is constant and reliable, responding to the patient's affects, not her own. Implied in holding has been the idea that, like the mother, the therapist maintains an emotionally protective setting in which the patient's affective experience is not challenged. It is important to note that the therapist, like the mother, is actively monitoring her own tensions and responses.

Winnicott (1960, 1969a) described certain characteristics of good mothering that are present in a good therapist. First, the mother he described presents the world to her baby, holding him while he explores the real things around him. Similarly, the therapist offers interpretations in such a way that the patient can either dismiss or accept them. The therapist is not in the position of a seer who knows all, but is an aid to his patient in the exploration of his problem. This maternal presence stands by and is also actively present in the endeavor. Second, the mother allows the baby to be alone with her, to foster a relaxed separateness within relatedness. This suggests the mother's capacity for judgments about timing and readiness. Similarly, the therapist must make decisions about when to leave the patient alone with himself, respecting the need for privacy. Third, there are legitimate reasons for mothers to hate their children, and in fact when the mother is comfortable with her hatred, her child becomes more comfortable with his. Winnicott (1947) lists the reasons one might hate one's child: he pukes, wakes her, isn't grateful, and so on, and Winnicott shows how some patients can be hated also. This is linked with the normalcy of countertransference phenomena. Both the mother and therapist must deal with their hatred so as to be maximally available to their child or patient, without masochistic acquiescence. Fourth, Winnicott's (1969b) mother requires a resilience that enables her to survive the child's attack and to recognize the potential for constructive aggression. Therapists working with borderline patients, in particular, try to hold their own with very rageful or sadistic people.

Some of Winnicott's concepts are not easy to digest. When I was teaching a class on Winnicott, a student cried because she felt guilty being in school when her baby was at home. Another time, when discussing hate in the countertransference and relating it to mothers, an indignant student shouted, "A mother cannot hate her child!" It has been very difficult to relinquish certain ideals of motherhood and move to a place where mothers are subjects with their own tumultuous needs and the necessity to contain them. Some have cautioned against carrying Winnicott too far. First (1994), a revisionist writer of Winnicott, states: "He was not saying that analysts are mothers, or patients babies, but that at a certain level of work the analyst tries to repair what mothers try to develop" (p. 148). She goes on to point out that a helpful comparison of mothers and analysts shows that both require an acceptance of their own ambivalence and even of their hatred. But she is careful to warn about a wholesale application of motherhood to therapy.

POST-WINNICOTT

By seeing the mother and infant as an integral unit, Winnicott has enabled us to move toward a more intersubjective stance. Concurrent with the recognition of a mother's active and complicated subjectivity, in which tensions must be held, there has been recognition that the therapist's subjectivity with all its tensions is integral to an understanding of the patient's dynamics. We are focused on the rich inner life of the therapist, which consists of aggression but also positive and sensual feelings, and we recognize the requirement that the therapist contain the tension of these feelings. It is important that along with this recognition there is an exploration of the patient's experience of his or her therapist's inner life.

But because of the impact of biological, social, and cultural influences, motherhood has very specific dynamics and inner emotional work, and is a specific constellation with a complicated subjectivity. Current object relations theorists have made us aware that we are constantly reacting to old images of our mother or to ourselves as mothers. First, we realize the consistent need to rework old maternal images. This was not an issue Winnicott addressed. Second, just as we recognize the flexibility but also the tensions involved in mothering, we have also become aware that there are difficulties in holding for a therapist. Far from a relaxed stance, holding requires constant monitoring (Slochower 1996). Third, we can understand that in our zeal to consider the early dyad we may miss vital oedipal issues having to do with competitive, conflict-charged rivalries and aggressions. Mitchell (1988) criticizes what he calls the maternal tilt. In clinical work this is evidenced by (1) the therapist's focus on early needs and infantile dynamics, (2) a tendency to have the therapist in the position of the good object and the patient the passive recipient, and (3) playing into the therapist's and patient's desire for a magical cure. In general, Mitchell believes there is not enough recognition of the adult patient's complicated development and capacities.

Certain of these criticisms can also be leveled at Daniel Stern's description of treatment implications stemming from what he calls the "motherhood constellation" (1995). He describes this constellation as a unique psychic organization triggered by pregnancy. It supersedes the oedipal configuration, with the baby as the focal point, the husband now an imminent father more than a sexual partner, and the grandmother more important than before. For Stern, the motherhood constellation has important implications for treatment. According to him, a special transference to the therapist occurs because the mother's major requirement is to be valued, supported, and taught by a maternal figure. It is comparable to a "grandmother transference," requiring the therapist to be active, giving, and to focus more on the patient's assets and abilities rather than on pathology. This is a very special, active holding of the maternal function. Stern believes a combination of interpretation and modeling helps liberate maternal functions. I have found this more active, positive approach helpful with mothers (and I will show this in a case further on). I believe Stern attempted a corrective to the prior analytic stance, which ignored the needs of the mother. However, he went overboard in not recognizing the importance of the father in the mother's internal and real world. Nor does he recognize how the pregnancy and/or the birth of a child reactivates competition, in sibling issues as well as oedipal love. In fact, unless Stern's motherhood constellation applies only to a small fragment of time, I think he has separated out the mothering aspects of women needlessly. Mothering does not exclude all other personality complexes and capacities.

A "grandmother" stance for the therapist is helpful, as an active and optimistic stance is helpful in many situations, especially in transitional phases. But it is difficult to separate one's beliefs about mothering from the patient's complicated requirements. It is tempting to impose one's own ideal of motherhood and also to infantilize the patient. By having a more balanced view, the therapist is able to see the patient's mature needs and hopes and can underline them for the patient. What is constructive is a heightened awareness of the maternal feelings and conflicts, and a respect for the constantly changing and influencing unconscious actors in the maternal dyad as well as in the therapeutic endeavor. A goal of the therapeutic situation includes the gradual relinquishment of old and extreme representations.

CASE EXAMPLES

Especially during pregnancy, when so much is disequilibrium and change, the old maternal relationship is revisited and a constant reworking of the maternal bond is required. Long-forgotten memories from the prospective mother's own childhood are triggered by pregnancy and birth. To encourage the evolution of the young mother's desires, of her vision of how she would like to be, requires that the therapist be active and encouraging. In this way the therapist is empowering the maternal function. The case described below illustrates how pregnancy requires work around the earlier maternal dyad as well as the changing father, sibling, and self-representations placed on the fetus. It illustrates a helpful therapeutic stance as well.

Sarah

Sarah, a young woman I have already written about (Rappaport 1994b), was married and in treatment when her brother died of a drug overdose. She wanted children, but following her sibling's death she miscarried and reacted in her habitual way—by cruelly devaluing herself and me. We had to work on her enormous guilt about being better off than her brother and surviving him. She did learn to question how tragic events made such a difference in her self-evaluation. A great deal of work was done around the image of her mother, which was multilayered. First, she was seen as all-powerful and perfect—but also a pathetic woman. Therefore, Sarah was afraid she would not be an entity in her own right. Also, when Sarah became pregnant the presence of her fetus evoked sibling hatreds and jealousies, as well as self-hatred when the baby represented herself. She was so overwhelmed by these feelings that I took a very active stance, reminding her of her deep desire to have a child to enable her to distance herself from regressive and tormenting feelings. Later, in her seventh month, she became frightened that the baby would require that she extinguish her identity. I encouraged her to consider ways that would help her validate her space. So, as time went on she worked through sibling issues and self-issues, as well as the powerful influence of her father, and finally the realization that she was not required to be the perfect mother. I was constantly working with her aggression and worries of destructiveness and there were times I almost didn't survive her onslaughts. But I was equally attentive to her aspirations for motherhood. I am an active therapist but I was especially so during her pregnancy (and this may be so of all critical periods). I emphasized her maternal desires and hopes and was the memory for desires that went underground with regression.

Though a woman may have worked out many problems in her therapy, childbearing can trigger some unresolved anxieties that require further therapy. Working with a pregnant woman can reveal how extreme images of self and other (baby) come from several developmental periods. Once the need for them no longer exists (due to increased ego strength and the ability to see the other as separate and as a subject in her own right), then these images become muted and take on human dimensions.

I think work around motherhood, whether it be pregnancy or miscarriage, requires a great deal of attunement to one's own countertransference. For example, when Sarah was trying to make a decision about whether to stay home with her baby or work, I needed to go beyond my own motherhood and daughterhood. I was enriched by my personal experiences but also by my readings in feminism and Winnicott. The former enabled me to understand the richness of the maternal subjectivity and its constant tensions. The latter helped me to be humble in my interpretations as well as teaching me about the necessity to endure.

Helen

Another example is that of an obsessional young woman, Helen, who never thought about children or imagined herself a mother. An interesting change occurred when her denial of her mother as a person began to break down. Heretofore, she had had trouble imagining her mother as part of a couple and was now surprised to consider ways that her father and mother interacted. Gradually she got in touch with a more realistic picture of her very depressed mother, who had suffered a still-birth when Helen was 1 year old. Then buried desires for children surfaced, though she quickly retracted them. Sensing her strong repressive measures, I was very actively inquiring and suggesting that we should consider her lack of interest in a family and see what would come of it. I believe many therapists are afraid of bringing up the issue of children or family, and that the absence of this discussion colludes with the anxieties of many women.

In thinking over this patient from the point of view of ideals or intersubjective tensions, I realize that Helen had a very superficial maternal representation and great difficulty deepening her feelings and attachments. Probably, because the major trauma was that her mother was preoccupied with mourning when she was so young, Helen had difficulty finding an emotional space for herself as a woman, and avoided intimate relationships so that she wouldn't be required to know her deep feelings. With treatment she became aware of a deep desire to have children.

An active and especially affirmative approach is helpful with mothers who become guilty and overburdened with their own angry and jealous feelings. The knowledge that mothers often have angry and ambivalent feelings evoking superego reprisals, changing self and object representations, and self-esteem fluctuations is essential. We must allow for a fuller emotional repertoire to come forth.

Betty

I remember treating a 40-year-old woman, Betty, with a complex obsessional neurosis no doubt exacerbated by the birth of her children and by a failed pregnancy fifteen years previous to her treatment with me. After her children were born, and because of excessive anxiety, she returned to her first therapist. The therapist's inability to allow her to articulate her concerns and his inflexible scheduling blocked discussion of her mothering needs. Had she been enabled to articulate her concerns, had the therapist been more attuned to how having children and miscarriages affected Betty, her illness might have been averted. While this may seem obvious, I do not believe many therapists are very sensitive to issues and difficulties around pregnancy and having children. This patient taught me a great deal about how the tensions in motherhood can trigger a regression. She was unable to progress through a miscarriage and was pulled back. Much of our work had to do with her earlier relationship with her mother, and finally with the guilt that destroyed her happiness.

I do want to add that there is some benefit in being a good mother in the transference. Many patients need to bathe in a benign atmosphere in order to feel secure enough to risk other kinds of fears and feelings. However, like the mother, the therapist's subjectivity is always under strain.

CONCLUSION

The evolving concept of motherhood goes hand in hand with the recognition of women's complex inner subjectivity. We realize that the ideal "good" mother, all-responsive and attuned, is an unrealistic expectation creating guilt and self-blame. Though Winnicott and other object relations theorists recognized the importance of the dyad and of the mother's responsiveness to her child, little attention was paid to the mother's singular and evolving subjectivity. Feminist theorists address this imbalance by describing the complicated richness of the maternal subjectivity.

We are becoming more appreciative of a mother's subjectivity with all its passions. What was once considered the ideal all-good mother has become transformed, as has the idea of the therapist. It is important for therapists to become more sensitive to the mother's inner work, and to recognize the internal tensions and the attempts to contain them. We need to examine the maternal feelings in ourselves, even the primitive and early sensuous longings, so we may enable our patients to realize their own infantile longings.

We have come to realize that the idealization—and consequently the blaming—of mothers has been part of a societal heritage. In addition, we have come to recognize that mother's work is affected by race and/or class, and that idealized or degraded representations are also affected by societal expectations. We are attuning ourselves to mothers having their own rich subjectivities that inform the mother–child dyad and are clearer in our recognition that mutuality between mother and child is present from the beginning. Over a period of time, the effects of mutuality could be a modification of the extreme representations of mothers. This could result in more balanced expectations and more societal supports for the care of children.

REFERENCES

Benjamin, J. (1994). The omnipotent mother: a psychoanalytic study of fantasy and reality. In *Representations of Motherhood*, ed. D. Bassin, M. Honey, and M. M. Kaplan, pp. 129–146. New Haven, CT: Yale University Press.

Bion, W. (1977). *Learning from Experience.* New York: Jason Aronson.

Chasseguet-Smirgel, J. (1985). *Female Sexuality.* London: Karnac.

Chodorow, N. (1978). *The Reproduction of Mothering.* Berkeley, CA: University of California Press.

——— (1989). *Feminism and Psychoanalytic Theory.* New Haven, CT: Yale University Press.

Cixous, H. (with Clement, C.) (1985). *The Newly Born Woman.* Minneapolis: University of Minnesota Press.

de Beauvoir, S. (1952). *The Second Sex.* New York: Knopf.

Deutsch, H. (1945). *The Psychology of Women.* New York: Grune & Stratton.

Domash, L. (1988). Motivation for motherhood and the nature of the self–object tie. In *Critical Psycho-Physical Passages in the Life of a Woman: A Psychodynamic Formulation*, ed. J. Offerman-Zuckerberg, pp. 93–101. New York: Plenum.

First, E. (1994). Mothering, hate, and Winnicott. In *Representations of Motherhood*, ed. D. Bassin, M. Honey, and M. Kaplan, pp. 147–161. New Haven, CT: Yale University Press.

Ireland, M. (1993). *Reconceiving Women.* New York: Guilford.

Irigary, L. (1985). *Speculum of the Other Woman.* Ithaca, NY: Cornell University Press.

Klein, M. (1937). Love, guilt and reparation. In *Love, Guilt and Reparation*, pp. 306–343. New York: Viking Penguin, 1963.

Kohut, H. (1977). *The Restoration of the Self.* New York: International Universities Press.

Kraemer, S. (1996). Betwixt the dark and the sunlight: some meditations on maternal subjectivity. *Psychoanalytic Dialogues* 6:765–791.

Kristeva, J. (1986). *The Kristeva Reader*, ed. T. Moi. Oxford, England: Basil Blackwell.

Langer, M. (1992). *Motherhood and Sexuality.* New York: Guilford.

Leach, P. (1990). *Your Baby and Child from Birth to Age 5*. New York: Knopf.

Mitchell, S. (1988). *Relational Concepts in Psychoanalysis*. Cambridge, MA: Harvard University Press.

Morrison, T. (1994). *Beloved*. Bergenfield, NJ: New American Library.

Rappaport, J. (1994a). Sibling suicide: its effects on the wish for a child and in the maternal transference/countertransference. *Journal of Clinical Psychoanalysis* 3, 94(2):241–258.

——— (1994b). Analytic work concerning motherhood. *Psychoanalytic Review* 81(4):695–716.

Rich, A. (1976). *Of Woman Born*. New York: Norton.

Ruddick, S. (1989). *Maternal Thinking*. New York: Ballantine.

Slochower, J. (1996). Holding the fate of the analyst's subjectivity. *Psychoanalytic Dialogues* 6(3):323–353.

Stern, D. (1995). *The Motherhood Constellation*. New York: Basic Books.

Tyler, A. (1995). *The Ladder of Years*. New York: Random House.

Welldon, E. (1988). *Mother, Madonna, Whore*. New York: Guilford.

Winnicott, D. W. (1947). Hate in the countertransference. In *Through Paediatrics to Psycho-Analysis*, pp. 194–203. New York: Basis Books.

——— (1956). Primary maternal preoccupation. In *Through Paediatrics to Psycho-Analysis*, pp. 300–305. New York: Basic Books.

——— (1960). The theory of parent–infant relationship. In *The Maturational Processes and the Facilitating Environment*, pp. 37–55. New York: International Universities Press.

——— (1962). Ego integration in child development. In *The Maturational Processes and the Facilitating Environment*, pp. 56–63. New York: International Universities Press.

——— (1969a). The mother–infant experience of mutuality. In *Psychoanalytic Explorations*, pp. 251–260. Cambridge, MA: Harvard University Press.

——— (1969b). The use of an object and relating through identifications. In *Playing and Reality*, pp. 101–111. New York: Penguin.

Wrye, H. K., and Welles, J. K. (1994). *The Narration of Desire*. Hillsdale, NJ: Analytic Press.

10

Transference Love, Eros, and Attachment

FLORENCE ROSIELLO

In one of the last sessions of Anna O's treatment with Josef Breuer in 1882, she revealed she was pregnant with his child (Freud 1932). One account of this day suggested that Breuer abruptly terminated the treatment, another stated it was Anna O, but nevertheless, Breuer learned that same evening his patient was in the throes of a hysterical childbirth. The next day, Breuer left Vienna with his wife for a second honeymoon.

Later, Freud wrote about Breuer's trauma to his own wife, Martha, who hoped this phenomenon would not happen to her husband. Freud admonished Martha for her vanity in thinking other women would fall in love with her husband, and denied *his* patients would ever fall in love with him (Jones 1953). Martha, on the other hand, had intuitively understood the universal nature of the problem. A short time later, Freud learned that Anna O's reaction to Breuer was more the rule than the exception—the "talking cure" in psychoanalysis inherently facilitated the development of erotic feelings (Person 1993).

It is my assertion that the erotic transference[1] can serve a facilitating function toward therapeutic "cure" in the sense of its being a special love or symbol of intimacy with the analyst. I am referring to patients who are able to immerse themselves in their own inner life through the development of transference love. The patient experiences this love as creating a very special intimacy that allows an exploration of self, as well as an experiencing of the self in relation to (an)other.

The unfolding of transference love in such patients is developed by their having a particular *symbolic attitude* (Deri 1984). This implies a paired stance vis-à-vis experience, where the patient feels an interpenetrating alternation of the *symbolic* with the *real* or actual. This way of thinking, conceived by Deri (1984), differs from Freud's thoughts on the nature of the mind. Freud (1923) envisioned the mind as a mental apparatus always at odds with itself. He gave the example of the horse as the id struggling with the rider, the ego. Deri (1984) argued that the mind could develop symbolic structures that functioned to unify conflict. She used the example of the *centaur* (p. 292) rather than the horse and rider to represent the different dimensions of the mind, as not merely a condensation as Freud would have considered it, but as a new structure that unified the conflict between ego and id—in other words, the mind as a complex whole rather than two antagonistic and conflicting parts.

I would like to use Deri's metaphor of the centaur to illustrate the symbolic along with the real or actual quality of transference love. The *symbolic* is the patient's fear and resistance against an emergence of incestuous wishes (represented by the horse), and the *real* or actual quality is the patient's wish to enact his or her love toward the analyst (represented as the rider). These two inimical representations make up— in the reorganization of the mind—a third entity, neither horse nor rider but centaur, that is, transference love.

---

1. For the purpose of this chapter, the term *erotic transference* is used interchangeably with the term *transference love*, which is in keeping with analytic literature on the subject. Transference love refers to a combination of sexual and tender feelings that a patient develops in relation to his or her analyst. This phenomenon can also encompass demands for physical and sexual relations, assaultive antagonisms, demands for approval, and dependent fears of object loss (Person 1985).

In my experience, this capacity on the part of some patients only partially overlaps with what is usually called *ego strength*. Yet there are so-called borderline patients who seem very able to work with a transference that is experienced as real, while there are so-called neurotic patients who, like Freud's rider on the horse, seem to need a clean distinction between transference fantasy and transference reality (Kaftal 1991).

But the patient does not function alone in transference love. The reparative effect of transference love matures in the analyst's *receptivity* and participation in a unique mutuality of affect in the therapeutic relationship. It is not only the patient but also the analyst who share in the responsibility and development of transference love, and therefore transference love is a two-person system (Gill 1993). It is within this intimate, erotic transference that there can be an integration of self through delicate, loving communication with the surrounding human environment, experienced by the self as part of its own wholeness. Thus, the erotic transference is not merely a resistance to the emergence of incestuous wishes, not just a sign of a structural deficit, not simply a real or unreal treatment phenomenon, not just a confusion between satisfactions or securities. The erotic transference is also an intimate facilitator of therapeutic action.

Our attitude about transference love should be guided by the theory of therapeutic action. Freud's main concept of therapeutic action was the analysis of resistance in order to bring unconscious needs into consciousness. Yet Freud continually vacillated on this concept with regard to the phenomenon of transference love. In his postscript to "Fragment of an Analysis of a Case of Hysteria" (1905), while he attributed the breakdown of Dora's treatment to his failure to interpret the transference, he also seems to wonder whether he could have kept Dora in treatment if he had exaggerated how important she was to him, in a sense actually providing her with a substitute for the affection she desired (Eickhoff 1993).

Another, perhaps more emphatic, comment on transference love is found in Freud's (1907) "Delusions and Dreams in Jensen's *Gradiva*" paper: "The process of cure is accomplished in a relapse into love, if we combine all the many components of the sexual instinct under the term 'love'; and such a relapse is indispensable, for [if] the symptoms on account of which the treatment has been undertaken are nothing other than precipitates of earlier struggles connected with repression or the return of the repressed, . . . [then] they can only be resolved and washed away by a fresh high tide of the same passions" (p. 90). I will repeat this part, because in it Freud addressed a crucial struggle for the analyst working with the erotic transference. In essence, he said, "The process of cure is accomplished in a relapse into love [which] . . . can only be resolved and washed away by a fresh high tide of the same passions."

In both these early papers, Freud presented the importance of the patient's perceiving the analyst as a "substitute" object. But what is the therapeutic action that creates or allows passionate unconscious currents to develop within the transference? Freud alluded to transference love as creating a reparative or facilitating opportunity to perceive the analyst in a particular manner where the patient's perception of the analyst can serve as a distinct psychic function toward cure. Unfortunately, Freud did not elaborate on this notion of reparation through a passionate love for an all-powerful substitute. Yet these early papers set a precedent for a continued analytic controversy—a controversy that the erotic transference highlights—regarding whether analysis is a one- or two-person psychology. In a one-person psychology, the analysand's endogenous fantasies are the predominant concern in treatment. In the two-person perspective, the patient's fantasies are seen as one part of the focus and the analyst's experiences and influences on the patient make up an additional focus. Freud often took one perspective and sometimes the other in the same paper (see Freud 1915, "Observations on Transference-Love").

Freud (1915) did allow for a two-person system, particularly regarding his original interest in the seduction theory, with its focus on memories of interpersonal consequences, but his theoretical work focused on the analyst as a blank screen, with treatment carried out in abstinence. Freud considered abstinence the driving power of therapeutic action in uncovering and bringing instinctual motivations of unconscious processes into consciousness. Freud stated that the analyst could not offer the patient anything other than a "substitute" object, who gratified her wishes and needs without eliminating inner conflict and motivations to change. Freud's theory of abstinence as a driving therapeutic action affirmed a primarily one-person psychology. It wasn't until Ferenczi's (1933) paper on the actuality of children being traumatized by adult misreading of what they meant that the concept of a two-person psychology was introduced—a concept that has been gaining the favor of contemporary analysts.

In continuing to look at Freud's early conflict between transference love as a facilitator and the analysis of transference love as a resistance, Freud said in his 1912 paper on technique, "The Dynamics of Transference," that if the individual's need for love does not find satisfaction in reality, when he meets new people he maintains hopeful conscious and unconscious libidinal ideas. Freud asserted that, in treatment, it was normal and expected that the unsatisfied libidinal cathexis would be held ready in anticipation and should be directed to the figure of the analyst. The libidinal cathexis resorts to prototypes already in the patient's psychic structure as the patient introduces the analyst into an already existing "psychical 'series' " (Freud 1912, p. 100). Freud argued that if the analyst did not stay distant, the early origin of conflict would not be recognized. He said that when the analysis uncovered the hiding place of the libido, a struggle developed that was imbued with all the forces that had caused the libido to regress. These forces rise up as resistances in order to preserve the patient's psychic homeostasis. Transference, then, appears as a weapon of resistance. "The *mechanism* of transference is dealt with when we have traced it back to the state of readiness of libido, which has remained in possession of infantile imagoes; but the part transference plays in the treatment can only be explained if we enter into its relations with resistance" (p. 104). In other words, the transference develops as a means of resistance (not as a means of direct reparation, but as an indirect, thwarted, [albeit] generative yet facilitating process) as it allows the patient to express or resist early wishful impulses with regard to the person of the analyst, to whom the impulse now appears to relate.

Freud (1912) maintained that the patient does not want to remember the painful unconscious impulses but wants "to reproduce them in accordance with the timelessness of the unconscious" (p. 108). The patient regards his unconscious impulses as real and attempts to put his feelings into action. The analyst puts these emotional impulses to intellectual consideration to understand their psychical value. There is a battle between analyst and patient, intellect and instinctual life, and understanding and enactment in the transference situation as the patient attempts to hide his forgotten erotic impulses. Freud's theory moved away from the idea of the analyst "playing a part" in the transference, and more and more he saw analysis as an intellectual process. In so doing, Freud further distanced himself from his wife's emotional intuition about the special love inherent in the talking cure.

I have been involved in a reading and study group for many years, and during one of those years we read literature pertaining to the erotic transference. My own clinical experience seemed quite different from that described in most of the articles I read, which focused on the erotic transference as a treatment resistance. There is a possibility that the notion of transference love as a facilitator of treatment was forced on me by my work with patients, since it is an essential part of my clinical experience. Certainly, I was influential and *evocative* in the erotic transference development through my receptivity of the patient's loving and sexual feelings. In addition, transference love was not just evoked by the analytic situation, but was also influenced by my character and persona. Did this mean it was all countertransference?

The idea of the analyst being evocative of and receptive to the erotic transference places emphasis on the analyst's part in treatment development. The analyst's countertransference was not traditionally a focus of analytic theory; instead, the literature highlighted the patient's transference. Searles (1959) was one of few exceptions, in his classic paper "Oedipal Love in the Countertransference," where he said it was "only the rare [analyst] who [publicly] acknowledged the presence of [erotic and romantic countertransference feelings] in himself" (p. 285). Certainly, public acknowledgment of erotic countertransference can often evoke professional criticism. Self-criticisms, however, are perhaps more damning, in that the analyst typically fears being a seductive, victimizing, powerful, incestuous parent. When the analyst is behind closed doors with a patient who is talking about erotic feelings, it seems safer and more theoretically familiar to genetically interpret the erotic transference as resistance, as negative therapeutic reaction, as solely the patient's

development of unreal love, than to freely move within a mutual transference–countertransference exploration.

The diversity between traditional and contemporary perspectives
in handling erotic material was brought home to me when I attended a
conference on transference love. During one of the workshops, I presented material on one of my patients to illustrate a mutually sexually
stimulating transference and countertransference development. Sean was
a very handsome man, blond, Irish, blue eyes, maybe 6 feet, 4 inches
tall, with a terrific body, and in his early forties. He quickly fell in love
in the treatment and asked if he could take me for a walk through the
park, since he wanted to point out his favorite places. He added that he
hoped we would end up, bodies intertwined, making love in a secluded
spot. This was quite moving—countertransferentially—in that I felt very
emotionally and sexually stimulated by his passions.

In the conference workshop, the group discussion of this material
focused largely on the question of interpretation—What should or could
I have said about Sean's fantasy? The workshop participants largely
agreed to the need to interpret Sean's wishes as infantile longings and
many of my colleagues stated the importance of making conscious Sean's
unconscious needs. Despite my colleagues' insistence on interpretations,
I stated that my experience with Sean had shown that efforts to make
genetic interpretations were felt by him as the verbal building of a re-
strictive emotional frame around his affective freedom. Sean responded
to genetic interpretations as though I were constructing walls between
us, and felt narcissistically wounded and emotionally abandoned if I
discussed an early incestuous wish or fear in relation to his transference love. Interpretations of this kind are a hallmark of a blank-screen
analyst who considers abstinence as motivating therapeutic action. Sean
was powerfully immersed in his feelings toward me and his immersion
could be traumatized by my emotional abstinence. This clinical material clearly poses the question of therapeutic action. Is therapeutic action facilitated by Sean's knowing the information that would make up
my interpretation, or is therapeutic action facilitated by Sean's emotional
experience in the erotic transference?

The reaction I experienced in this workshop is fairly typical of the
larger analytic community where most analysts perceive the erotic trans-

ference as a resistance to bringing unconscious material into consciousness, as an unreal phenomenon, and/or as a transitional phase in treatment. I believe these are valid understandings of the erotic transference, but I also feel transference love can be understood as a facilitator of a deeper analytic intimacy.

A second problem with the traditional approach to understanding the erotic transference as a treatment obstacle rests with Freud's theory of narcissism. Freud's perception of the therapeutic value of the analyst as love-object, which is still adhered to by the traditional analysts I just mentioned, is inconsequential in the light of his interpretation of the role of narcissism in the configuration of libido (Canestri 1993). In "On Narcissism: An Introduction" (1914) Freud said:

> He [the patient] then seeks a way back to narcissism from his prodigal expenditure of libido upon objects, by choosing a sexual ideal after the narcissistic type which possesses the excellences to which he cannot attain. This is the cure by love, which he generally prefers to cure by analysis. Indeed, he cannot believe in any other mechanism of cure; he usually brings expectations of this sort with him to treatment and directs them toward the person of the physician. The patient's incapacity for love resulting from his extensive repressions naturally stands in the way of a therapeutic plan of this kind. [p. 101]

A central part of the traditional concept of therapeutic action was that "cure by love" did not work because it was so narcissistic and different from real love. But Freud realized it was not so different from real love and yet was confused about the difference between real love and transference love.

Finally, in Freud's 1915 paper, "Observations on Transference-Love," he suggested that an analysis of the complexities and vicissitudes of the transference neurosis can encourage the development of intense erotic transferences, which manifest as demands for love and gratification.

> The patient, whose sexual repression is of course not yet removed but merely pushed into the background, will then feel safe enough to allow all her preconditions for loving, all the phantasies spring-

ing from her sexual desires, all the detailed characteristics of her state of being in love, to come to light; and from these she will herself open the way to the infantile roots of her love. [p. 166].

Freud was now saying that psychoanalysis enabled the ego to grow within and from transference love into a mature capacity to love. Also in this paper, Freud took a one-person perspective, that the transference was the patient's doing, as well as alluding to a two-person perspective: " . . . [the analyst] has evoked this love by instituting analytic treatment . . . " (pp. 168–169).

There is a problem in this section of Freud's paper, because he created a vagueness in his discussion on the distinction between "genuine love" and transference love. In this part, he characterized all transference love as unreal and suggested it was always overly intensified by the analytic situation, and then added that the emotional features of erotic love are different from other inner or outer manifestations within the analytic situation. Therefore, Freud implied, the analyst saw only the patient's primitive, narcissistic love, and the analyst differentiated this from the genuine love the analyst experienced in his or her own personal life. Yet, in erotic transferences, patients experience their own love as authentic and, equally important, they have come to analysis because of their difficulties in loving. It would seem that the transference has offered up a rather pristine opportunity and not just an expression of narcissistic pathology.

Throughout most of this paper Freud considered transference love as an impersonal treatment resistance that arose in response to the patient's emotional defense against painful repressed memory. But if we read the last few pages, we again hear Freud's struggle with the paradoxical vicissitudes inherent in transference love. He commented:

I think we have told the patient the truth, but not the whole truth regardless of the consequences. The part played by resistance in transference-love is unquestionable and very considerable. Nevertheless the resistance did not, after all, create this love; it finds it ready at hand, makes use of it and aggravates its manifestations. Nor is the genuineness of the phenomenon disproved by the resistance. It is true that the love consists of new editions of old traits and that it repeats infantile reactions. . . . Transference-love

has perhaps a degree less of freedom than the love which appears
in ordinary life and is called normal; it displays its dependence
on the infantile pattern more clearly and is less adaptable and capable of modification; but that is all, and not what is essential.
[1915, p. 168]

In this quote, Freud breaks from his earlier stated conviction that
transference love is merely a form of resistance. It is in these last few
pages that Freud gives transference love the rank of a specific type of
love.

The ego psychologists had an understanding of therapeutic action
similar to Freud's, that is, of its making the unconscious conscious. But
the ego psychologists did not have to speculate on the analyst's role,
while Freud clearly did. By this time, the ego psychologists' notion of
the detached analyst had become dogma. Ego psychologists argued
against "cure by love" or cure through a corrective emotional experience. The erotic transference was considered a treatment resistance that
replaced a workable transference neurosis.

In the erotization of the transference, the breakdown of distinction
between the analyst and parent meant that the patient had an impairment of ego function, reality testing, and critical judgment (Blitsten,
personal communication, in Rappaport 1956, p. 515). The successful
erotization was a sequence of narcissistic, borderline, or psychotic functioning (Blum 1973, Gitelson 1952, Rappaport 1956, 1959). Ego psychologists handled the erotic transference in a harsh way. The analyst
was not to engage in the patient's distortions or to duplicate the qualities
of either the pathogenic parent or the desired one. According to Rappaport
(1956), these patients "should be told that they are playing a cheap bur-
lesque and that their behavior is delusive . . . their delusional omnipotence [should be] . . . carefully undermined [and] they can be encouraged
to learn something they had never known before, namely self-respect
and self-esteem" (p. 527). Ferenczi's experiments (Rappaport 1956)
with the analytic role were considered a function of the analyst's inability to control his own narcissism, leading to an unsuccessful treatment.

The shortcomings of this ego psychological, one-person perspective on erotic transference truncated an understanding of its vicissitudes
and clinical implications, since a one-person psychology contends that

the analyst holds a true perception of the analytic relationship, and the patient holds a distorted view. In conceptualizing the transference as a distortion, the analyst has used his or her own construction of psychic reality. Yet, since the analyst already has a sexualized view of human development, at least from didactic training, we must wonder about a bias in the construct of the analyst's psychic reality.

The two-person perspective is an innovative approach to cure, as it tends to emphasize the influence of both analyst and patient operating in a new relational experience, and the fact that the relational experience is the primary vehicle of the therapeutic action. The erotic transference is such a new relational experience (and therefore a transference vehicle) that it moves or allows the patient to have a different attitude than he or she formerly had. What was once considered too personally intimate for analytic consideration is now made public and accessible within the therapeutic relationship.

Most of the traditional literature on transference love prior to the 1970s was written by male analysts about female patients. Those articles that were written by female analysts said their male patients did not develop erotic transferences, with the exception of Bibring-Lehner's case example in 1936 where an "eroticized" transference was discussed toward a female analyst. Lester (1985) stated there were almost no references in the literature in which male patients were reported to have developed intense erotic transferences toward their female analysts. In general, erotic transferences from male patients toward female analysts were considered to be less overt, unconsciously experienced or dreamt, short-lived, or muted, or were merely enacted triangulated wishes and were expressed as a wish for sex rather than a longing for love (Person 1985).

Within the last decade, however, contemporary female analysts, influenced by the current feminist perspective on sexuality, have begun writing about their male patients' erotic transferences (Davies 1994, Goldberger and Holmes 1993, Karme 1993, Kulish and Mayman 1993, Lester 1993, Marcus 1993, and Wrye 1993). Not surprisingly, some of these female authors were the same therapists who wrote prior to the acceptance of feminist thought in psychoanalysis. Certainly, the patients' pathology hasn't changed; however, society's attitudes on women's

sexuality have greatly altered both gender role expectations and receptivity to sexual expression in the last few decades.

As women become more in possession of their own sexuality and
feel less guilty about playing an active sexual role in the world, it is
important to consider if female analysts, or analysts in general, feel more
receptive (as well as more able analytically) to evoking an erotic transference in their patients. Of course, a great deal of work needs to be
done to distinguish an analytic evocation of an erotic transference from
the analyst's being sexually seductive. If we accept the importance of
the analyst's person and gender as influential in treatment, we are again
returned to the concept of a two-person psychology.

A very salient influence on therapeutic action and on the new relational approach to treatment was Kohut's (1971) psychology of the
self, since it led to major revisions in analytic attitudes in the 1970s.
While Kohut felt his clinical observations altered his perception of the
drives, he no longer saw sexuality as a motivator of human *interrelatedness* (Kaftal 1983); rather, he saw development as stemming from
the psychic need for self-cohesion. Kohut's psychology of the self was
developed as a one-person psychology. Yet Kohut also understood (1971,
1977) that one person uses an aspect of another's personality as an
essential, functional component of the self—this is his concept of the
relationship of the self to the selfobject. He wrote (Kohut 1984) that
the "I–You" experience had a selfobject frame of reference, as well as
a mutual influence frame of two intertwining sets of experience" (pp.
52–53), and he added, " . . . object love strengthens the self . . . [and]
a strong self enables us to experience love and desire more intensively"
(p. 53).

For many years, I used a classical Kohutian perspective. I found
it very helpful, particularly with narcissistic patients. I believe it provided an opportunity to understand my patients in a very different and
very real way, as the analyst steps into the shoes of the patient and
responds empathically. This means not just using empathy, which all
perspectives use, but rather using empathy as "vicarious introspection"
(Kohut 1959), which means the capacity to think and feel the inner life
of another person.

Kohut's theory addressed the analytic battle of whether psychoanalysis could have elements of a "cure by love" as opposed to its being a "cure through love" (Kohut 1984, p. 102). Both notions are often associated with cultism by the scientific community. Still, Kohut (1973) likened the analyst's empathic attunement to the patient's inner experience as a "cure by a special love" (p. 705). Therefore, Kohut's concept of empathy encompassed the elements of the "special love" that Freud had previously addressed as a factor in therapeutic action.

Self psychologists are currently struggling with a change in the concept of the nature of the relationship between self and objects, brought about, perhaps, by Kohut's own ambiguities on the concept of cure (1977, 1984). In his last book, *How Does Analysis Cure?* (1984), Kohut stated that empathy or vicarious introspection was not in itself curative, and that therapeutic action was also facilitated through a phase of understanding, followed by a phase of explanation or interpretation. This understanding phase, and particularly the interpretative phase, creates a need for "negotiation" between the two psychic realities of the two participants (Goldberg 1988). Did Kohut's theory of the self only temporarily accept the patient's experience with the eventuality of including a reciprocal relationship between the self and object? Was Kohut struggling with the notion of therapeutic action facilitated by a mutually reciprocal relationship? I believe, and many will disagree, that Kohut, as did Freud, moved between one- and two-person psychologies.

THE VICISSITUDES OF AN EROTIC TRANSFERENCE: AN ILLUSTRATION

The erotic transference is not just simply a love relationship between two people; it can also encompass profound feelings of hatred and anger between . . . a few people. This was made very clear to me when I ran an AIDS psychotherapy group for gay men. In this group, I experienced the erotic transference as an aggressive penetration of hateful rage. When therapists work with extremes, such as patients who are dying or those who are sexually demanding, there can be an elevation of passions from everyone involved. In group work, these passions can arise between individual group members, as well as between the therapist and particular group members. I found that this intimate group relationship, with its focus on life, death, and sex, placed a demand on me, as the analyst, to be receptive to and reciprocate intense, passionate feelings. An analyst who remained an "outsider" would only exacerbate to an intolerable level the real future of isolation, abandonment, loss, and death in these individuals.

In the AIDS group, the emotional demands to relate on a mutual level were instantly powerful. I was expected to find a similarity with them or be "killed off" by their rejection of my differences. For instance, in the first session one of the group members began to eliminate all "different" group members, those who were too ill, those who were not analytically insightful, those who would not disclose their intimate emotions, and so on, as well as the one very different, straight, healthy, uninfected, female therapist. This one particular group member, John, a social worker who ran AIDS groups in a hospital setting, quickly developed a rageful narcissistic transference, which I realized was exacerbated by my early interpretations of the psychic motivations for his behavior. For instance, I interpreted that he was angry at being infected and that exerting control in the group meant feeling powerful against the virus. With hindsight, I wonder if I could have worked with my awareness of being attracted to John. My countertransference feelings were an indicator of an empathic resonance or attunement to John's innermost, secret feelings toward me. I thought he was attracted to me because he would often stare at me and study my mannerisms while he preened and stroked his body. He identified with me professionally, and I felt he was also furious about being attracted to me. And he was rageful that I was more powerful in the group and in better health. I addressed his anger—it was overwhelming—and for a long time it covered his wish for my love and approval.

In addition, the other group members were in full support of John's rage, perhaps also in defense of their loving feelings. John served as the group's "ego ideal" (Freud 1921), something that occurs when individuals in a group identify themselves with a chosen subject whom they imbue with special abilities and allow him to express the forbidden wishes of the individuals in the group.

The group now seemed to want to kill me, and to infect me with the hate they felt about their having contracted the HIV virus. They were aware of a group wish to murder me and so validate their power in life and over life. When John, early on, stated he wanted to have sex with me, he said he wanted a murderous experience. Later when he said he wanted sex it felt like he wanted my life encased within his skin, or wanted to have me in his life in another way. Within these emotional requests, the group demanded a mutuality in the treatment that changed my work, and that, more importantly, was integral in the alteration of the rageful transference into an erotic one. The group needed a mutual flow of affect among all of us, and I found this reciprocal relationship began to encourage insights. But it was not just insight that made the group experience more intimate; it was not just the group members' feeling understood within the context of an empathic milieu. The therapeutic action hinged, in my view, on our mutual interaction and on how we shaped each other in the treatment. We understood the psychic reality of the other—the group members needed to feel and provide love—and this emotional experience far outweighed insight and empathy in bringing about change. As I openly struggled to alter my analytic attitude to a more emotionally reciprocal one, the group members likened my struggle to theirs and we experienced a shared bond that felt passionately reparative. I remember that upon nearing the end of this struggle John aggressively asked me to have sex with him—and this time I replied that I knew I sexually aroused him. I told him I knew it because I had experienced his penetration when he looked at me and felt both his anger and love . . . my experience highlighted his.

It was at this point and within the erotic transference that these group members reached a pinnacle in the intimacy of loving desires and wishes among each other and with me. I took an intense journey into the emotional experiences of these men that led to passionate material. My receptivity created a group intimacy that they said allowed them a sense of cohesion, often to their last moments alive. This experience made me a little fearless about working with patients' profound transference reactions, and helped bring the realization that I could tolerate difficult, passionate countertransference emotions. The construction I made from this group experience was that therapeutic action was facilitated from passionate feelings—both by my patients who experienced their emotions as intimate and reparative, and by me in my receptivity and evocation of the transference.

A number of analysts have delineated the erotic transference as serving a reparative purpose. Goldberg (1975), Stolorow and Atwood (1984, 1992), Stolorow and Lachmann (1979), and Stolorow et al. (1987) are intersubjectivists (a theoretical branch of classical self psychology that incorporates a two-person perspective) who describe the function of sexuality in the transference as restoring a precarious sense of self. The erotic transference is conceptualized as a reaction to an empathic break in the self-sustaining relationship with the analyst. In other words, the erotic transference served as the patient's reparative attempt if the patient felt the analyst had created a narcissistic injury. The erotic transference is the patient's attempt to repair a fragmenting self through loving feelings that replace an unsteady selfobject experience (Gould 1994, Stolorow 1986, and Tropp 1988), that is, it is a therapeutic action originating from the reparative selfobject function.

This view of erotic transference as facilitating therapeutic action in being restorative and self-enhancing, yet still having resistant aspects as a line of interpretation, is derived from Ferenczi (1933). Ferenczi's mutual analysis highlighted particular issues that are now being discussed by contemporary psychoanalysis—specifically that countertransference reaction plays a critical part in treatment, that the analyst must be comfortable with countertransference and analyze it, and that there needs to be a creative, therapeutic way to express countertransference with the patient. Ferenczi took his "active technique" of psychoanalysis, which included relaxation experiments as well as exchanging physical embraces that were symbolic of the mother–child relationship, and attempted to repair his patient *through* love (Aron and Harris 1993). He experimented with his technique in the hope that his investigations would lead to theoretical revision, believing that "analytic technique has never been, nor is it now, something finally settled" (Ferenczi 1931, p. 135). Ferenczi (1913) made the first and most important shift in psychoanalytic theory from a one-person model to a two-person model and felt that transference developed within the framework of countertransference, and that resistance arose in response to the analyst's empathic failures.

AN EROTIC
TRANSFERENCE–COUNTERTRANSFERENCE
CLINICAL ILLUSTRATION

When I first interviewed June a little over a year ago, I thought, "She mine." My countertransference was immediate, in that I felt there was a very early, powerful bond between us. I felt she was sexually attracted to me in the way she studied my appearance and smiled seductively as she did so. For myself, I was receptive to what I felt was an early development of an erotic transference. It is important to wonder what part my countertransference feelings played in evoking June's early transference development, and vice versa. It was also significant to consider if her erotic transference was an initial resistance to the treatment. A month into the treatment June wrote the first of many letters; it read: "I feel better already. I think I express more of my sexual feelings toward you in letters than in person. The reasons are obvious. I probably do want to control you. I don't think my past therapists could possibly have evoked all of this sexual stuff. Why? Well, we'll speak about it in detail when I see you."

In this short letter, June made a meaningful point—she felt I had evoked "all this sexual stuff." She later defined this, saying she was attracted to my personal presentation, my manner of dressing, and my humor—all of which can have a sexual edge. Certainly, my countertransference played a part in evoking her sexual feelings, since I must have been responsive and given receptive nonverbal clues that further evoked her sexual material and relatedness. In addition, I was very encouraging of her sexual comments about her self and her lovers, as well as her remarks about my person. I decided not to provide oedipal interpretations of her sexual material, but rather allowed the transference to unfold by encouraging her to discuss her sexual wishes and desires in the hopes of deepening the eroticism. This is not to say that I did not discuss her feelings about her mother or father, but rather I did not use genetic material to explain her sexual attraction to others since this seemed to shame her. I found June's comments about her sexual wishes facilitated therapeutic action as it led her to discussing her inner experiences and intimacies. For instance, after great hesitation, she let me know about her daily sobbing spells where she ended up in a fetal position under her sink for protection. Her need for protection, in a womblike environment, involved her fears and wishes of merger with women, which led her to express a long-held shameful secret wish to have sex with her mother.

One day she said, "I had three dreams about you. I don't remember two of them, but in the third dream I'm sucking on your breast. I've also been fantasizing about you, you know, sexually. It's not easy to talk about this stuff, but since I think about it all the time and I think about you all the time—sexually—then it seems like I would need to talk about this. I never mentioned this stuff in my other therapies, you know, I just told them what I did between sessions, they might have asked, but . . . you know . . . I didn't 'have' to tell them because I could distract them and we'd go off on other topics. Anyway, the last time I fantasized I was thinking about your body. How do your breasts look, you know. . . . I wondered how you looked naked. (she paused) Oh, do I really have to tell you more?"

Her question was understood as asking permission to tell more, rather than as an appeal to stop. I asked if she felt I was torturing her to get this fantasy. She laughed and said I wasn't torturing her—she was torturing herself.

She continued to let me in to her illusion, "Okay, the fantasy I have takes place in here, in your office. I fantasize you're standing at your desk, right in front of it and you've bent over the desk and I touch you, sexually. I also have the fantasy of watching you have sex with someone else."

I did not interpret her comment as a resistance regarding infantile incestuous longings because I believed it would truncate and concretize her answer. Instead, I wondered aloud if that didn't make her feel left out. "No," she answered. "It makes me feel more like I'm part of the couple. I wish I had been able to see my parents have sex." This was the infantile wish I might have interpreted, but instead I focused on her sexual feelings as the vehicle toward further insights.

June quietly admitted to feeling ashamed of her wish to watch her parents have sex. I was not sure, however, if she was ashamed of her wish or ashamed to admit it. Since this was a long-held secret fantasy, I decided her conflict around its existence must have been mutated over the years or else she would have worked against its continued creation. From her vantage point, her wish was titillating, and I therefore pursued it as such, asking her what she experienced in her sexual fantasy about her parents. June then described the placement of bodies, and how her fantasy included an observation of her own masturbation while she watched her mother sexually climax. She seemed surprised she was telling me these secrets since they were never mentioned in her earlier treatments.

June's erotic response in a mutual association to my erotic countertransference created a special intimacy in which she felt cohesive in the expression of her deepest secret wishes. This was different than it had been in her previous treatments, and different than it was in her life, where she mostly felt fragile and fragmented through loss of others and loss of self in relation. Over time, experience like this is reparative, in that the sexualized and loving bond matures through a special mutuality of affect and receptivity of her innermost feelings.

I asked about her wish to merge using a shared sensuality as the vehicle for insights. I said, "You have an exquisite means of getting in, don't you?"

She answered that she was like a puppeteer—not of puppets on a string, but of hand puppets. "I make the bodies perform the way I want. It's all my show."

Then I said, "Am I one of the puppets you're manipulating in your fantasy of bending me over the desk? Are you verbally masturbating me when you tell your sexual fantasies?"

"That's how I function," she said. "I'm always thinking about everyone in a sexual way. I want to be in people. And you let me in to you when you let me say what I want sexually."

June's sexual feelings toward me now facilitated her discussion about her other relationships. I then learned about her desires with her current lover. She spoke about being aroused by the scars on her lover's skin and how she saw the scars as vulnerable junctures and opportunities to enter her lover. She would masturbate on the scars and feel infused by her lover. After she said her lover didn't even need to participate, she associated her experience with her lover to her thoughts about her mother's self-preoccupations and obsessions.

I then asked if June felt she was required to participate in her mother's obsessions. "Do you enter or merge with your mother when she is most vulnerable and preoccupied in her obsessions? Do you manipulate her with mutual obsessions and feel a closeness with her?"

"Yes," June answered.

"Are mutual obsessions the only means of relating to your mother? Do you ever feel penetrated by your mother's needs and manipulations? Is your mother the ultimate puppeteer?"

She responded, "Oh, definitely. You'd be talking to her and she'd be off in her own world. You know what being with her was like . . . she spent half her time rearranging furniture. I'd go home from school and the house would look entirely different when I got there. But you couldn't say anything because she would feel criticized and rearrange it again."

"Do you worry that one day I'll move the couch?" I asked.

June said, "I'm worried that you'll be like my mother and you'll get fed up with me and leave me behind. That's what I fear you'll do. But the fact that you let me write to you and call you and you call me back, and that you're here every time I come here, and you listen to me . . . well, that's very different from my mother. So, the difference between you and my mother is that I kind of know that you're not going to leave me. You even seem okay with my secret sexual thoughts . . . nobody else knows that stuff. I actually feel pretty dependent on you and it happened pretty quick, too. I didn't feel this dependent on my other shrinks. How did I get to the point of feeling almost entirely dependent on you?"

What appears most clearly in this excerpt is that June's loving and sexual feelings serve as a vehicle that leads the analyst to a treatment level that might not have been achieved had June's sexual feelings been interpreted as a defensive maneuver. Rather, my receptivity allowed June to move freely, using her sexual feelings as a vehicle for insights and intimate feelings. There was no attempt to create an oedipal interpretation about June's feelings for the analyst as infantile longings, no attempt made to address them as an unreal phenomenon, or as transferred oedipal feelings. The intimacy June and I attained though the erotic transference led to more analytic work that might not have been discovered had I heard her erotic material as resistance. This relational concept of therapeutic action means that a new kind of relationship makes insight possible. June and I formed a cohesive mutual bond in our first session that allowed the development of an erotic transference. Was this just projective identification? If it was, then I believe my receptive response to her would have been problematic and the treatment would have been different. We see in her treatment that mutuality in the erotic transference was more than resistance.

SUMMARY

The erotic transference facilitates and gives form to the development of the analytic relationship as it cuts across oedipal and preoedipal boundaries, in that it need not be treated as purely real or unreal, and that it is not merely a resistance or defense against decompensation or self-fragmentation. The erotic transference can serve a facilitating function toward therapeutic "cure" when it is perceived as being a special love or symbol of intimacy with the analyst. The reparative effect of transference love develops in the analyst's evocation, receptivity, and participation in a distinctive mutuality of affect in the therapeutic relationship. It is within the intimate, erotic transference that there can be a synthesis of self through sensitive, erotic, and loving communication within an intimate environment, which is experienced by the self as part of its own completeness—and the struggle for self-completeness is the purpose of therapeutic action.

REFERENCES

Aron, L., and Harris, A., eds. (1993). *The Legacy of Sandor Ferenczi.* Hillsdale, NJ: Analytic Press.

Bibring-Lehner, G. (1936). A contribution to the subject of transference resistance. *International Journal of Psycho-Analysis* 17:181–189.

Blum, H. (1973). The concept of erotized transference. *Journal of the American Psychoanalytic Association* 21:61–76.

Canestri, J. (1993). A cry of fire: some considerations on transference love. In *On Freud's "Observations on Transference-Love,"* ed. E. S. Person, A. Hagelin, and P. Fonagy, pp. 146–164. New Haven, CT: Yale University Press.

Davies, J. M. (1994). Love in the afternoon: a relational reconsideration of desire and dread in the countertransference. *Psychoanalytic Dialogues* 4:153–170.

Deri, S. K. (1984). *Symbolization and Creativity*. New York: International Universities Press.

Eickhoff, F. W. (1993). A reading of "Transference-Love." In *On Freud's "Observations on Transference-Love,"* ed. E. S. Person, A. Hagelin, and P. Fonagy, p. 36. New Haven, CT: Yale University Press.

Ferenczi, S. (1913). To whom does one relate one's dreams? In *Further Contributions to the Theory and Technique of Psycho-Analysis*, ed. J. Richman, trans. J. Suttie, pp. 213–239. London: Karnac, 1980.

——— (1931). Child analysis in the analysis of adults. In *Final Contributions to the Problems and Methods of Psycho-Analysis*, ed. M. Balint, trans. E. Mosbacher, pp. 126–142. London: Karnac, 1980.

——— (1933). Confusion of tongues between adult and child. In *Final Contributions to Problems and Methods of Psychoanalysis*, ed. M. Balint, trans. E. Mosbacher, pp. 156–167. London: Karnac, 1980.

Freud, S. (1905). Fragment of an analysis of a case of hysteria. *Standard Edition* 7:15–124.

——— (1907). Delusions and dreams in Jensen's *"Gradiva."* *Standard Edition* 9:3–93.

——— (1912). The dynamics of transference. *Standard Edition* 12:97–109.

——— (1914). On narcissism: an introduction. *Standard Edition* 14:73–104.

——— (1915). Observations on transference-love. *Standard Edition* 12:157–171.

——— (1921). Group psychology and the analysis of the ego. *Standard Edition* 18:69–144.

——— (1923). The ego and the id. *Standard Edition* 19:13–68.

——— (1932). Letter to Stefan Zweig, 2 June. In *Freud: Biologist of the Mind*, ed. F. Sulloway, p. 80. New York: Basic Books, 1979.

Gill, M. M. (1993). One-person and two-person perspectives: Freud's "Observations on transference-love." In *On Freud's "Observations on Transference-Love,"* ed. E. S. Person, A. Hagelin, and P. Fonagy, pp. 114–129. New Haven, CT: Yale University Press.

Gitelson, M. (1952). The emotional position of the analyst in the psychoanalytic situation. *International Journal of Psycho-Analysis* 33:1–10.

Goldberg, A. (1975). A fresh look at perverse behavior. *International Journal of Psycho-Analysis* 56:335–342.

——— (1988). *A Fresh Look at Psychoanalysis*. Hillsdale, NJ: Analytic Press.

Goldberger, M., and Holmes, D. E. (1993). Transferences in male patients with female analysts: an update. *Psychoanalytic Inquiry* 13:173–191.

Gould, E. (1994). A case of erotized transference in a male patient: formations and transformations. *Psychoanalytic Inquiry* 14:558–571.

Jones, E. (1953). *The Life and Work of Sigmund Freud, Vol. I: The Formative Years and the Great Discoveries*, pp. 1856–1900. New York: Basic Books.

Kaftal, E. (1983). Self psychology and psychological interrelatedness. *Contemporary Psychotherapy Review* 1:20–46.

——— (1991). *The surprising patient*. Paper presented at the American Psychoanalytic Association Conference, Philadelphia, PA, April.

Karme, L. (1993). Male patients and female analysts: erotic and other psychoanalytic encounters. *Psychoanalytic Inquiry* 13:192–205.

Kohut, H. (1959). Introspection, empathy and psychoanalysis. In *The Search for the Self*, vol. 1, ed. P. Ornstein, pp. 205–232. New York: International Universities Press, 1978.

——— (1971). *The Analysis of the Self*. New York: International Universities Press.

——— (1973). The psychoanalyst in the community of scholars. In *The Search for the Self*, vol. 2, ed. P. Ornstein, pp. 685–724. New York: International Universities Press.

——— (1977). *The Restoration of the Self*. New York: International Universities Press.

——— (1984). *How Does Analysis Cure?* Chicago: University of Chicago Press.

Kulish, N., and Mayman, M. (1993). Gender-linked determinants of transference and countertransference in psychoanalytic psychotherapy. *Psychoanalytic Inquiry* 13:286–305.

Lester, E. P. (1985). The female analyst and the erotized transference. *International Journal of Psycho-Analysis* 66:283–293.

——— (1993). Boundaries and gender: their interplay in the analytic situation. *Psychoanalytic Inquiry* 13:153–172.

Marcus, B. F. (1993). Vicissitudes of gender identity in the female therapist/male patient dyad. *Psychoanalytic Inquiry* 13:258–269.

Person, E. S. (1985). The erotic transference in women and in men: differences and consequences. *Journal of the American Academy of Psychoanalysis* 11:159–180.

——— (1993). Introduction. In *On Freud's "Observations on Transference-Love,"* ed. E. S. Person, A. Hagelin, and P. Fonagy, pp. 1–14. New Haven, CT: Yale University Press.

Rappaport, E. (1956). The management of an erotized transference. *Psychoanalytic Quarterly* 26:515–529.

——— (1959). The first dream in an erotized transference. *International Journal of Psycho-Analysis* 40:240–245.

Searles, H. F. (1959). Oedipal love in the countertransference. In *Collected Papers on Schizophrenia and Related Subjects*, pp. 284–303. London: Hogarth, 1965.

Stolorow, R. D. (1984). Aggression in the psychoanalytic situation: an intersubjective viewpoint. *Contemporary Psychoanalysis* 20:643–651.

———— (1986). Critical reflections on the theory of self psychology: an inside view. *Psychoanalytic Inquiry* 6:387–402.

Stolorow, R., and Atwood, G. (1984). *Structures of Subjectivity: Explorations in Psychoanalytic Phenomenology*. Hillsdale, NJ: Analytic Press.

———— (1992). *Contexts of Being: The Intersubjective Foundations of Psychological Life*. Hillsdale, NJ: Analytic Press.

Stolorow, R. D., Atwood, G., and Brandchaft, B. (1987). *Psychoanalytic Treatment: An Intersubjective Approach*. Hillsdale, NJ: Analytic Press.

Stolorow, R. D., and Lachmann, F. (1979). *Faces in a Cloud: Subjectivity in Personality Theory*. New York: Jason Aronson.

Tropp, J. L. (1988). Erotic and eroticized transference—a self psychology perspective. *Psychoanalytic Psychology* 5:269–284.

Wrye, H. K. (1993). Erotic terror: male patients' horror of the early maternal erotic transference. *Psychoanalytic Inquiry* 13:240–257.

Index